MARY, THE MOTHER OF JESUS.

GOODALL, *Pinx.*   JEHENNE, *Lith.*

WOMAN

IN

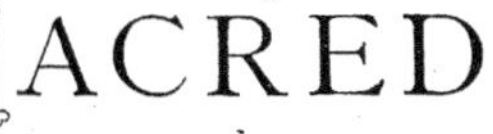

SACRED HISTORY

A SERIES OF SKETCHES

DRAWN FROM SCRIPTURAL, HISTORICAL, AND LEGENDARY SOURCES

BY

HARRIET BEECHER STOWE

Illustrated

WITH TWENTY-FIVE CHROMO-LITHOGRAPHS, AFTER PAINTINGS BY RAPHAEL, BATONI, HORACE VERNET, GOODALL, LANDELLE, KOEHLER. PORTAËLS, VERNET-LECOMTE, BAADER, MERLE, AND BOULANGER AND OTHERS; PRINTED BY MONROCQ, FROM STONES EXECUTED BY JEHENNE, PARIS.

NEW YORK
J. B. FORD AND COMPANY

TO

ALL CHRISTIAN WOMEN

WHO LOVE AND REVERENCE

The Bible

THESE SKETCHES ARE AFFECTIONATELY DEDICATED

BY

THE AUTHOR.

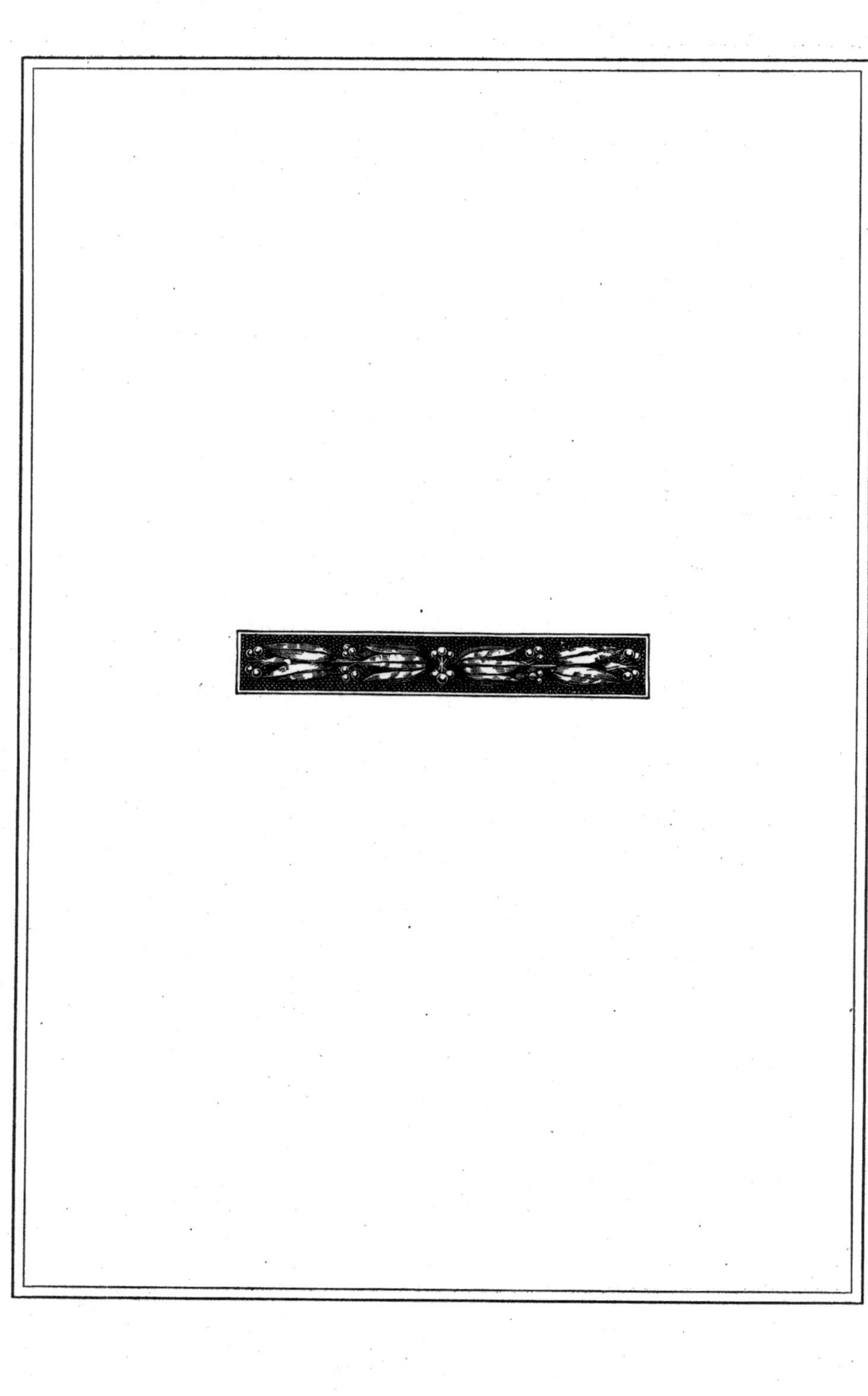

CONTENTS.

CONTENTS.

CONTENTS.

LIST OF ILLUSTRATIONS.

PAST AND FUTURE.

REFT of thy sons, amid thy foes forlorn,
Mourn, widowed Queen, forgotten Sion, mourn!
Is this thy place, sad city, this thy throne,
Where the wild desert rears its craggy stone;
While sons unblest their angry luster fling,
And way-worn pilgrims seek the scanty spring?—
Where now thy pomp, which kings with envy viewed?
Where now thy might, which all those kings subdued?
No martial myriads muster in thy gate;
No suppliant nations in thy Temple wait;
No prophet bards, thy glittering courts among,
Wake the full lyre, and swell the tide of song:
But lawless force and meager want are there,
And the quick-darting eye of restless fear,
While cold oblivion, 'mid thy ruins laid,
Folds his dank wing beneath the ivy shade.
Ye guardian saints! ye warrior sons of Heaven,
To whose high care Judæa's state was given!
O, wont of old your mighty watch to keep,
A host of gods, on Sion's towery steep!
If e'er your secret footsteps linger still
By Siloa's fount, or Tabor's echoing hill;
If e'er your song on Salem's glories dwell,
And mourn the captive land you loved so well
(For oft, 't is said, in Kedron's palmy vale
Mysterious harpings swell the midnight gale,
And, blest as balmy dews that Hermon cheer,
Melt in soft cadence on the pilgrim's ear);
Forgive, blest spirits, if a theme so high
Mock the weak notes of mortal minstrelsy!
Yet, might your aid this anxious breast inspire
With one faint spark of Milton's seraph fire,
Then should my muse ascend with bolder flight,
And wave her eagle plumes exulting in the light.

PAST AND FUTURE.

O, happy once in Heaven's peculiar love,
Delight of men below, and saints above!
Though, Salem, now the spoiler's ruffian hand
Has loosed his hell-hounds o'er thy wasted land;
Though weak, and whelmed beneath the storms of fate,
Thy house is left unto thee desolate;
Though thy proud stones in cumbrous ruins fall,
And seas of sand o'ertop thy mouldering wall;
Yet shall the Muse to fancy's ardent view
Each shadowy trace of faded pomp renew:
And as the seer on Pisgah's topmost brow
With glistening eye beheld the plain below,
With ardor drank the scented gale,
And bade the opening glades of Canaan hail;
Her eagle eye shall scan the prospect wide,
From Carmel's cliffs to Almotana's tide,—
The flinty waste, the cedar-tufted hill,
The liquid health of smooth Ardeni's rill;
The grot, where, by the watch-fire's evening blaze,
The robber riots or the hermit prays;
Or where the tempest rives the hoary stone,
The wintry top of giant Lebanon.

. . . . .

O Thou, their Guide, their Father, and their Lord,
Loved for thy mercies, for thy power adored!
If at thy name the waves forgot their force,
And refluent Jordan sought his trembling source;
If at thy name like sheep the mountains fled,
And haughty Sirion bowed his marble head;—
To Israel's woes a pitying ear incline,
And raise from earth thy long-neglected vine!
Her rifled fruits behold the heathen bear,
And wildwood boars her mangled clusters tear.
Was it for this she stretched her peopled reign
From far Euphrates to the western main?
For this o'er many a hill her boughs she threw,
And her wide arms like goodly cedars grew?
For this, proud Edom slept beneath her shade,
And o'er th' Arabian deep her branches played?
O, feeble boast of transitory power!
Vain, fruitless trust of Judah's happier hour!
Not such their hope, when through the parted main

The cloudy wonder led the warrior train;
Not such their hope, when through the fields of night
The torch of heaven diffused its friendly light;
Not, when fierce conquest urged the onward war,
And hurled stern Canaan from his iron car;
Nor, when five monarchs led to Gibeon's fight,
In rude array, the harnessed Amorite:
Yes,—in that hour, by mortal accents stayed,
The lingering sun his fiery wheels delayed;
The moon, obedient, trembled at the sound,
Curbed her pale car, and checked her mazy round!
  Let Sinai tell,—for she beheld His might,
And God's own darkness veiled her mystic height
(He, cherub-born, upon the whirlwind rode,
And the red mountain like a furnace glowed),—
Let Sinai tell,—but who shall dare recite
His praise, His power, eternal, infinite?—
Awe-struck, I cease; nor bid my strains aspire,
Or serve His altar with unhallowed fire.
  Such were the cares that watched o'er Israel's fate,
And such the glories of their infant state.
—Triumphant race! and did your power decay?
Failed the bright promise of your early day?
No;—by that sword which, red with heathen gore,
A giant spoil, the stripling champion bore;
By him, the chief to farthest India known,
The mighty master of the ivory throne;
In Heaven's own strength, high towering o'er her foes,
Victorious Salem's lion banner rose;
Before her footstool prostrate nations lay,
And vassal tyrants crouched beneath her sway.
  And he, the kingly sage, whose restless mind
Through nature's mazes wandered unconfined;
Who every bird and beast and insect knew,
And spake of every plant that quaffs the dew;
To him were known—so Hagar's offspring tell—
The powerful vigil and the starry spell,
The midnight call, hell's shadowy legions dread,
And sounds that burst the slumbers of the dead.
Hence all his might; for who could these oppose?
And Tadmor thus, and Syrian Balbec rose.
Yet e'en the works of toiling Genii fall,

And vain was Eslakhar's enchanted wall.
In frantic converse with the mournful wind,
There oft the houseless Santon rests reclined;
Strange shapes he views, and drinks with wondering ears
The voices of the dead and songs of other years.
  Such, the faint echo of departed praise,
Still sound Arabia's legendary lays;
And thus their fabling bards delight to tell
How lovely were thy tents, O Israel!
  For thee his ivory load Behemoth bore,
And far Sofala teemed with golden ore;
Thine all the arts that wait on wealth's increase,
Or bask and wanton in the beam of peace.
When Tiber slept beneath the cypress gloom,
And silence held the lonely woods of Rome;
Or e'er to Greece the builder's skill was known,
Or the light chisel brushed the Parian stone;
Yet here fair Science nursed her infant fire,
Fanned by the artist aid of friendly Tyre.
Then towered the palace, then in awful state
The Temple reared its everlasting gate:
No workman steel, no ponderous axes rung!
Like some tall palm the noiseless fabric sprung.
Majestic silence!—then the harp awoke,
The cymbal clanged, the deep-voiced trumpet spoke;
And Salem spread her suppliant arms abroad,
Viewed the descending flame, and blessed the present God.
  Nor shrunk she then, when, raging deep and loud,
Beat o'er her soul the billows of the proud.
E'en they who, dragged to Shinar's fiery sand,
Tilled with reluctant strength the stranger's land;
Who sadly told the slow-revolving years,
And steeped the captive's bitter bread with tears;—
Yet oft their hearts with kindling hopes would burn,
Their destined triumphs, and their glad return,
And their sad lyres, which, silent and unstrung,
In mournful ranks on Babel's willows hung,
Would oft awake to chant their future fame,
And from the skies their lingering Saviour claim.
His promised aid could every fear control;
This nerved the warrior's arm, this steeled the martyr's soul!
Nor vain their hope;—bright beaming through the sky,

Burst in full blaze the Dayspring from on high;
Earth's utmost isles exulted at the sight,
And crowding nations drank the orient light;
Lo, star-led chiefs Assyrian odors bring,
And bending Magi seek their infant King!
Marked ye where, hovering o'er his radiant head,
The dove's white wings celestial glory shed?
Daughter of Sion! virgin queen! rejoice!
Clap the glad hand, and lift the exulting voice!
He comes, — but not in regal splendor drest,
The haughty diadem, the Tyrian vest;
Not armed in flame, all-glorious from afar,
Of hosts the chieftain, and the lord of war:
Messiah comes! — let furious discord cease;
Be peace on earth before the Prince of Peace!
Disease and anguish feel his blest control,
And howling fiends release the tortured soul;
The beams of gladness hell's dark caves illume,
And Mercy broods above the distant gloom.
  Thou palsied earth, with noonday night o'erspread!
Thou sickening sun, so dark, so deep, so red!
Ye hovering ghosts, that throng the starless air,
Why shakes the earth? why fades the light? declare!
Are those his limbs, with ruthless scourges torn?
His brows, all bleeding with the twisted thorn?
His the pale form, the meek forgiving eye
Raised from the cross in patient agony?
— Be dark, thou sun, — thou noonday night, arise,
And hide, O hide, the dreadful sacrifice!
  Ye faithful few, by bold affection led,
Who round the Saviour's cross your sorrows shed,
Not for His sake your tearful vigils keep; —
Weep for your country, for your children weep!
— Vengeance! thy fiery wing their race pursued;
Thy thirsty poniard blushed with infant blood.
Roused at thy call, and panting still for game,
The bird of war, the Latian eagle, came.
Then Judah raged, by ruffian Discord led,
Drunk with the steamy carnage of the dead:
He saw his sons by dubious slaughter fall,
And war without, and death within the wall.
Wide-wasting plague, gaunt famine, mad despair,

And dire debate, and clamorous strife were there;
Love, strong as death, retained his might no more,
And the pale parent drank her children's gore.
Yet they, who wont to roam the ensanguined plain,
And spurn with fell delight their kindred slain;
E'en they, when, high above the dusty fight,
Their burning Temple rose in lurid light,
To their loved altars paid a parting groan,
And in their country's woes forgot their own.

. . . . .

Still o'er her sky the clouds of anger roll,
And God's revenge hangs heavy on her soul.
Yet shall she rise; — but not by war restored,
Not built in murder, — planted by the sword:
Yes! Salem, thou shalt rise: thy Father's aid
Shall heal the wound His chastening hand has made;
Shall judge the proud oppressor's ruthless sway,
And burst his brazen bonds, and cast his cords away.
Then on your tops shall deathless verdure spring.
Break forth, ye mountains, and ye valleys, sing!
No more your thirsty rocks shall frown forlorn,
The unbeliever's jest, the heathen's scorn;
The sultry sands shall tenfold harvests yield,
And a new Eden deck the thorny field.
E'en now, perchance, wide waving o'er the land,
That mighty Angel lifts his golden wand,
Courts the bright vision of descending power,
Tells every gate, and measures every tower;
And chides the tardy seals that yet detain
Thy Sion, Judah, from his destined reign.

From "PALESTINE," by *Bishop Heber.*

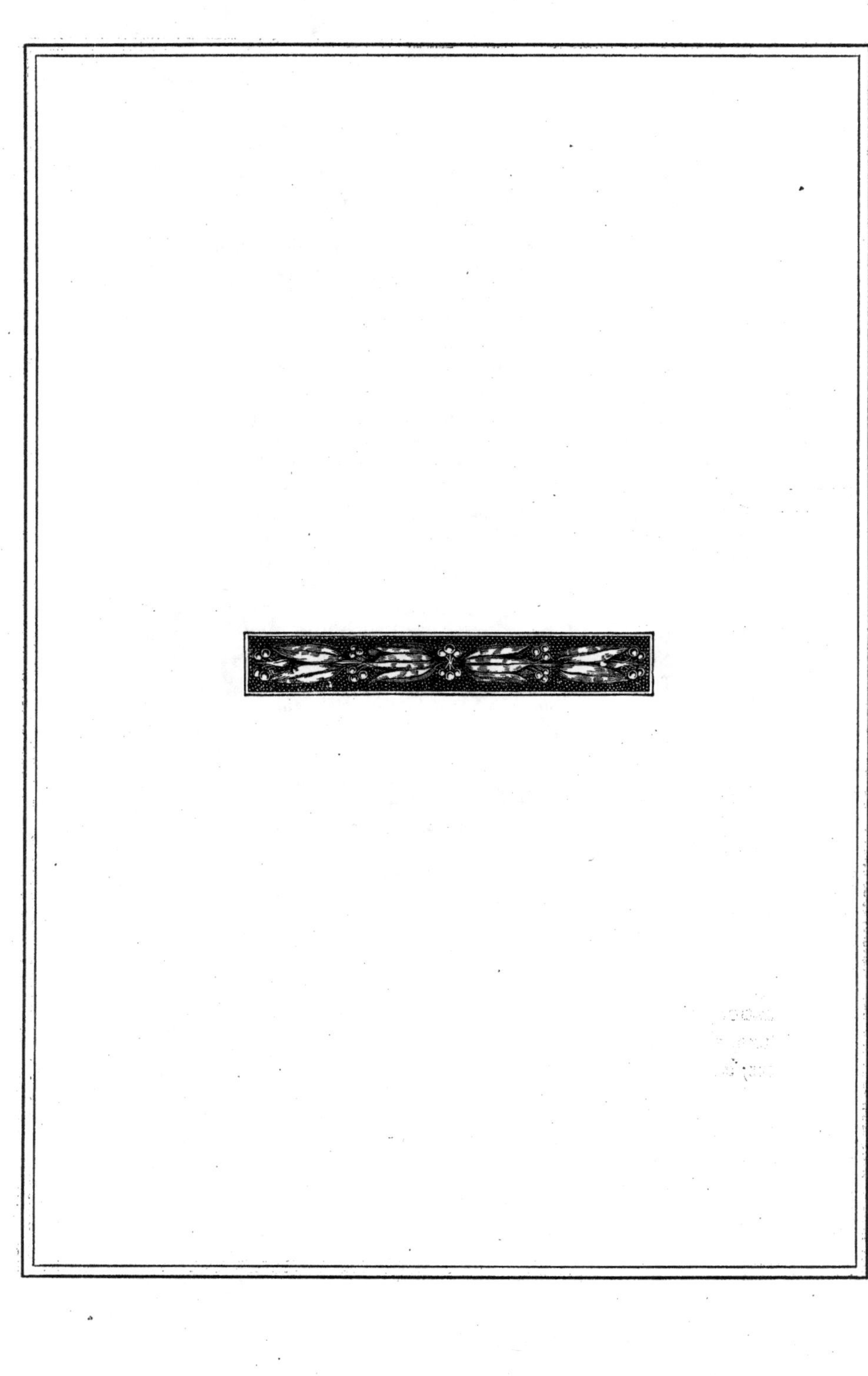

WOMAN IN SACRED HISTORY.

INTRODUCTION.

THE object of the following pages will be to show, in a series of biographical sketches, a history of WOMANHOOD UNDER DIVINE CULTURE, tending toward the development of that high ideal of woman which we find in modern Christian countries.

All the characters comprised in these sketches belong to one nationality. They are of that mysterious and ancient race whose records begin with the dawn of history; who, for centuries, have been sifted like seed through all the nations of the earth, without losing either their national spirit or their wonderful physical and mental vigor.

By this nation the Scriptures, which we reverence, were written and preserved. From it came all the precepts and teachings by which our lives are guided in things highest and holiest; from it came HE who is at once the highest Ideal of human perfection and the clearest revelation of the Divine.

We are taught that the Creator revealed himself to man, not at once, but by a *system* progressively developing from age to age. Selecting one man, he made of his posterity a sacerdotal nation, through which should gradually unfold a religious literature, and from which should come a succession of religious teachers, and the final development, through Jesus, of a religion whose ultimate triumphs should bring complete blessedness to the race.

In tracing the Bible narrative from the beginning, it is interesting to mark the effect of this great movement in its relation to women. The characters we have selected will be arranged for this purpose in a series, under the following divisions: —

I. Women of the Patriarchal Ages.
II. Women of the National Period.
III. Women of the Christian Period.

We understand by the patriarchal period the interval between the calling of Abraham and the public mission of Moses. The pictures of life at this time are interesting, because they give the clearest idea of what we may call the raw material on which the educational system of the Divine Being began to work. We find here a state of society the elements of which are in some respects peculiarly simple and healthful, and in others exhibiting the imperfections of the earth's childhood. Family affection appears to be the strongest force in it, yet it is family affection with the defects of an untaught, untrained morality. Polygamy, with its well-known evils, was universal in the world. Society was broken into roving tribes, and life was a constant battle, in which artifice and deception were the only refuge of the quiet and peace-loving spirit. Even within the bounds of the family, we continually find fraud, artifice, and deception. Men and women, in that age of the world, seem to have practiced deceit and spoken lies, as children do, from immaturity and want of deep reflection. A certain childhood of nature, however, is the redeeming charm in all these pictures. There is an honest simplicity in the narrative, which refreshes us like the talk of children.

We have been so long in the habit of hearing the Bible read in solemn, measured tones, in the hush of churches, that we are apt to forget that these men and women were really flesh and blood, of the same human nature with ourselves. A factitious solemnity invests a Bible name, and some good people seem to feel embarassed by the obligation to justify all the proceedings of patriarchs and prophets by the advanced rules of Christian morality. In this respect, the modern fashion of treating the personages of sacred story with the same freedom of inquiry as the characters of any other history has its advantages. It takes them out of a false, unnatural light, where they lose all hold on our sympathies, and brings them before us as real human beings. Read in this way, the ancient sacred history is the purest naturalism, under the benevolent guidance of the watchful Father of Nations.

Pascal very wisely says, "The whole succession of men during the long course of ages ought to be considered as a single man, who exists and learns from age to age." Considered in this light, it is no more difficult to conceive of an infinite Father tolerating an imperfect childhood of morals in the whole human race, than in each individual of that race. The patriarchs are to be viewed as the first pupils in the great training-school whence the world's teachers in morals were to come, and they are shown to us in all the crudity of early pupilage. The great virtue of which they are presented as the pattern is the virtue of the child and the scholar — FAITH.

Faith, the only true reason for weak and undeveloped natures, was theirs, and as the apostle says, "it was counted to them for righteousness." However imperfect and uncultured one may be, if he has implicit trust in an infallible teacher, he is in the way of all attainment.

The faith of which Abraham is presented as the example is not the blind, ignorant superstition of the savage. Not a fetish, not a selfish trust in a Patron Deity for securing personal advantages, but an enlightened, boundless trust in the Supreme power, wisdom, and rectitude. "The Judge of all the earth will *do right.*" In this belief, Abraham trusts him absolutely. To him he is willing to surrender the deepest and dearest hopes of his life, and sacrifice even the son in whom center all the nerves of joy and hope, "accounting," as the Apostle tells us, "that God was able to raise him from the dead."

Nor was this faith bounded by the horizon of this life. We are informed by the Apostle Paul, who certainly well understood the traditions of his nation, that Abraham looked forward to the same heavenly home which cheers the heart of the Christian. "By faith Abraham, when he was called to go out into a place which he should after receive for an inheritance, obeyed; and he went out, not knowing whither he went. By faith he sojourned in the land of promise, as in a strange country, dwelling in tabernacles with Isaac and Jacob, the heirs with him of the same promise: *for he looked for a city that hath foundations,* whose builder and maker is God. They — the patriarchs — desired a better country, even an heavenly: wherefore God is not ashamed to be called their God." (Heb. xi. 8–10, 16.)

We are further told that this faith passed as a legacy through the patriarchal families to the time of Moses, and that the inspiring motive of his life was the invisible God and the future world beyond the grave. "By faith Moses, when he was come to years, refused to be called the son of Pharaoh's daughter, choosing rather to suffer affliction with the people of God, than to enjoy the pleasures of sin for a season; esteeming the reproach of Christ greater riches than the treasures of Egypt, for he had respect unto the recompense of reward. By faith he forsook Egypt, not fearing the wrath of the great king; for he endured as seeing him who is invisible." (Heb. xi. 24–27.) It has been blindly asserted that the hope of a future life was no part of the working force in the lives of these ancient patriarchs. Certainly, no one ever sacrificed more brilliant prospects of things seen and temporal, for the sake of things unseen and eternal, than Moses.

Finally, one remarkable characteristic of all these old patriarchs was the warmth of their affections. Differing in degree as to moral worth, they were all *affectionate* men. So, after all that Christianity has done for us, after all the world's growth and progress, we find no pictures of love in family life more delicate and tender than are given in these patriarchal stories. No husband could be more loyally devoted to a wife than Abraham; no lover exhibit less of the eagerness of selfish passion and more of enduring devotion than Jacob, who counted seven years of servitude as nothing, for the love he bare his Rachael; and, for a picture of parental tenderness, the story of Joseph stands alone and unequalled in human literature.

In the patriarchal families, as here given, women seem to have reigned as queens of the interior. Even when polygamy was practiced, the monogamic affection was still predominant. In the case of Abraham and Jacob, it appears to have been from no wandering of the affections, but from a desire of offspring, or the tyranny of custom, that a second wife was imposed.

Female chastity was jealously guarded. When a young prince seduced Dinah, the daughter of Jacob, although offering honorable marriage, with any amount of dowry, the vengeance of the brothers could only be appeased by blood; and the history of Joseph shows that purity was regarded as a virtue in man as well as in woman. Such, then, was the patriarchal stock, — the seed-form of the great and chosen nation. Let us now glance at the influences which nourished it through the grand growth of the prophetic or national period, up to the time of its consummate blossom and fruit in the Christian era.

Moses was the great lawgiver to mold this people into a nation. His institutes formed a race of men whose vital force has outlived conquest, persecution, dispersion, and every possible cause which could operate to destroy a nationality; so that, even to our time, talent and genius spring forth from the unwasted vigor of these sons and daughters of Abraham. The remarkable vigor and vitality of the Jewish race, their power of adaptation to every climate, and of bearing up under the most oppressive and disadvantageous circumstances, have attracted the attention of the French government, and two successive commissions of inquiry, with intervals of three or four years between, have been instituted, "on the causes of the health and longevity of the Jewish race."

In the "Israelite" of February 9, 1866, we have, on this subject, the report of M. Legoyt, chief of a division of the ministry of commerce and public works, one of the first statisticians of France. He says: "We have seen that all the documents put together are affirmative of an exceptional vitality of the Jews. How can this phenomenon be explained? Dietrici, after having demonstrated its existence in Prussia, thinks it is to be attributed to greater temperance, a better regulated life, and purer morals. This is likewise the opinion of Drs. Neufville, Glatter, and Meyer.

Cases of drunkenness, says Dietrici, frequent among the Christians, occur very rarely among the Jews. This regularity and discipline, and greater self-control, of Jewish life is confirmed by the criminal statistics of Prussia, which show fewer Jews condemned for crime."

M. Legoyt goes on to account for this longevity and exceptional vitality of the Jews by the facts of their family life: that early marriages are more common; that great care is taken to provide for the exigencies of marriage; that there are fewer children born, and thus they are better cared for; that family feeling is more strongly developed than in other races; that the Jewish mother is the nurse of her own infant, and that great care and tenderness are bestowed on young children.

It is evident that the sanitary prescriptions of the Mosaic law have an important bearing on the health. If we examine these laws of Moses, we shall find that they consist largely in dietetic and sanitary regulations, in directions for detecting those diseases which vitiate the blood, and removing the subjects of them from contact with their fellows.

But the greatest peculiarity of the institutes of Moses is their care of family life. They differed from the laws of all other ancient nations by making the family the central point of the state. In Rome and Greece, and in antiquity generally, the ruling purpose was war and conquest. War was the normal condition of the ancient world. The state was for the most part a camp under martial law, and the interests of the family fared hardly. The laws of Moses, on the contrary, contemplated a peaceful community of land-holders, devoted to agriculture and domestic life. The land of Canaan was divided into homesteads; the homestead was inalienable in families, and could be sold only for fifty years, when it reverted again to the original heirs. All these regulations gave a quality of stability and perpetuity to the family. We have also some striking laws which show how, when brought into immediate comparison, family life is always considered the first; for instance, see Deuteronomy xxiv. 5: "When a man hath taken a new wife he shall not go out to war, neither shall he be charged with any business; but he shall be free at home one year, and shall cheer up his wife which he hath taken." What can more strongly show the delicate care of woman, and the high regard paid to the family, than this? It was more important to be a good husband and make his wife happy than to win military glory or perform public service of any kind.

The same regard for family life is shown, in placing the father and the mother as joint objects of honor and veneration, in the Ten Commandments: "Honor thy father and thy mother, that thy days may be long in the land that the Lord thy God giveth thee." Among the Greeks, the wife was a nonentity, living in the seclusion of the women's apartments, and never associated publicly with her husband as an equal. In Rome, the father was all in all in the family, and held the sole power of life and death over his wife and children. Among the Jews, the wife was the co-equal queen of the home, and was equally honored and obeyed with her husband. Lest there should be any doubt as to the position of the mother, the command is solemnly reiterated, and the mother placed first in order: "And the Lord spake to Moses, speak unto the children of Israel and say unto them, Ye shall be holy, for I the Lord your God am holy. Ye shall fear every man his MOTHER and his father. I am the Lord." (Lev. xix. 3.) How solemn is the halo of exaltation around the mother in this passage, opened with all the authority of God, — calling to highest holiness, and then exalting the mother and the father as, next to God, objects of reverence!

Family government was backed by all the authority of the state, but the power of life and death was not left in the parents' hands. If a son proved stubborn and rebellious, utterly refusing domestic discipline, then the father and the mother were to unite in bringing him before the civil magistrates, who condemned him to death. But the *mother* must appear and testify, before the legal act was accomplished, and thus the power of restraining the stronger passions of the man was left with her.

The laws of Moses also teach a degree of delicacy and consideration, in the treatment of women taken captives in war, that was unparalleled in those ages. With one consent, in all other ancient nations, the captive woman was a slave, with no protection for chastity. Compare with this the spirit of the law of Moses: "If thou seest among thy captives a beautiful woman, and hast a desire unto her that thou wouldst have her to wife, then thou shalt bring her to thy house, and she shall remain in thy house and bewail her father and mother a full month; and after that thou shalt go in unto her and be her husband, and she shall be thy wife." Here is consideration, regard to womanly feeling, and an opportunity for seeking the affection of the captive by kindness. The law adds, furthermore, that if the man change his mind, and do not wish to marry her after this time for closer acquaintance, then he shall give her her liberty, and allow her to go where she pleases: "Thou shalt not sell her at all for money, thou shalt not make merchandise of her, because thou hast humbled her."

The laws of Moses did not forbid polygamy, but they secured to the secondary wives such respect and attention as made the maintenance of many of them a matter of serious difficulty. Everywhere we find Moses interposing some guard to the helplessness of the woman, softening and moderating the harsh customs of ancient society in her favor. Men were not allowed to hold women-servants merely for the gratification of a temporary passion, without assuming the obligations of a husband. Thus we find the following restraint on the custom of buying a handmaid or concubine: "If a man sell his daughter to be a maid-servant, she shall not go out to work as the men-servants do, and, if she please not her master which hath betrothed her to himself, then shall he let her be redeemed; he shall have no power to sell her unto a stranger, seeing he hath dealt deceitfully with her. And if he have betrothed her to his son, he shall deal with her as a daughter. And if he take another wife, her food and her raiment, and her duty of marriage shall he not diminish. And if he do not these three things unto her, then shall she go out free without money." (Ex. xxi. 7.) This law, in fact, gave to every concubine the rights and immunities of a legal wife, and in default of its provisions she recovered her liberty. Thus, also, we find a man is forbidden to take two sisters to wife, and the feelings of the first wife are expressly mentioned as the reason: "Thou shalt not take unto thy wife her sister to vex her during her lifetime."

In the same manner it was forbidden to allow personal favoritism to influence the legal rights of succession belonging to children of different wives. (Deut. xxi. 15.) "If a man have two wives, one beloved and the other hated, and they have both borne him children, and if the firstborn son be hers that is hated, then, when he maketh his sons to inherit, he may not make the son of the beloved firstborn, but he shall acknowledge the son of the hated for the firstborn."

If a man slandered the chastity of his wife before marriage, she or her relations had a right to bring him before a tribunal of the elders, and, failing to substantiate his accusations, he was heavily fined and the right of divorce taken from him.

By thus hedging in polygamy with the restraints of serious obligations and duties, and making every concubine a wife, entitled to claim all the privileges of a wife, Moses prepared the way for its gradual extinction. For since it could not be a mere temporary connection involving no duty on the man's part, since he could not sell or make merchandise of the slave when he was tired of her, since the children had a legal claim to support, — it became a serious matter to increase the number of wives. The kings of Israel were expressly forbidden to multiply wives; and the disobedience of Solomon, who followed the custom of Oriental sovereigns, is mentioned with special reprobation, as calling down the judgments of God upon his house.

The result of all this was, that in the course of time polygamy fell into disuse among the Jews; and, after the Babylonian captivity, when a more strenuous observance of the laws of Moses was enforced, it almost entirely ceased.* In the time of Christ and the Apostles, the Jews had become substantially a monogamic nation.

Another peculiarity in the laws of Moses is the equality of the treatment of man and woman. Among other nations, adultery was punished severely in the wife, and lightly, if at all, in the

* Michaelis, Laws of Moses, III. 5, § 95.

husband. According to the Jewish law, it was punished by the death of both parties. If a man seduced a girl, he was obliged to marry her; and forcible violation was punished by death.

While in many other nations, prostitution, in one form or other, formed part of the services of the temple and the revenues of the state, it was enacted that the wages of such iniquity should not be received into the treasury of the Lord; and, finally, it was enjoined that there should be no prostitute among the daughters of Israel. (Deut. xxiii. 17, 18.)

In all that relates to the details of family life, the laws of Moses required great temperance and government of the passions; and, undoubtedly, these various restraints and religious barriers raised by the ceremonial law around the wife and mother are one great reason of the vigor of the Jewish women and the uncorrupted vitality of the race.

The law of Moses on divorce, though expressly spoken of by Christ as only a concession or adaptation to a low state of society, still was, in its day, on the side of protection to women. A man could not put his wife out of doors at any caprice of changing passion: a legal formality was required, which would, in those times, require the intervention of a Levite to secure the correctness of the instrument. This would bring the matter under the cognizance of legal authority, and tend to check the rash exercise of the right by the husband. The final result of all this legislation, enforced from age to age by Divine judgments, and by the warning voices of successive prophets, was, that the Jewish race, instead of sinking into licentiousness, and losing stamina and vigor, as all the other ancient nations did, became essentially a chaste and vigorous people, and is so to this day.

The comparison of the literature of any ancient nation with that of the Jews strikingly demonstrates this. The uncleanness and obscenity of much of the Greek and Roman literature is in wonderful contrast to the Jewish writings in the Bible and Apocrypha, where vice is never made either ludicrous or attractive, but mentioned only with horror and reprobation.

If we consider now the variety, the elevation, and the number of female characters in sacred history, and look to the corresponding records of other nations, we shall see the results of this culture of women. The nobler, the heroic elements were developed among the Jewish women by the sacredness and respect which attached to family life. The veneration which surrounded motherhood, and the mystic tradition coming down through the ages that some Judæan mother should give birth to the great Saviour and Regenerator of mankind, consecrated family life with a devout poetry of emotion. Every cradle was hallowed by the thought of that blessed child who should be the hope of the world.

Another cause of elevation of character among Jewish women was their equal liability to receive the prophetic impulse. A prophet was, by virtue of his inspiration, a public teacher, and the leader of the nation, — kings and magistrates listened to his voice; and this crowning glory was from time to time bestowed on women.

We are informed in 2 Kings xxii. 14, that in the reign of King Josiah, when a crisis of great importance arose with respect to the destiny of the nation, the king sent a deputation of the chief priests and scribes to inquire of the word of the Lord from Huldah the prophetess, and that they received her word as the highest authority. This was while the prophet Jeremiah was yet a young man.

The prophetess was always a poetess, and some of the earliest records of female poetry in the world are of this kind. A lofty enthusiasm of patriotism also distinguishes the Jewish women, and in more than one case in the following sketches we shall see them the deliverers of their country. Corresponding to these noble women of sacred history, what examples have we in polished Greece? The only women who were allowed mental culture — who studied, wrote, and enjoyed the society of philosophers and of learned men — were the courtesans. For chaste wives and mothers there was no career and no record.

In the Roman state we see the influence upon woman of a graver style of manhood and a more equal liberty in the customs of society. In Rome there were sacred women, devoted to religion, and venerated accordingly. They differed, however, from the inspired women of Jewish history in being entirely removed from the experiences of family life. The vestal virgins were bound by cruel penalties to a life of celibacy. So far as we know, there is not a Jewish prophetess who is not also a wife, and the motherly character is put forward as constituting a claim to fitness in public life. "I, Deborah, arose a mother in Israel." That pure ideal of a sacred woman springing from the bosom of the family, at once wife, mother, poetess, leader, inspirer, prophetess, is peculiar to sacred history.

WOMEN OF THE PATRIARCHAL AGES.

INVOCATION.

AS the tired voyager on stormy seas
Invokes the coming of bright birds from shore,
To waft him tidings with the gentler breeze,
Of dim sweet woods that hear no billow's roar;
So from the depth of days, when earth yet wore
Her solemn beauty and primeval dew,
I call you, gracious Forms! O, come, restore
Awhile that holy freshness, and renew
Life's morning dreams! Come with the voice, the lyre,
Daughters of Judah! with the timbrel rise!
Ye of the dark prophetic eastern eyes,
Imperial in their visionary fire;
O, steep my soul in that old glorious time,
When God's own whisper shook the cedars of your clime!

Felicia Hemans.

SARA, THE PRINCESS.

BROCHART, *Pinx.* JEHENNE, *Lith.*

SARAH THE PRINCESS.

ONE woman in the Christian dispensation has received a special crown of honor. Sarah, the wife of Abraham, mother of the Jewish nation, is to this day an object of traditional respect and homage in the Christian Church. Her name occurs in the marriage service as an example for the Christian wife, who is exhorted to meekness and obedience by St. Peter, "Even as Sarah obeyed Abraham, calling him lord; whose daughters ye are, so long as ye do well, and are not subject to a slavish fear."

In turning to the narrative of the Old Testament, however, we are led to feel that in setting Sarah before wives as a model of conjugal behavior, no very alarming amount of subjection or submission is implied.

The name Sarah means "princess"; and from the Bible story we infer that, crowned with the power of eminent beauty, and fully understanding the sovereignty it gave her over man, Sarah was virtually empress and mistress of the man she called "lord." She was a woman who understood herself and him, and was too wise to dispute the title when she possessed the reality of sway; and while she called Abraham "lord," it is quite apparent from certain little dramatic incidents that she expected him to use his authority in the line of her wishes.

In going back to these Old Testament stories, one feels a ceaseless admiration of the artless simplicity of the primitive period of which they are the only memorial. The dew of earth's early morning lies on it, sparkling and undried; and the men and women speak out their hearts with the simplicity of little children.

In Abraham we see the man whom God designed to be the

father of a great sacerdotal nation; through whom, in the fullness of time, should come the most perfect revelation of himself to man, by Jesus Christ. In choosing the man to found such a nation, the Divine Being rejected the stormy and forcible characters which command the admiration of rude men in early ages, and chose one of gentler elements.

Abraham was distinguished for a loving heart, a tender domestic nature, great reverence, patience, and fidelity, a childlike simplicity of faith, and a dignified self-possession. Yet he was not deficient in energy or courage when the event called for them. When the warring tribes of the neighborhood had swept his kinsman, Lot, into captivity, Abraham came promptly to the rescue, and, with his three hundred trained servants, pursued, vanquished, and rescued. Though he loved not battle, when roused for a good cause he fought to some purpose.

Over the heart of such a man, a beautiful, queenly woman held despotic sway. Traveling with her into the dominions of foreign princes, he is possessed by one harassing fear. The beauty of this woman, — will it not draw the admiration of marauding powers? And shall I not be murdered, or have her torn from me? And so, twice, Abraham resorts to the stratagem of concealing their real relation, and speaking of her as his sister. The Rabbinic traditions elaborate this story with much splendor of imagery. According to them, Abraham being obliged by famine to sojourn in Egypt, rested some days by the river Nile; and as he and Sarah walked by the banks of the river, and he beheld her wonderful beauty reflected in the water, he was overwhelmed with fear lest she should be taken from him, or that he should be slain for her sake. So he persuaded her to pass as his sister; for, as he says, "she was the daughter of my father, but not of my mother." The legend goes on to say, that, as a further precaution, he had her placed in a chest to cross the frontier; and when the custom-house officers met them, he offered to pay for the box whatever they might ask, to pass it free.

"Does it contain silks?" asked the officers.

"I will pay the tenth as of silk," he replied.

"Does it contain silver?" they inquired.

"I will pay for it as silver," answered Abraham.

"Nay, then, it must contain gold."

"I will pay for it as gold."

"May be it contains most costly gems."

"I will pay for it as gems," he persisted.

In the struggle the box was broken open, and in it was seated a beautiful woman whose countenance illumined all Egypt. The news reached the ears of Pharaoh, and he sent and took her.

In comparing these Rabinnic traditions with the Bible, one is immediately struck with the difference in quality, — the dignified simplicity of the sacred narrative contrasts forcibly with the fantastic elaborations of tradition.

The Rabbinic and Alcoranic stories are valuable, however, as showing how profound an impression the personality of these characters had left on mankind. The great characters of the Biblical story, though in themselves simple, seemed, like the sun, to raise around them many-colored and vaporous clouds of myth and story. The warmth of their humanity kept them enwreathed in a changing mist of human sympathies.

The falsehoods which Abraham tells are to be estimated not by the modern, but by the ancient standard. In the earlier days of the world, when physical force ruled, when the earth was covered with warring tribes, skill in deception was counted as one of the forms of wisdom. "The crafty Ulysses" is spoken of with honor through the "Odyssey" for his skill in dissembling; and the Lacedemonian youth were punished, not for stealing or lying, but for performing these necessary operations in a bungling, unskillful manner.

In a day when it was rather a matter of course for a prince to help himself to a handsome woman wherever he could find her, and kill her husband if he made any objections, a weaker party entering the dominions of a powerful prince was under the laws of war.

In our nineteenth century we have not yet grown to such maturity as not to consider false statements and stratagem as legitimate war policy in dealing with an enemy. Abraham's *ruse* is not, therefore, so very far behind even the practice of modern Christians. That he should have employed the same fruitless stratagem twice, seems to show that species of infatuation on the one subject of a beloved woman, which has been the "last infirmity" of some otherwise strong and noble men, — wise everywhere else, but weak there.

The Rabbinic legends represent Sarah as being an object of ardent admiration to Pharaoh, who pressed his suit with such vehemence that she cried to God for deliverance, and told the king that she was a married woman. Then — according to this representation — he sent her away with gifts, and even extended his complacency so far as to present her with his daughter Hagar as a handmaid, — a legend savoring more of national pride than of probability.

In the few incidents related of Sarah she does not impress us as anything more than the beautiful princess of a nomadic tribe, with many virtues and the failings that usually attend beauty and power.

With all her advantages of person and station, Sarah still wanted what every woman of antiquity considered the crowning glory of womanhood. She was childless. By an expedient common in those early days, she gives her slave as second wife to her husband, whose child shall be her own. The Rabbinic tradition says that up to this time Hagar had been tenderly beloved by Sarah. The prospect, however, of being mother to the heir of the family seems to have turned the head of the handmaid, and broken the bonds of friendship between them.

In its usual naïve way, the Bible narrative represents Sarah as scolding her patient husband for the results which came from following her own advice. Thus she complains, in view of Hagar's insolence: "My wrong be upon thee. I have given my maid unto thy bosom, and when she saw that she had conceived, I was despised in her eyes. The Lord judge between thee and me."

We see here the eager, impulsive, hot-hearted woman, accustomed to indulgence, impatient of trouble, and perfectly certain that she is in the right, and that the Lord himself must think so. Abraham, as a well-bred husband, answers pacifically: "Behold, thy maid is in thy hand, to do as pleaseth thee." And so it pleased Sarah to deal so hardly with her maid that she fled to the wilderness.

Finally, the domestic broil adjusts itself. The Divine Father, who watches alike over all his creatures, sends back the impetuous slave from the wilderness, exhorted to patience, and comforted with a promise of a future for her son.

Then comes the beautiful idyl of the three angels, who announce the future birth of the long-desired heir. We could wish all our readers, who may have fallen out of the way of reading the Old Testament, to turn again to the eighteenth chapter of Genesis, and see the simple picture of those olden days. Notice the beautiful hospitality of reception. The Emir rushes himself to his herd to choose the fatted calf, and commands the princess to make ready the meal, and knead the cakes. Then comes the repast. The announcement of the promised blessing, at which Sarah laughs in incredulous surprise; the grave rebuke of the angels, and Sarah's white lie, with the angel's steady answer, — are all so many characteristic points of the story. Sarah, in all these incidents, is, with a few touches, made as real flesh and blood as any woman in the pages of Shakespeare, — not a saint, but an average mortal, with all the foibles, weaknesses, and variabilities that pertain to womanhood, and to womanhood in an early age of imperfectly developed morals.

We infer from the general drift of the story, that Sarah, like most warm-hearted and passionate women, was, in the main, a kindly, motherly creature, and that, when her maid returned and submitted, she was reconciled to her. At all events, we find that the son of the bondwoman was born and nurtured under her roof, along with her own son Isaac. It is in keeping with our conception of Sarah, that she should at times have overwhelmed Hagar with kindness, and helped her through the trials of motherhood, and petted the little Ishmael till he grew too saucy to be endured.

The Jewish mother nursed her child three years. The weaning was made a great *fête*, and Sarah's maternal exultation at this crisis of her life, displayed itself in festal preparations. We hear her saying: "God hath made me to laugh, so that all that hear will laugh with me. Who would have said unto Abraham that Sarah should have given children suck? for I have borne him a son in his old age."

In the height of this triumph, she saw the son of the Egyptian woman mocking, and all the hot blood of the woman, mother, and princess flushed up, and she said to her husband: "Cast out this bondwoman and her son; for the son of this bondwoman shall not be heir with my son, even with Isaac."

We are told "the thing was very grievous in Abraham's sight because of his son." But a higher power confirms the hasty, instinctive impulse of the mother. The God of nations saw in each of these infant boys the seed-forms of a race with a history and destiny apart from each other, and Abraham is comforted with the thought that a fatherly watch will be kept over both.

Last of all we come to the simple and touching announcement of the death of this woman, so truly loved to the last. "And Sarah was a hundred and seven and twenty years old: these were the years of the life of Sarah. And Sarah died in Kirjath-arba; the same is Hebron in the land of Canaan; and Abraham came to mourn for Sarah, and to weep for her." It is a significant token of the magnificent physical vigor with which that early age was endowed, that now, for the first time, the stroke of death has fallen on the family of Abraham, and he is forced to seek a burial-place. Sarah, the beautiful princess, the crowned mother of a great nation, the beloved wife, is dead; and Abraham, constant lover in age as youth, lays her away with tears. To him she is ever young; for love confers on its object eternal youth.

A beautiful and peculiar passage in the history describes the particulars of the purchase of this burial-place. All that love can give to the fairest, most beautiful, and dearest is a tomb; and Abraham refuses to take as a gift from the nobles of the land so sacred a spot. It must be wholly his own, bought with his own money. The sepulchre of Machpelah, from the hour it was consecrated by the last sleep of the mother of the tribe, became the calm and sacred resting-place to which the eyes of children's children turned. So Jacob, her grandson, in his dying hour, remembered it:—

"Bury me with my fathers in the cave that is in the field of Ephron the Hittite. There they buried Abraham and Sarah his wife; there they buried Isaac and Rebekah his wife, and there I buried Leah."

Two powerful and peculiar nations still regard this sepulchre with veneration, and cherish with reverence the memory of Sarah the Princess.

THE CAVE OF MACHPELAH.

CALM is it in the dim cathedral cloister,
Where lie the dead all couched in marble rare,
Where the shades thicken, and the breath hangs moister
Than in the sunlit air.

Where the chance ray that makes the carved stone whiter,
Tints with a crimson or a violet light
Some pale old bishop with his staff and mitre,
Some stiff crusading knight!

Sweet is it where the little graves fling shadows
In the green churchyard, on the shaven grass,
And a faint cowslip fragrance from the meadows
O'er the low wall doth pass!

More sweet, more calm in that fair valley's bosom
The burial-place in Ephron's pasture-ground,
Where the oil-olive shed her snowy blossom,
And the red grape was found;

When the great pastoral prince, with love undying,
Rose up in anguish from the face of death,
And weighed the silver shekels for its buying
Before the sons of Heth.

Here, when the measure of his days was numbered, —
Days few and evil in this vale of tears! —
At Sarah's side the faithful patriarch slumbered,
An old man full of years:

THE CAVE OF MACHPELAH.

Here, holy Isaac, meek of heart and gentle,
  And the fair maid who came to him from far,
And the sad sire who knew all throes parental,
  And meek-eyed Leah, are.

She rests not here, the beautiful of feature,
  For whom her Jacob wrought his years twice o'er,
And deemed them but as one, for that fair creature,
  --So dear the love he bore,—

Nor Israel's son beloved,* who brought him sleeping
  With a long pomp of woe to Canaan's shade,
Till all the people wondered at the weeping
  By the Egyptians made.

Like roses from the same tree gathered yearly,
  And flung together in one vase to keep,—
Some, but not all who loved so well and dearly,
  Lie here in quiet sleep.

What though the Moslem mosque be in the valley,
  Though faithless hands have sealed the sacred cave,
And the red Prophet's children shout "El Allah!"
  Over the Hebrews' grave;

Yet a day cometh when those white walls shaking
  Shall give again to light the living dead,
And Abraham, Isaac, Jacob, reawaking,
  Spring from their rocky bed.

Mrs. C. F. Alexander.

* "And the bones of Joseph buried they in Shechem."—JOSH. xxiv. 32.

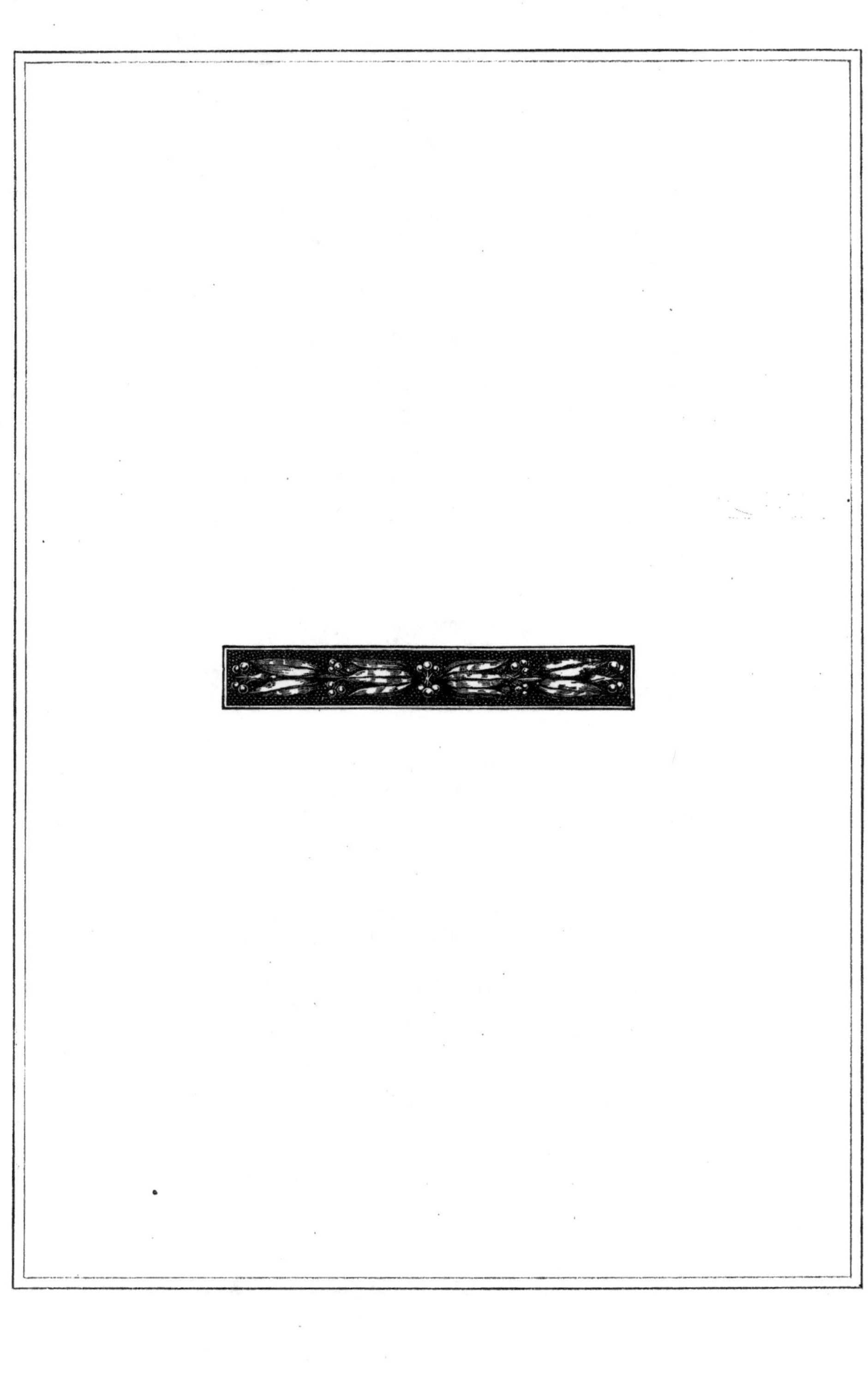

HAGAR AND ISHMAEL.

KOEHLER, *Pinx.* JEHENNE, *Lith.*

HAGAR THE SLAVE.

A STRIKING pendant to the picture of Sarah the Princess is that of Hagar the Slave.

In the Bible narrative she is called simply Hagar the Egyptian; and as Abraham sojourned some time in the land of Egypt, we are to suppose that this acquisition to the family was then made. Slavery, in the early patriarchal period, had few of the horrors which beset it in more modern days. The condition of a slave more nearly resembled that of the child of the house than that of a modern servant. The slave was looked upon, in default of children, as his master's heir, as was the case with Eliezer of Damascus, the confidential servant of Abraham; the latter, when speaking to God of his childless condition says: "Lo! one born in my house is mine heir." In like manner there is a strong probability in the legend which represents Hagar as having been the confidential handmaid of Sarah, and treated by her with peculiar tenderness.

When the fear of being childless seized upon her, Sarah was willing to exalt one, who was as a second self to her, to the rank of an inferior wife, according to the customs of those early days; intending to adopt and treat as her own the child of her handmaid. But when the bondwoman found herself thus exalted, and when the crowning honor of prospective motherhood was conferred upon her, her ardent tropical blood boiled over in unseemly exultation, — "her mistress was despised in her eyes."

Probably under the flapping curtains of the pastoral tent, as under the silken hangings of palaces, there were to be found flatterers and mischief-makers ready to fill the weak, credulous ear with their suggestions. Hagar was about to become mother of the prince and heir of the tribe; her son one day should be their chief and ruler, while Sarah, childless and uncrowned, should sink to a secondary rank. Why should she obey the commands of Sarah?

Our idea of Sarah is that of a warm-hearted, generous, bountiful woman, with an intense sense of personal dignity and personal rights,—just the woman to feel herself beyond measure outraged by this unexpected result of what she must have looked upon as unexampled favor. In place of a grateful, devoted creature, identified with her interests, whose child should be to her as her own child, she finds herself confronted with an imperious rival, who lays claim to her place and position.

The struggle was one that has been witnessed many a time since in families so constituted, and with such false elements. Abraham, peace-loving and quiet, stands neutral; confident, as many men are, of the general ability of the female sex, by inscrutable ways and methods of their own, to find their way out of the troubles they bring themselves into. Probably he saw wrong on both sides; yet Hagar, as the dependent, who owed all the elevation on which she prided herself to the good-will of her mistress, was certainly the more in fault of the two; and so he dismisses the subject with: "Thy maid is in thy hand; do with her as pleaseth thee."

The next we hear of the proud, hot-hearted, ungoverned slave-girl, is her flight to the wilderness in a tumult of indignation and grief, doubtless after bitter words and hard usage from the once indulgent mistress. But now comes into the history the presence of the Father God, in whose eye all human beings are equal, and who looks down on the boiling strifes and hot passions of us all below, as a mother on the quarrels of little children in the nursery. For this was the world's infancy, and each character in the drama represented a future nation for whom the All-Father was caring.

So when the violent, desolate creature had sobbed herself weary in the lonesome desert, the story says: "And the angel of the Lord found her by a fountain of water, in the way to Shur. And he said, Hagar, Sarah's maid, whence camest thou? and whither wilt thou go? And she said, I flee from the face of my mistress, Sarah."

In this calm question there is a reminder of duty violated, and in the submissive answer is an acknowledgment of that duty. The angel calls her "Sarah's maid," and she replies, "my mistress, Sarah."

"And the angel of the Lord said unto her, Return to thy mistress, and submit thyself under her hands." Then, as with awe and submission she rises to go, she is comforted with promises of gracious tenderness. The All-Father does not take part with her in her rebellious pride, nor in her haughty desire to usurp the station and honors of her mistress, and yet he has sympathy for that strong, awakening feeling of motherhood which makes the wild girl of the desert begin at once to crave station and place on earth for the son she is to bring into it. So the story goes on: "And the angel of the Lord said unto her, I will multiply thy seed exceedingly, that it shall not be numbered for multitude. And the angel of the Lord said unto her, Behold, thou art with child, and shalt bear a son, and shalt call his name Ishmael, because the Lord hath heard thy affliction. And he will be a wild man; his hand will be against every man, and every man's hand against him; and he shall dwell in the presence of all his brethren. And she called the name of the Lord that spake unto her, Thou God seest me: for she said, Have I also here looked after him that seeth me?"

This little story is so universally and beautifully significant of our every-day human experience, that it has almost the force of an allegory.

Who of us has not yielded to despairing grief, while flowing by us were unnoticed sources of consolation? The angel did not *create* the spring in the desert: it was there all the while, but Hagar was blinded by her tears. She was not seeking God, but he was seeking her. How often may we, all of us, in the upliftings and deliverances of our life, say as she did, "Have I here looked after him that seeth me?"

The narrative adds, "Wherefore the spring was called *The Well of Him that Liveth and Seeth Me.*"

That spring is still flowing by our daily path.

So, quieted and subdued and comforted, Hagar returns to her

mistress and her home, and we infer from the story, that, with submission on her part, kindness and bounty returned on the part of her mistress. She again becomes a member of the family. Her son is born, and grows up for twelve years under the shadow of Abraham's tent, and evidently, from the narrative, is fondly beloved by his father, and indulgently treated by his foster-mother.

In an hour of confidential nearness the Divine Father announces to Abraham that a son shall be given him by the wife of his heart.

"As for Sarah, thy wife, I will bless her, and give thee a son of her, and she shall be a mother of nations; kings of people shall be of her. Then Abraham fell upon his face and laughed, and said in his heart: Shall a child be born to him that is an hundred years old, and shall Sarah, that is ninety years old, bear?" Yet, in this moment of triumphant joy, his heart yearns after Ishmael; "And Abraham said unto God: O that Ishmael might live before thee!" And the Divine answer is: "As for Ishmael, I have heard thee. Behold, I have blessed him, and will make him fruitful, and will multiply him exceedingly; twelve princes shall he beget, and I will make him a great nation."

But now comes the hour long waited for, of Sarah's triumph, — the fulfillment of the desires of her life. A generous heart would have sympathized in her triumph. A mother who had known the blessedness of motherhood would have rejoiced when the mistress who had done so much for her was made so joyful. If her own son be not the heir in succession, yet an assured future is promised to him. But the dark woman and her wild son are of untamable elements. They can no more become one in spirit with the patriarchal family, than oil can mix with water. When the weaning feast is made, and all surround the little Isaac, when the mother's heart overflows with joy, she sees the graceless Ishmael mocking; and instantly, with a woman's lightning prescience, she perceives the dangers, the impossibilities of longer keeping these aliens under the same roof, — the feuds, the jealousies, the fierce quarrels of the future.

"Cast out this bondwoman and her son," she says, with the

air of one accustomed to command and decide; "for the son of this bondwoman shall not be heir with my son, even with Isaac."

It appears that Abraham had set his heart on the boy, and had hoped to be able to keep both in one family, and divide his inheritance between them; but it was otherwise decreed. "And God said to Abraham, Let it not be grievous in thy sight, because of the lad and because of thy bondwoman: in all that Sarah hath said unto thee, hearken unto her voice; for in Isaac shall thy seed be called. And also of the son of the bondwoman will I make a nation, because he is thy seed. And Abraham arose up early, and took bread and a bottle of water and gave it to Hagar, putting it on her shoulder, and sent her away with the child; and she departed and wandered in the wilderness of Beersheba." Probably she was on the road towards Egypt. "And the water was all spent in the bottle, and she cast the child under one of the shrubs; and she went away and sat her down over against him a good way off, as it were a bow-shot, for she said, Let me not see the death of the child; and she lifted up her voice and wept."

Poor, fiery, impatient creature! — moaning like a wounded leopardess, — apparently with no heart to remember the kindly Power that once before helped her in her sorrows; but the story goes on: "And God heard the voice of the lad; and the angel of the Lord called to Hagar out of heaven, and said unto her, What aileth thee, Hagar? Fear not, for God hath heard the voice of the lad where he is. Arise, lift up the lad, and hold him in thy hand; for I will make of him a great nation. And God opened her eyes, and she saw a well of water; and she went and filled the bottle with water and gave the lad drink. And God was with the lad, and he grew, and dwelt in the wilderness and became an archer. And he dwelt in the wilderness of Paran; and his mother took him a wife out of the land of Egypt."

In all this story, nothing impresses us so much as the absence of all modern technical or theological ideas respecting the God who is represented here as sowing the seed of nations with a wise foresight of the future. As a skillful husbandman, bent on perfecting a certain seed, separates it from all others, and grows it by itself, so the Bible tells us that God selected a certain stock to be trained and cultivated into the sacerdotal race, through which should come his choicest revelations to man. Of this race in its final outcome and perfected flowering was to spring forth Jesus, spoken of as the BRANCH of this sacred tree. For the formation of this race, we see a constant choice of the gentler and quieter elements of blood and character, and the persistent rejection of that which is wild, fierce, and ungovernable. Yet it is with no fond partiality for the one, or antipathy to the other, that the Father of both thus decides. The thoughtful, patient, meditative Isaac is chosen; the wild, hot-blooded, impetuous Ishmael is rejected, — not as in themselves better or worse, but as in relation to their adaptation to a great purpose of future good to mankind. The ear of the All-Father is as near to the cry of the passionate, hot-tempered slave, and the moans of the wild, untamable boy, as to those of the patriarch. We are told that God was with Ishmael in his wild growth as a hunter in the desert, — his protector from harm, the guardian of his growing family, according to the promise made to Abraham.

When the aged patriarch is gathered to his fathers at the age of a hundred and seventy-five years, it is recorded: "And Abraham gave up the ghost in a good old age, an old man and full of years; and his sons, Isaac and Ishmael, buried him in the cave of Machpelah, in the field that Abraham purchased of the sons of Heth; there was Abraham buried, and Sarah his wife."

The subsequent history of the nation which Ishmael founded, shows that the promises of God were faithfully kept.

The Arab race has ever been a strongly marked people. They have been worshipers of the one God, and, at one time, under the califs, rose to a superiority in art, science, and literature beyond that of so-called Christian nations.

The race of Ishmael is yet as vigorous and as peculiar, and as likely to perpetuate itself, as the race of Isaac and Jacob; and as God was near to the cries and needs of the wild mother of the race and her wild offspring, so, doubtless, he has heard the prayer that has gone up from many an Arab tent in the desert.

The besetting sin of a select people is the growth of a spirit of haughty self-sufficiency among them. In time the Jews came to look upon themselves as God's only favorites, and upon all other nations as outcasts. It is this spirit that is rebuked by the prophet Amos (ix.) when, denouncing the recreant children of Israel, he says, in the name of the Lord: "Are ye not as children of the Ethiopians unto me, O children of Israel? saith the Lord. Have not I brought up Israel out of the land of Egypt? and the Philistines from Caphtor, and the Syrians from Kir?"

There is a deep comfort in this record of God's goodness to a poor, blinded, darkened, passionate slave-woman, nowise a model for imitation, yet tenderly watched over and succored and cared for in her needs. The Father unsought is ever seeking. He who said, "What aileth thee, Hagar?" is he who, in later times, said that he came to seek and to save the lost. Not to the saintly and the righteous only, or mostly, but to the wayward, the sinful, the desperate, the despairing, to those whose troubles come of their own folly and their own sin, is the angel sent to console, to promise, to open the blind eyes upon the fountain which is ever near us in life's desert, though we cannot perceive it.

HAGAR IN THE WILDERNESS.

THE morning broke. Light stole upon the clouds
With a strange beauty. Earth received again
Its garment of a thousand dyes; and leaves,
And delicate blossoms, and the painted flowers,
And everything that bendeth to the dew
And stirreth with the daylight, lifted up
Its beauty to the breath of that sweet morn.

All things are dark to sorrow; and the light
And loveliness and fragrant air were sad
To the dejected Hagar. The moist earth
Was pouring odors from its spicy pores,
And the young birds were singing as if life
Were a new thing to them; but oh! it came
Upon her heart like discord, and she felt
How cruelly it tries a broken heart,
To see a mirth in anything it loves.
She stood at Abraham's tent. Her lips were pressed
Till the blood started; and the wandering veins
Of her transparent forehead were swelled out,
As if her pride would burst them. Her dark eye
Was clear and tearless, and the light of heaven,
Which made its language legible, shot back
From her long lashes, as it had been flame.
Her noble boy stood by her, with his hand
Clasped in her own, and his round, delicate feet,
Scarce trained to balance on the tented floor,
Sandaled for journeying. He had looked up
Into his mother's face until he caught
The spirit there, and his young heart was swelling
Beneath his dimpled bosom, and his form
Straightened up proudly in his tiny wrath,
As if his light proportions would have swelled,
Had they but matched his spirit, to the man.

HAGAR IN THE WILDERNESS.

Why bends the patriarch as he cometh now
Upon his staff so wearily? His beard
Is low upon his breast, and his high brow,
So written with the converse of his God,
Beareth the swollen vein of agony.
His lip is quivering, and his wonted step
Of vigor is not there; and, though the morn
Is passing fair and beautiful, he breathes
Its freshness as it were a pestilence.
O, man may bear with suffering: his heart
Is a strong thing, and godlike, in the grasp
Of pain that wrings mortality; but tear
One chord affection clings to — part one tie
That binds him to a woman's delicate love —
And his great spirit yieldeth like a reed!

He gave to her the water and the bread,
But spoke no word, and trusted not himself
To look upon her face, but laid his hand
In silent blessing on the fair-haired boy,
And left her to her lot of loneliness.

Should Hagar weep? May slighted woman turn
And, as a vine the oak hath shaken off,
Bend lightly to her leaning trust again?
O no! by all her loveliness, by all
That makes life poetry and beauty, no!
Make her a slave; steal from her rosy cheek
By needless jealousies; let the last star
Leave her a watcher by your couch of pain;
Wrong her by petulance, suspicion, all
That makes her cup a bitterness, — yet give
One evidence of love, and earth has not
An emblem of devotedness like hers.
But oh! estrange her once — it boots not how —
By wrong or silence, — anything that tells
A change has come upon your tenderness, —
And there is not a feeling out of heaven
Her pride o'ermastereth not.

She went her way with a strong step and slow, —
Her pressed lip arched, and her clear eye undimmed,

As if it were a diamond, and her form
Borne proudly up, as if her heart breathed through.
Her child kept on in silence, though she pressed
His hand till it was pained; for he had caught,
As I have said, her spirit, and the seed
Of a stern nation had been breathed upon.

The morning past, and Asia's sun rode up
In the clear heaven, and every beam was heat.
The cattle of the hills were in the shade,
And the bright plumage of the Orient lay
On beating bosoms in her spicy trees.
It was an hour of rest! but Hagar found
No shelter in the wilderness, and on
She kept her weary way, until the boy
Hung down his head, and opened his parched lips
For water; but she could not give it him.
She laid him down beneath the sultry sky, —
For it was better than the close, hot breath
Of the thick pines, — and tried to comfort him;
But he was sore athirst, and his blue eyes
Were dim and bloodshot, and he could not know
Why God denied him water in the wild.
She sat a little longer, and he grew
Ghastly and faint, as if he would have died.
It was too much for her. She lifted him
And bore him farther on, and laid his head
Beneath the shadow of a desert shrub;
And, shrouding up her face, she went away,
And sat to watch, where he could see her not,
Till he should die; and, watching him, she mourned: —

"God stay thee in thine agony, my boy!
I cannot see thee die; I cannot brook
Upon thy brow to look,
And see death settle on my cradle joy.
How have I drunk the light of thy blue eye!
And could I see thee die?

"I did not dream of this when thou wast straying,
Like an unbound gazelle, among the flowers;
Or wiling the soft hours,

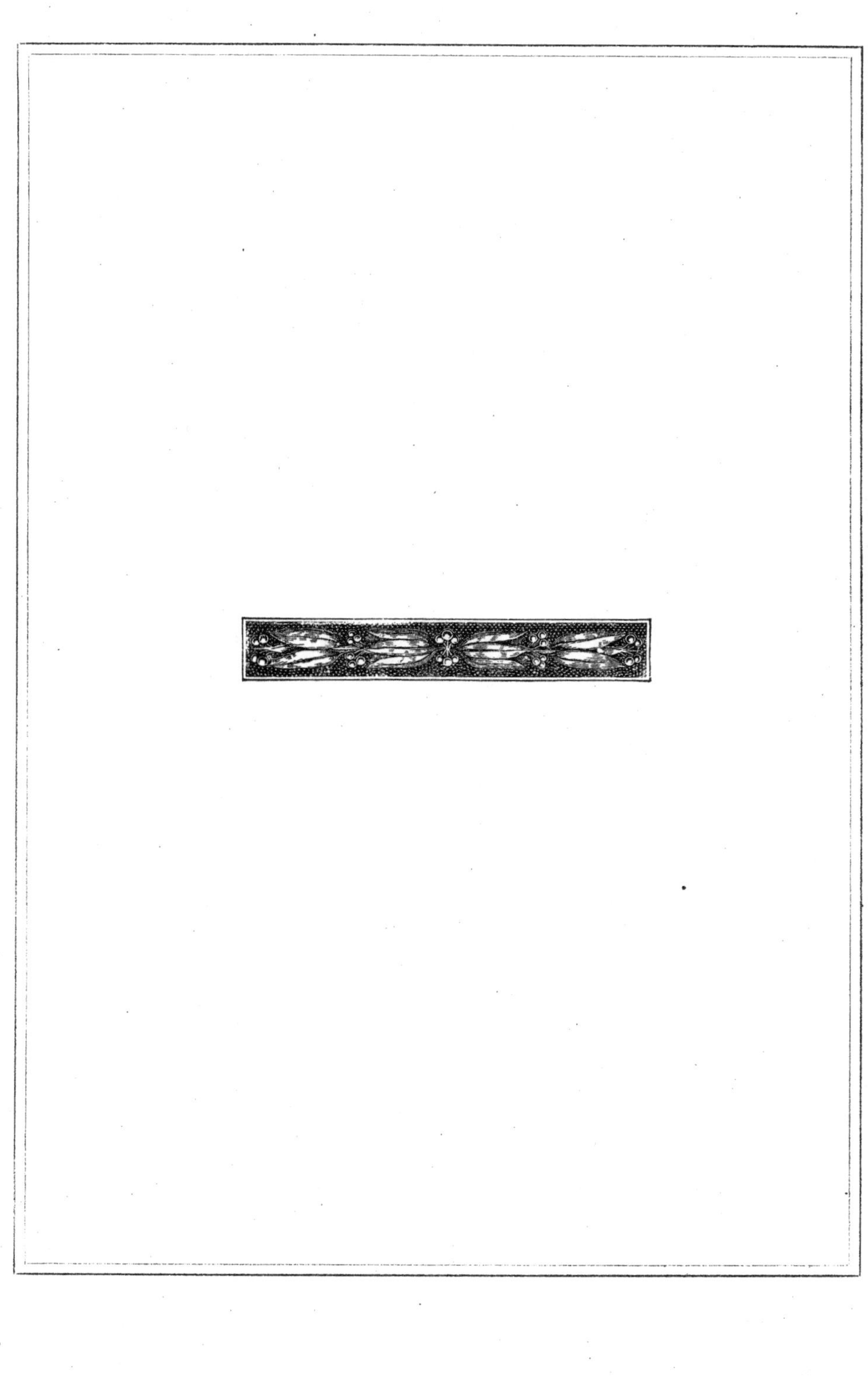

HAGAR IN THE WILDERNESS.

By the rich gush of water-sources playing,
Then sinking weary to thy smiling sleep,
So beautiful and deep.

"O no! and when I watched by thee the while,
And saw thy bright lip curling in thy dream,
And thought of the dark stream
In my own land of Egypt, the far Nile,
How prayed I that my father's land might be
A heritage for thee!

"And now the grave for its cold breast hath won thee,
And thy white, delicate limbs the earth will press;
And O, my last caress
Must feel thee cold, for a chill hand is on thee.
How can I leave my boy, so pillowed there
Upon his clustering hair!"

She stood beside the well her God had given
To gush in that deep wilderness, and bathed
The forehead of her child until he laughed
In his reviving happiness, and lisped
His infant thought of gladness at the sight
Of the cool plashing of his mother's hand.

Nathaniel P. Willis.

REBEKAH.

Landelle, *Pinx.* Jehenne, *Lith.*

REBEKAH THE BRIDE.

IN the pictures which the Bible opens to us of the domestic life of the patriarchal ages, we have one perfectly characteristic and beautiful idyl of a wooing and wedding, according to the customs of those days. In its sweetness and sacred simplicity, it is a marvelous contrast to the wedding of our modern fashionable life.

Sarah, the beautiful and beloved, has been laid away in the dust, and Isaac, the cherished son, is now forty years old. Forty years is yet early youth, by the slow old clock of the golden ages, when the thread of mortal life ran out to a hundred and seventy-five or eighty years. Abraham has nearly reached that far period, and his sun of life is dipping downwards toward the evening horizon. He has but one care remaining, — to settle his son Isaac in life before he is gathered to his fathers.

The scene in which Abraham discusses the subject with his head servant sheds a peculiar light on the domestic and family relations of those days. "And Abraham said unto his eldest servant of his house, that ruled over all that he had, Put, I pray thee, thy hand under my thigh: and I will make thee swear by the Lord, the God of heaven, and the God of the earth, that thou shalt not take a wife unto my son of the daughters of the Canaanites, among whom I dwell: but thou shalt go unto my country, and to my kindred, and take a wife unto my son Isaac. And the servant said unto him, Peradventure the woman will not be willing to follow me unto this land: must I needs bring thy son again unto the land from whence thou camest? And Abraham said unto him, Beware that thou bring not my son thither again. The Lord God of heaven, which took me from my father's house, and from the land of my kindred, and which spake unto me, and sware unto me, saying, Unto thy seed will I give this land;

he shall send his angel before thee; and thou shalt take a wife unto my son from thence. And if the woman will not be willing to follow thee, then thou shalt be clear from this my oath: only bring not my son thither again."

Here it is remarkable that the servant is addressed as the legal guardian of the son. Abraham does not caution Isaac as to whom he should marry, but cautions the old servant of the house concerning the woman to whom he should marry Isaac. It is apparently understood that, in case of Abraham's death, the regency in the family falls into the hands of this servant.

The picture of the preparations made for this embassy denotes a princely station and great wealth. "And the servant took ten camels of the camels of his master, and departed; for all the goods of his master were in his hand; and he arose, and went to Mesopotamia, unto the city of Nahor."

Now comes a quaint and beautiful picture of the manners of those pastoral days. "And he made his camels to kneel down without the city by a well of water, at the time of the evening, even the time that women go out to draw water."

Next, we have a specimen of the kind of prayer which obtained in those simple times, when men felt as near to God as a child does to its mother. Kneeling, uncovered, in the evening light, the gray old serving-man thus talks to the invisible Protector: — "O Lord God of my master Abraham, I pray thee, send me good speed this day, and show kindness unto my master Abraham. Behold, I stand here by the well of water; and the daughters of the men of the city come out to draw water: and let it come to pass that the damsel to whom I shall say, Let down thy pitcher, I pray thee, that I may drink; and she shall say, Drink, and I will give thy camels drink also: let the same be she that thou hast appointed for thy servant Isaac; and thereby shall I know that thou hast showed kindness unto my master."

This is prayer. Not a formal, ceremonious state address to a monarch, but the talk of the child with his father, asking simply and directly for what is wanted here and now. And the request was speedily granted, for thus the story goes on: "And it came to pass, before he had done speaking, that, behold, Rebekah came out, who was born to Bethuel, son of Milcah, the wife of Nahor, Abraham's brother." It is noticeable, how strong is the sensibility to womanly beauty in this narrative. This young Rebekah is thus announced: "And the damsel was very fair to look upon, and a virgin, and she went down to the well, and filled her pitcher, and came up." Drawn by the bright eyes and fair face, the old servant hastens to apply the test, doubtless hoping that this lovely creature is the one appointed for his young master. "And the servant ran to meet her, and said, Let me, I pray thee, drink a little water of thy pitcher. And she said, Drink, my lord: and she hastened, and let down her pitcher upon her hand, and gave him drink." She gave with a will, with a grace and readiness that overflowed the request; and then it is added: "And when she had done giving him drink, she said, I will draw water for thy camels also, until they have done drinking. And she hasted and emptied her pitcher into the trough, and ran again unto the well to draw water, and drew for all his camels." Let us fancy ten camels, all on their knees in a row, at the trough, with their long necks, and patient, careworn faces, while the pretty young Jewess, with cheerful alacrity, is dashing down the water from her pitcher, filling and emptying in quick succession, apparently making nothing of the toil; the gray-haired old servant looking on in devout recognition of the answer to his prayer, for the story says: "And the man wondering at her, held his peace, to wit [know] whether the Lord had made his journey prosperous or not."

There was wise penetration into life and the essentials of wedded happiness in this prayer of the old servant. What he asked for his young master was not beauty or talent, but a ready and unfailing outflow of sympathy and kindness. He sought not merely for a gentle nature, a kind heart, but for a heart so rich in kindness that it should run even beyond what was asked, and be ready to anticipate the request with new devices of helpfulness. The lively, light-hearted kindness that could not be content with waiting on the thirsty old man, but with cheerful alacrity took upon herself the care of all the ten camels, this was a gift beyond that of beauty; yet when it came in the person of a maiden exceedingly fair to look upon, no marvel that the old man wondered joyously at his success.

When the camels had done drinking, he produced from his treasury a golden earring and bracelets, with which he adorned the maiden. "And he said to her, Whose daughter art thou? tell me, I pray thee; is there room in thy father's house for us to lodge in? And she said unto him, I am the daughter of Bethuel the son of Milcah, which she bare to Nahor. She said, moreover, unto him, We have both straw and provender enough, and room to lodge in. And the man bowed down his head, and worshiped the Lord. And he said, Blessed be the Lord God of my master Abraham, who hath not left destitute my master of his mercy and his truth: I being in the way, the Lord led me to the house of my master's brethren."

We may imagine the gay delight with which the pretty maiden ran to exhibit the gifts of jewelry that had thus unexpectedly descended upon her. Laban, her brother, does not prove either a generous or hospitable person in the outcome of the story; but the ambassador of a princely relative, traveling with a caravan of ten camels, and showering gold and jewels, makes his own welcome. The narrative proceeds: — "And it came to pass when he saw the earring, and the bracelets upon his sister's hands, and when he heard the words of Rebekah his sister, saying, Thus spake the man unto me; that he came unto the man; and, behold, he stood by the camels at the well. And he said, Come in, thou blessed of the Lord; wherefore standest thou without? for I have prepared the house, and room for the camels. And the man came into the house: and he ungirded the camels, and gave straw and provender for the camels, and water to wash his feet, and the men's feet that were with him. And there was set meat before him to eat: but he said, I will not eat, till I have told my errand. And he said, Speak on. And he said, I am Abraham's servant, and the Lord hath blessed my master greatly, and he is become great: and he hath given him flocks, and herds, and silver, and gold, and men-servants, and maid-servants, and camels, and asses."

After this exordium he goes on to tell the whole story of his oath to his master, and the purport of his journey; of the prayer that he had uttered at the well, and of its fulfillment in a generous-minded and beautiful young maiden; and thus he ends his story: "And I bowed down my head, and worshiped the Lord, and blessed the Lord God of my master Abraham, which hath led me in the right way to take my master's brother's daughter unto his son. And now, if ye will deal kindly and truly with my master, tell me: and if not, tell me; that I may turn to the right hand or to the left. Then Laban and Bethuel answered and said, The thing proceedeth from the Lord: we cannot speak unto thee bad or good. Behold, Rebekah is before thee; take her, and go, and let her be thy master's son's wife, as the Lord hath spoken. And it came to pass, that when Abraham's servant heard their words, he worshiped the Lord, bowing himself to the earth."

And now comes a scene most captivating to female curiosity. Even in patriarchal times the bridegroom, it seems, provided a *corbeille de mariage;* for we are told: "And the servant brought forth jewels of silver, and jewels of gold, and raiment, and gave them to Rebekah; he gave also to her brother and to her mother precious things." The scene of examining jewelry and garments and rich stuffs in the family party would have made no mean subject for a painter. No wonder such a suitor, sending such gifts, found welcome entertainment. So the story goes on: "And they did eat and drink, he and the men that were with him, and tarried all night; and they rose up in the morning; and he said, Send me away unto my master. And her brother and her mother said, Let the damsel abide with us a few days, at the least ten, and after that she shall go. And he said unto them, Hinder me not, seeing the Lord hath prospered my way; send me away, that I may go to my master. And they said, We will call the damsel and inquire at her mouth. And they called Rebekah, and said unto her, Wilt thou go with this man? And she said, I will go. And they sent away Rebekah their sister, and her nurse, and Abraham's servant and his men. And they blessed Rebekah, and said unto her, Thou art our sister; be thou the mother of thousands of millions, and let thy seed possess the gate of those which hate them." The idea of being a mother of nations gives a sort of dignity to the married life of these patriarchal women, — it was the motherly instinct made sublime.

Thus far, this wooing seems to have been conceived and conducted in that simple religious spirit recognized in the words of the old prayer: "Grant that all our works may be begun, continued, and ended in thee." The Father of Nations has been a never-failing presence in every scene.

The expectant bridegroom seems to have been a youth of a pensive, dreamy, meditative nature. Brought up with the strictest notions of filial submission, he waits to receive his wife dutifully from his father's hand. Yet, as the caravan nears the encampment, he walks forth to meet them. "And Isaac went out to meditate in the field at the eventide: and he lifted up his eyes, and saw, and, behold, the camels were coming. And Rebekah lifted up her eyes, and when she saw Isaac, she lighted off the camel. For she had said unto the servant, What man is this that walketh in the field to meet us? And the servant had said, It is my master: therefore she took a veil, and covered herself."

In the little that is said of Rebekah, we see always that alert readiness, prompt to see and do what is to be done at the moment. No dreamer is she, but a lively and wide-awake young woman, who knows her own mind exactly, and has the fit word and fit action ready for each short turn in life. She was quick, cheerful, and energetic in hospitality. She was prompt and unhesitating in her resolve; and yet, at the moment of meeting, she knew the value and the propriety of the *veil.* She covered herself, that she might not unsought be won.

With a little touch of pathos, the story ends: "And Isaac brought her into his mother Sarah's tent, and took Rebekah, and she became his wife; and he loved her: and Isaac was comforted after his mother's death." We see here one of those delicate and tender natures that find repose first in the love of a mother, and, when that stay is withdrawn, lean upon a beloved wife.

So ideally pure, and sweet, and tenderly religious has been the whole inception and carrying on and termination of this wedding, that Isaac and Rebekah have been remembered in the wedding ritual of the catholic Christian churches as models of a holy marriage according to the Divine will. "Send thy blessing upon these thy servants, this man and this woman, whom we bless in thy name; that as Isaac and Rebekah lived faithfully together, so these persons may surely perform and keep the vow and covenant between them."

In the subsequent history of the family, the dramatic individuality of the characters is kept up: Isaac is the gentle, thoughtful, misty dreamer, lost in sentiment and contemplation; and Rebekah the forward, cheerful, self-confident manager of external things. We can fancy it as one of the households where all went as the mother said. In fact, in mature life, we see these prompt and managing traits, leading the matron to domestic artifices which could only be justified to herself by her firm belief that the end pursued was good enough to sanctify the means. Energetic, lively, self-trustful young women do sometimes form just such managing and diplomatic matrons.

Isaac, the husband, always dreamy and meditative, becomes old and doting; conceives an inordinate partiality for the turbulent son Esau, whose skill in hunting supplies his table with the meat he loves. Rebekah has heard the prophetic legend, that Jacob, the younger son, is the chosen one to perpetuate the sacred race; and Jacob, the tender, the care-taking, the domestic, is the idol of her heart.

Now, there are some sorts of women that, if convinced there was such a Divine oracle or purpose in relation to a favorite son, would have rested upon it in quiet faith, and left Providence to work out its ends in its own way and time. Not so Rebekah. The same restless activity of helpfulness that led her to offer water to all the camels, when asked to give drink for the servant, now led her to come to the assistance of Providence. She proposes to Jacob to make the oracle sure, and obtain the patriarchal blessing by stratagem. When Jacob expresses a humble doubt whether such an artifice may not defeat itself and bring on him the curse rather than the blessing of his father, the mother characteristically answers: "Upon me be the curse, my son:

only obey my voice." Pages of description could not set a character before us more sharply and distinctly than this one incident, and nothing can show more dramatically in whose hands was the ruling power in that family.

The managing, self-reliant Rebekah, ready to do her full share in every emergency, and to run before every occasion with her busy plannings, is not a character of patriarchal ages merely. Every age has repeated it, and our own is no exception. There are not wanting among us cheerful, self-confident, domestic managers, who might take a lesson from the troubles that befell the good-hearted, but too busy and officious Rebekah, in consequence of the success of her own schemes. The account of this belongs to our next chapter.

ISAAC MEDITATING.

"And Isaac went out to meditate in the field at the eventide: and he lifted up his eyes, and saw, and, behold, the camels were coming. And Rebekah lifted up her eyes, and when she saw Isaac, she lighted off the camel. For she had said unto the servant, What man is this that walketh in the field to meet us? And the servant had said, It is my master: therefore she took a vail, and covered herself. And the servant told Isaac all things that he had done. And Isaac brought her into his mother Sarah's tent, and took Rebekah, and she became his wife; and he loved her: and Isaac was comforted after his mother's death." — GEN. xxiv. 63-67.

IN the lone field he walks at eventide,
To meditate beneath the open sky,
Where born on lighter wings prayers upward fly,
And down from Heaven sweet answers swiftly glide.
But as he glanced around that landscape wide,
Far off a train of camels meets his eye,
And as they nearer come he can descry
A maiden vailed, — his unseen, God-sent bride.
Thus while to Heaven thought after thought was rising,
The fair Rebekah step by step drew nigh,
With life's chief joy the prayerful saint surprising:
For those who think of Him God still is thinking,
With tender condescension from on high,
Some comfort ever to some duty linking.

Rev. R. Wilton.

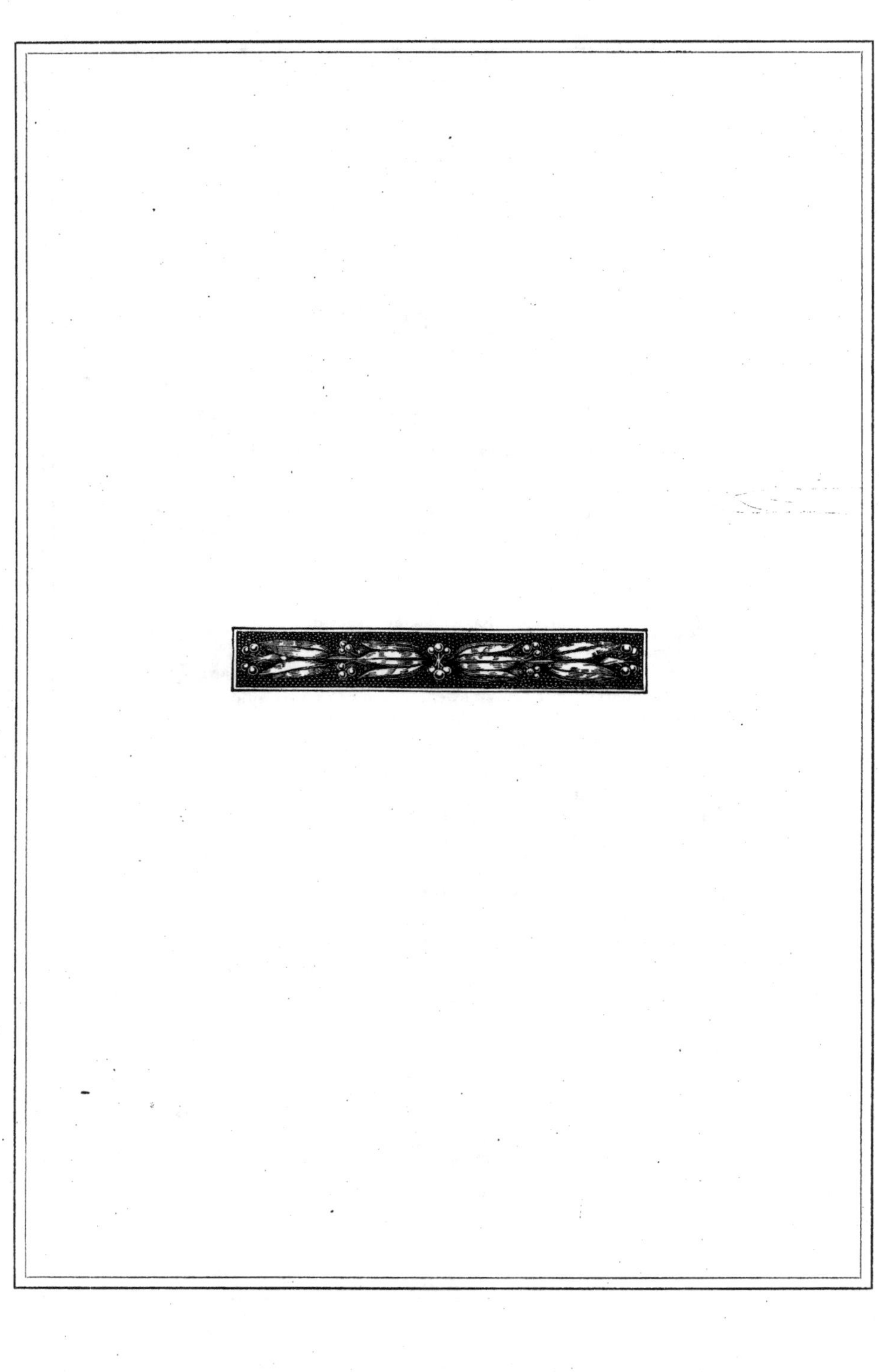

LEAH AND RACHEL.

PORTAELS, *Pinx.* JEHENNE, *Lith.*

LEAH AND RACHEL.

IN the earlier portions of the Old Testament we have, very curiously, the history of the deliberate formation of an influential race, to which was given a most important mission in the world's history. The principle of *selection*, much talked of now in science, is the principle which is represented in the patriarchal history as operating under a direct Divine guidance. From the calling of Abraham, there seems to have been this continued watchfulness in selecting the party through whom the chosen race was to be continued. Every marriage thus far is divinely appointed and guided. While the Fatherly providence and nurture is not withdrawn from the rejected ones, still the greatest care is exercised to separate from them the chosen. The latter are selected apparently not so much for moral excellence in itself considered, as for excellence in relation to stock. The peaceable, domestic, prudent, and conservative elements are uniformly chosen, in preference to the warlike and violent characteristics of the age.

The marriage of Isaac and Rebekah was more like the type of a Christian marriage than any other on record. No other wife shared a place in his heart and home; and, even to old age, Isaac knew no other than the bride of his youth. From this union sprang twin boys; between whom, as is often the case, there was a remarkable difference. The physical energy and fire all seemed to go to one, the gentler and more quiet traits to the other. Esau was the wild huntsman, the ranger of the mountains, delighting in force, — precisely adapted to become the chief of a predatory tribe. Jacob, the patient, the prudent, the submissive, was the home child, the darling of his mother. Now, with every constitutional excellency and virtue is inevitably connected, in our imperfect humanity, the liability to a fault. The peace-loving and prudent, averse to strife, are liable to sins of artifice and deception, as stronger natures are to those of force and violence. Probably, in the calm eye of Him who sees things just as they are, the one kind of fault is no worse than the other. At all events, the sacred narrative is a daguerreotype of character; it reflects every trait and every imperfection without comment. The mild and dreamy Isaac, to save his wife from a rapacious king, undertakes to practice the same artifice that his father used before him, saying, "She is my sister"; and the same evil consequence ensues. The lesson of artifice once taught in the family, the evil spreads. Rebekah, when Isaac is old and doting, commands Jacob to personate his older brother, and thus gain the patriarchal blessing, which in those days had the force of a last will and testament in our times. Yet, through all the faults and errors of the mere human actors runs the thread of a Divine guidance. Before the birth of Jacob it was predicted that he should be the chosen head of the forming nation; and by his mother's artifice, and his own participation in it, that prediction is fulfilled. Yet the natural punishment of the action follows. Esau is alienated, and meditates murder in his heart; and Jacob, though the mother's darling, is driven out from his home a hunted fugitive, parted from her for life. He starts on foot to find his way to Padan-Aram, to his father's kindred, there to seek and meet and woo the wife appointed for him.

It is here that the history of the patriarch Jacob becomes immediately helpful to all men in all ages. And its usefulness consists in just this, — that Jacob, at this time in his life, was no saint or hero. He was not a person distinguished either by intellect or by high moral attainment, but simply such a raw, unformed lad as life is constantly casting adrift from the shelter of homes. He is no better and no worse than the multitude of boys, partly good and partly bad, who, for one reason or another, are forced to leave their mothers and their fathers; to take staff in hand and start out on the great life-journey alone. He had been religiously brought up; he knew that his father and his mother had a God, — the Invisible God of Abraham and Isaac; but then, other gods and lords many were worshiped in the tribes around him, and how did he know, after all, which was the right one? He wanders on over the wide, lonesome Syrian plains, till dark night comes on, and he finds himself all alone, an atom in the great silent creation,—alone, as many a sailor-boy has found himself on the deck of his ship, or hunter, in the deep recesses of the forest. The desolate lad gathers a heap of stones for a pillow and lies down to sleep. Nothing could be more sorrowfully helpless than this picture; the representative portrait of many a mother's boy to-day, and in all days. We cannot suppose that he prayed or commended his soul to God. We are told distinctly that he did not even remember that God was in that place. He lies down, helpless and forlorn, on his cold stone pillow, and sinks, overcome with fatigue, to prayerless slumber. And now, in his dreams, a glorious light appears; a luminous path opens upward to the skies,—angels are passing to and fro upon it, and above, in bright benignity, stands a visible form, and says: "I am the Lord God of Abraham thy father, and the God of Isaac: the land whereon thou liest, to thee will I give it, and to thy seed; and thy seed shall be as the dust of the earth; and thou shalt spread abroad to the west, and to the east, and to the north, and to the south; and in thee and in thy seed shall all the families of the earth be blessed. And, behold, I am with thee, and will keep thee in all places whither thou goest, and will bring thee again unto this land; for I will not leave thee, until I have done that which I have spoken to thee of. And Jacob awaked out of his sleep, and he said, Surely the Lord is in this place; and I knew it not. And he was afraid, and said, How dreadful is this place! This is none other but the house of God, and this is the gate of heaven. And Jacob arose up early in the morning, and took the stone that he had put for his pillow, and set it up for a pillar, and poured oil upon the top of it. And Jacob vowed a vow, saying, If God will be with me, and will keep me in this way that I go, and will give me bread to eat, and raiment to put on, so that I come again to my father's house in peace, then shall the Lord be my God: and this stone, which I have set for a pillar, shall be God's house: and of all that Thou shalt give me I will surely give the tenth unto thee."

In one night how much is born in that soul! The sentiment of reverence, awe of the Divine, — a conviction of the reality of God and an invisible world, — and the beginning of that great experiment by which man learns practically that God is his father. For, in the outset, every human being's consciousness of God must be just of this sort. Have I a Father in heaven? Does he care for me? Will he help me? Questions that each man can only answer as Jacob did, by casting himself upon God in a matter-of-fact, practical way in the exigencies of this present life. And this history is the more valuable because it takes man in his earlier stages of imperfection. We are apt to feel that it might be safe for Paul, or Isaiah, or other great saints, to expect God to befriend them; but here a poor, untaught shepherd boy, who is not religious, avows that, up to this time, he has had no sense of God; and yet between him and heaven there is a pathway, and about him in his loneliness are ministering spirits; and the God of Abraham and of Isaac is ready to become his friend. In an important sense, this night dream, this gracious promise of God to Jacob, are not merely for him, but for all erring, helpless, suffering sons of men. In the fatherly God thus revealed to the patriarch, we see the first fruits of the promise that through him all nations should be blessed.

The next step of the drama shows us a scene of sylvan simplicity. About the old well in Haran, shepherds are waiting with their flocks, when the stripling approaches: "And Jacob said unto them, My brethren, whence be ye? And they said, Of Haran are we. And he said unto them, Know ye Laban the son of Nahor? And they said, We know him. And he said unto them, Is he well? And they said, He is well: and, behold, Rachel his daughter cometh with the sheep. And he said, Lo, it is yet high day, neither is it time that the cattle should be gathered together. Water ye the sheep, and go and feed them. And they said, We cannot, until all the flocks be gathered together, and till they roll the stone from the well's mouth; then we water the sheep. And while he yet spake with them Rachel came with her father's sheep; for she kept them. And it came to pass, when Jacob saw Rachel, the daughter of Laban, his mother's brother, and the sheep of Laban, his mother's brother, that Jacob went near, and rolled the stone from the well's mouth, and watered the flock of Laban, his mother's brother. And Jacob kissed Rachel, and lifted up his voice, and wept; and Jacob told Rachel that he was her father's brother, and that he was Rebekah's son: and she ran and told her father. And it came to pass, when Laban heard the tidings of Jacob, his sister's son, that he ran to meet him, and embraced him, and kissed him, and brought him to his house."

In the story of Isaac, we have the bridegroom who is simply the submissive recipient of a wife at his father's hands; in that of Jacob, we have the story of love at first sight. The wanderer, exiled from home, gives up his heart at once to the keeping of his beautiful shepherdess cousin, and so, when the terms of service are fixed with the uncle, the narrative says: "And Laban had two daughters; the name of the elder was Leah, and the name of the younger was Rachel. Leah was tender-eyed; but Rachel was beautiful and well-favored. And Jacob loved Rachel, and said, I will serve thee seven years for Rachel, thy younger daughter. And Jacob served seven years for Rachel, and they seemed unto him but a few days, for the love he had to her."

But when the wedding comes, in the darkness and secrecy of the night a false bride is imposed on the lover. And Jacob awoke, and behold it was Leah. Not the last man was he who has awakened, after the bridal, to find his wife was not the woman he had taken her to be. But the beloved one is given as a second choice, and seven years more of service are imposed as her price.

The characteristics of these two sisters, Leah and Rachel, are less vividly given than those of any of the patriarchal women. Sarah, Hagar, and Rebekah are all sharply defined characters, in and of themselves; but of Leah and Rachel almost all that can be said is that they were Jacob's wives, and mothers of the twelve tribes of Israel.

The character of their father Laban was narrow, shrewd, and hard, devoid of any generous or interesting trait, and the daughters appear to have grown up under a narrowing and repressing influence. What we learn of them in the story shows the envies, the jealousies, the bickerings and heart-burnings of poorly developed natures. Leah, the less beloved one, exults over her handsomer and more favored sister because she has been made a fruitful mother, while to Rachel the gift of children is denied. Rachel murmurs and pines, and says to her husband, "Give me children, or I die." The desire for offspring in those days seemed to be an agony. To be childless, was disgrace and misery unspeakable. At last, however, Rachel becomes a mother and gives birth to Joseph, the best-beloved of his father. The narrative somehow suggests that charm of personal beauty and manner which makes Rachel the beloved one, and her child dearer than all the rest. How many such women there are, pretty and charming, and holding men's hearts like a fortress, of whom a biographer could say nothing only that they were much beloved!

When Jacob flees from Laban with his family, we find Rachel secretly taking away the images which her father had kept as household gods. The art by which she takes them, the effrontery with which she denies the possession of them, when her father comes to search for them, shows that she had little moral elevation. The belief in the God of her husband probably was mixed up confusedly in her childish mind with the gods of her father. Not unfrequently in those dim ages, people seemed to alternate from one to the other, as occasions varied. Yet she seems to have held her husband's affections to the last; and when, in giving birth to her last son, she died, this son became the darling of his father's old age. The sacred poet has made the name of this beloved wife a proverb, to express the strength of the motherly instinct, and "Rachel weeping for her children" is a line that immortalizes her name to all time.

Whatever be the faults of these patriarchal women, it must be confessed that the ardent desire of motherhood which inspired them is far nobler than the selfish, unwomanly spirit of modern times, which regards children only as an encumbrance and a burden. The motherly yearning and motherly spirit give a certain dignity to these women of primitive ages, which atones for many faults of imperfect development.

Twenty-one years elapse, and Jacob, a man of substance, father of a family of twelve children, with flocks and herds to form a numerous caravan, leaves the service of his hard master to go back to his father. The story shows the same traits in the man as in the lad. He is the gentle, affectionate, prudent, kindly, care-taking family-man, faithful in duty, and evading oppression by quiet skill rather than meeting it with active opposition. He has become rich, in spite of every effort of an aggressive master to prevent it.

When leaving Laban's service, he thus appeals to him: "These twenty years have I been with thee: thy ewes and thy she-goats have not cast their young, and the rams of thy flock have I not eaten. That which was torn of beasts I brought not unto thee; I bare the loss of it. Thus was I: in the day the drought consumed me, and the frost by night, and my sleep departed from mine eyes. Thus have I been twenty years in thy house. I served thee fourteen years for thy two daughters, and six years for thy cattle; and thou hast changed my wages ten times. Except the God of my father, the God of Abraham, and the fear of Isaac, had been with me, surely thou hadst sent me away now empty. God hath seen my affliction and the labor of my hands, and rebuked thee yesternight."

To the last of the history of Jacob, we see the same man, —careful, patient, faithful, somewhat despondent, wrapped up in family ties and cares, and needing at every step to lean on a superior power. And the Father on whom he seeks to lean is never wanting to him, as he will never be to any of us, however weak, or faulty, or blind. As the caravan nears home, news is brought that Esau, with an army of horsemen, is galloping to meet him. Then says the record: "Jacob was greatly afraid and distressed: and Jacob said, O God of my father Abraham, the God of my father Isaac, the Lord which saidst unto me, Return unto thy country and to thy kindred, and I will deal well with thee: I am not worthy of the least of all the mercies and of all the truth which thou hast showed unto thy servant: for with my staff I passed over this Jordan; and now I am become two bands. Deliver me, I pray thee, from the hand of my brother, from the hand of Esau; for I fear him, lest he will come and smite me, and the mother with the children. And thou saidst, I will surely do thee good, and make thy seed as the sand of the sea, which cannot be numbered for multitude." The prayer is not in vain. That night a mysterious stranger meets Jacob in the twilight shadows of morning. He seeks to detain him; but, as afterwards, when the disciples met an unknown Friend on the way to Emmaus, he made as though he would go farther. So now this stranger struggles in the embrace of the patriarch. Who, then, is this?—is it the Divine One? The thought thrills through the soul as Jacob strives to detain him. There is something wildly poetic in the legend. "And he said, Let me go, for the day breaketh. And he said, I will not let thee go, except thou bless me. And he said unto him, What is thy name? And he said, Jacob. And he said, Thy name shall be called no more Jacob, but Israel: for as a prince hast thou power with God and with men, and hast prevailed. And Jacob asked him: Tell me, I pray thee, thy name. And he said, Wherefore dost thou ask after my name? And he blessed him there. And Jacob called the name of the place Peniel, for he said, I have seen God face to face, and my life is preserved." God's love to man, the power of man's weakness and sorrow over the Father-heart, were never more beautifully shown than in this sacred idyl. The God of Abraham, Isaac, and Jacob; the God of the weak, the sinful, the despondent, the defenceless, the helper of the helpless,—He is the God of this sacred story; and so long as man is erring, and consciously frail, so long as he needs an ever-present and ever-loving Friend and Helper, so long will this story of Jacob be dear to the human heart.

JACOB'S DREAM.

THE sun was sinking on the mountain zone
  That guards thy vales of beauty, Palestine!
And lovely from the desert rose the moon,
  Yet lingering on the horizon's purple line,
Like a pure spirit o'er its earthly shrine.
  Up Bethel's rocky height abrupt and bare
A pilgrim toiled, and oft on day's decline
  Looked pale, then paused for eve's delicious air;
The summit gained, he knelt, and breathed his evening prayer.

He spread his cloak, and slumbered; darkness fell
  Upon the twilight hills; a sudden sound
Of silver trumpets o'er him seemed to swell,
  Clouds heavy with the tempest gathered round;
Yet was the whirlwind in its cavern bound;
  Still deeper rolled the darkness from on high,
Gigantic volume upon volume wound;—
  Above, a pillar shooting to the sky;
Below, a mighty sea that spread incessantly.

Voices are heard, a choir of golden strings,
  Low winds, whose breath is loaded with the rose:
Then chariot-wheels, the nearer rush of wings;
  Pale lightning round the dark pavilion glows.
It thunders; the resplendent gates unclose;
  Far as the eye can glance, on height o'er height
Rise fiery waving wings, and star-crowned brows,
  Millions on millions, brighter and more bright,
Till all is lost in one supreme, unmingled light.

But two beside the sleeping pilgrim stand,
  Like cherub kings, with lifted, mighty plume,
Fixed, sun-bright eyes, and looks of high command:
  They tell the Patriarch of his glorious doom;
Father of countless myriads that shall come,
  Sweeping the land like billows of the sea,
Bright as the stars of heaven from twilight's gloom,
  Till HE is given whom angels long to see,
And Israel's splendid line is crowned with Deity.

Rev. George Croly.

JACOB'S PILLOW.

THE bed was earth, the raisèd pillow stones,
  Whereon poor Jacob rests his head, his bones;
  Heaven was his canopy; the shades of night
Were his drawn curtains, to exclude the light.

Poor state for Israel's heir! it seems to me
His cattle found as soft a bed as he:
Yet God appearèd there, his joy, his crown;
God is not always seen in beds of down.

O, if that God shall please to make my bed,
I care not where I rest my bones, my head;
With Him, my wants can never prove extreme;
With Jacob's pillow give me Jacob's dream.

Philip Quarles.

DIRGE OF RACHEL.

(Gen. xxxv. 19.)

AND Rachel lies in Ephrath's land,
Beneath her lonely oak of weeping;
With mouldering heart, and withering hand,
The sleep of death forever sleeping.

The Spring comes smiling down the vale,
The lilies and the roses bringing;
But Rachel never more shall hail
The flowers that in the world are springing.

The Summer gives his radiant day,
And Jewish dames the dance are treading;
But Rachel, on her couch of clay,
Sleeps all unheeded and unheeding.

The Autumn's ripening sunbeam shines,
And reapers to the field are calling;
But Rachel's voice no longer joins
The choral song at twilight's falling.

The Winter sends his drenching shower,
And sweeps his howling blast around her;
But earthly storms possess no power
To break the slumber that hath bound her.

Thus round and round the Seasons go,
But joy or grief no more betide her;
For Rachel's bosom could not know,
Though friends were housed in death beside her.

Yet Time shall come, as prophets say,
  Whose dreams with glorious things are blended,
When Seasons, on their changeful way,
  Shall wend not as they long have wended.

Yes, Time shall come, when flowers that bloom
  Shall meet no storm their bloom to wither;
When friends, rejoicing from the tomb,
  Have gone to heavenly climes together.

William Knox.

WOMEN OF THE NATIONAL PERIOD.

UNIV.
OF
MICH.

MIRIAM AND MOSES.

DELAROCHE, *Pinx.* JEHENNE, *Lith.*

MIRIAM, SISTER OF MOSES.

IT has been remarked by Montalembert that almost all the great leading men in history have been intimately associated with superior women. If we look on Moses in a merely human light, and judge him by what he accomplished, as we do other historic characters, he is in certain respects the greatest man of antiquity. The works of the legislators, kings, and conquerors of ancient history were perishable. Their cities have crumbled, their governments and commonwealths have dissolved as waves of the sea. Moses alone founded a nation that still lives with an imperishable vitality, — a people whose religious literature still expresses the highest aspirations of the most cultivated nations of the earth.

His advent, therefore, forms an era in the history of humanity, and the very opening of his career presents us with pictures of imposing and venerable female characters. The mother of Moses is mentioned, in the epistle to the Hebrews, as one of those worthies of ancient time, who triumphed over things seen by the power of a sublime faith in the invisible God and his promises. The very name of the mother (Exodus vi. 20), Jochebed, — "the glory of Jehovah," — shows that a deep spirit of religious enthusiasm and trust was the prevailing impulse in the family. She was of that moral organization whence, through the laws of descent, might spring the prophet and prophetess. By *faith* she refused to obey the cruel order of the king, and for three months hid the beautiful child.

And here comes in the image of the first, and one of the most revered, of the race of Hebrew prophetesses, Miriam, the elder sister of Moses. According to the Rabbinic tradition, the gift of prophecy descended upon her even in childhood. The story is that Miriam's mother, Jochebed, was one of the midwives to whom Pharaoh gave the command to destroy the children, and that when the child Miriam heard it, being then only five years old, her face flushed scarlet, and she said in anger: "Woe to this man! God will punish him for his evil deeds." After this the tradition says that when the decree went forth for the destruction of every male child, Amram separated himself from his wife Jochebed, lest he should bring on her the anguish of fruitless motherhood. After three years, the spirit of prophecy came on Miriam as she sat in the house, and she cried out suddenly: "My parents shall have another son, who shall deliver Israel out of the hands of the Egyptians." The angel Gabriel guided Amram back to find his wife, whom he found blooming in all the beauty of youth, though more than a hundred years old. When she found herself with child, she feared that it might prove a boy, to be cruelly slain. Then the Eternal One spake in a dream to the father, bidding him be of good cheer, for he would protect the child, and all nations should hold him in honor.

The tradition goes on to say that the boy was born without pain, and that when he was born the whole house was filled with a light as of bright sunshine. The mother's anxiety was increased when she saw the beauty of the child, who was lovely as an angel of God. The parents called him Tobias, "God is good," to express their thankfulness, and Amram kissed Miriam on the brow and said: "Now know I that thy prophecy is come true."

In contrast to this ornate narrative is the grave and chaste simplicity of the Scripture story. It is all comprised in two or three verses of the second chapter of Exodus. "And there went a man of the house of Levi, and took to wife a daughter of Levi. And the woman conceived, and bare a son: and when she saw him that he was a goodly child she hid him three months. And when she could no longer hide him, she took for him an ark of bulrushes, and daubed it with slime and with pitch, and put the child therein and laid it in the flags by the river's brink. And his sister stood afar off to see what would be done to him. And the daughter of Pharaoh came down to wash herself at the river; and her maidens walked along the river's side: and when she saw the ark among the flags, she sent her maid to fetch it. And when she had opened it, she saw the child: and behold, the babe wept. And she had compassion on him and said: This is one of the Hebrew children. Then said his sister to Pharaoh's daughter, Shall I go and call to thee a nurse of the Hebrew women, that she may nurse the child for thee? And Pharaoh's daughter said unto her, Go. And the maid went and called the child's mother. And Pharaoh's daughter said, Take this child away, and nurse it for me, and I will give thee thy wages; and the woman took the child and nursed it. And the child grew, and she brought him unto Pharaoh's daughter, and she called his name Moses: and she said, Because I drew him out of the water."

To this, we may add the account which St. Stephen gives when standing before the Jewish council. "In which time Moses was born, who was exceeding fair,* and nourished up in his father's house three months. And when he was cast out, Pharaoh's daughter took him up and nourished him for her own son. And Moses was learned in all the wisdom of the Egyptians, and was mighty in words and deeds."

Such are the extremely brief notices of a great event and of a group of characters whose influence on mankind every one of us feels to-day. For, the Jewish nation, in being chosen of God to be a sacerdotal race, was to pass through a history which should embody struggles, oppressions, agonies, victories, and deliverances, such as should represent to all time the sorrows and joys, the trials and hopes, of humanity. To this day, the events of Jewish history so well express universal experiences, that its literature in all languages, and under all difference of climate and custom, has an imperishable hold on the human heart. It has been well said that nations struggling for liberty against powerful oppressors flee as instinctively to the Old Testament as they do to mountain ranges. The American slave universally called his bondage Egypt, and read the history of the ten plagues and the crossing of the Red Sea as parts of his own experience. In the dark days of slavery, the history of Moses was sung at

* The marginal translation reads "fair to God."

night, and by stealth, on plantations, with solemn rhythmic movements, reminding one of old Egyptian times. It was the Marseillaise of a rude people, forbidden by the master, and all the dearer to the slave.

We must take the full force of the anguish, the ignominy, the oppression of slavery acting on noble and sensitive natures, elevated by faith in a high national destiny, and looking with earnestness and prayer for its evolution, in order to get a full idea of the character of Miriam. Such periods produce children with that highly exalted organization which is predisposed to receive the prophetic impulse. The Rabbinic traditions with regard to Miriam, which we have added, are detailed at length by Josephus in his history, and show how strong is the impression which the personality of this woman made on those of her time, in connection with the life of their great lawgiver.

The Bible account of the birth and preservation of Moses has the usual quality of Scripture narratives; it is very brief and very stimulating to the imagination. Who of us has not seen in childhood the old Nile with its reeds and rushes, its background of temples and pyramids? We have shared the tremors of the mother and sister while the little one was launched in the frail ark. Probably some report of the kindness of the Princess had inspired a trembling hope. The mother dares not stay to guard her treasure, lest she draw cruel eyes upon it; but the little Miriam, as a child playing among the tall reeds, can remain on the watch without attracting attention. In the scene where the helpless stranger is discovered by the Princess, we have, in the movements of the sister, all the characteristics, in miniature, of the future leader of Israel. Prompt, fearless, with an instantaneous instinct as to the right thing to be done at the critical moment, we can see the little Hebrew maid press forward amid the throng surrounding the alarmed and crying child. The tradition is that an Egyptian woman, at the command of the Princess, tried to quiet him at her breast, and that the young prophet indignantly rejected the attempt, — a statement which we who know babies, whether prophetic or otherwise, may deem highly probable. Then spoke up the little Miriam: "Shall I go and call thee a nurse of the Hebrew women, that she may nurse the child for thee? This was a bold proposal, but it succeeded. Perhaps the small speaker had some of the wonderful beauty of her infant brother to set off her words: at all events, the Princess seems at once to have trusted her with the commission. We may readily believe the little feet had not far to go. The child comes back to his mother's bosom as a royal ward.

We see here in the child Miriam great self-poise and self-confidence. She is not afraid of royalty, and, though of an enslaved and despised race, is ready to make suggestions to a queen. These are the traits of a natural leader, and we shall see them reappearing later in the history of Miriam. It was customary among the Oriental races to prolong the period of nursing two or three years, and Moses was thus in the care of his mother and elder sister for a long time.

Josephus gives the tradition current among the Jews, that the child was a wonderfully attractive one, — so beautiful, that every one who beheld him turned to look at him. The mother and sister looked upon him as the visible pledge of God's mercy to their suffering people, as well as the visible answer to prayer. The God of Abraham, and Isaac, and Jacob, in whose hand are all hearts, had made a refuge for the young Deliverer in the very family of the destroying tyrant!

The intercourse thus established between the court of Pharaoh and these two women must have materially advanced their position. We see in the Princess indications of a gracious and affable nature, and in Miriam a quick readiness to turn every favorable indication to good account. It is, therefore, quite probable that Miriam may have shared the liberal patronage of the Princess. Evidently she continued to influence the mind of her brother after he had gone into the family of Pharaoh, since we see her publicly associated with him at the great period of the national deliverance.

In the history of Moses, and in his laws and institutes, we see a peculiar and almost feminine tenderness and consideration for whatever is helpless and defenceless. Perhaps the history of his own life, — the story of the forlorn helplessness of his own cradle, and the anguish of his mother and sister, — operating on a large and generous nature, produced this result. For example, among the laws of the great lawgiver, we find one which forbids the caging of a free bird (Deut. xxii. 6, 7); thus it was allowed to take the young who might easily be reconciled to captivity, but forbidden to take those accustomed to freedom. Whoever has seen the miserable struggles of a free bird brought suddenly into captivity, can appreciate the compassionateness of the man who made such a law for a great people. In the same spirit another law forbids the muzzling of the ox when he treads the grain, and commands every man to stop and help an overburdened ass that falls beneath his load; and it particularly adds, that the ass of an enemy shall be helped, no matter how great the unwillingness.

In fact, the strongest impulse in the character of Moses appears to have been that of protective justice, with regard to every helpless and down-trodden class. The laws of Moses, if carefully examined, are a phenomenon, — an exception to the laws of either ancient or modern nations in the care they exercised over women, widows, orphans, paupers, foreigners, servants, and dumb animals. Of all the so-called Christian nations there is none but could advantageously take a lesson in legislation from them. There is a plaintive, pathetic tone of compassion in their very language, which seems to have been learned only of superhuman tenderness. Not the gentlest words of Jesus are more compassionate in their spirit than many of these laws of Moses. Some of them sound more like the pleadings of a mother than the voice of legal statutes. For example: "If thou lend money to any that is poor by thee, thou shalt not lay upon him usury. If thou at all take thy neighbor's garment to pledge, thou shalt deliver it unto him by that the sun goeth down, for that is his covering, it is his raiment for his skin; wherein shall he sleep? and it shall come to pass that when he crieth unto me I will hear, for I am gracious." "Thou shalt not oppress a hired servant that is poor and needy, whether he be of thine own brethren or of strangers that are within thy gates. At his day shalt thou give him his wages, neither shall the sun go down upon it, for he is poor and setteth his heart upon it, lest he cry unto the Lord against thee." "Thou shalt not pervert the judgment of the stranger nor of the fatherless, nor take the widow's raiment as pledge; thou shalt remember that thou wast a bondman in Egypt, and the Lord thy God redeemed thee, therefore I command thee to do this thing." "When thou cuttest down thy harvest and hast forgot a sheaf in the field, thou shalt not go again to fetch it, it shall be for the stranger, the fatherless, and the widow. When thou beatest thine olive-tree, thou shalt not go over it again; when thou gatherest the grapes of thy vineyard, thou shalt not glean it afterward, it shall be for the stranger, the fatherless, and the widow."

In all this, we see how deep was the impression made on the mind of Moses by the enslaved and helpless condition of his people. He had felt for the struggles of the enslaved, and it made him tender to the wild bird of the desert beating against its cage, to the overloaded ass fainting under his burden, to the hungry ox toiling to procure food which he was restricted from enjoying.

Of the period including the time that Moses left his mother and sister to dwell in the palace of the Pharaohs, and receive the education of an Egyptian prince, we have no record in the sacred narrative, except the declaration of Stephen in the book of Acts, that he was learned in all the wisdom of the Egyptians, and mighty in word and deed.

In Smith's Dictionary of the Bible there is a brief *résumé* of what is said by ancient authors of this period of his life. According to Strabo, he was educated at Heliopolis, and grew up there as a priest, under his Egyptian name of Osariph. According to Philo, he was taught the whole range of Greek, Chaldee, and Assyrian literature. From the Egyptians, especially, he learned mathematics, to train his mind for the unprejudiced reception of truth. He invented boats, engines for building, instruments of war and of hydraulics, and also understood hieroglyphics and mensuration of land. He taught Orpheus, and is thence called by the Greeks Musæus, and by the Egyptians Hermes. According to Josephus, he was sent as general of the Egyptian army on an expedition against Ethiopia. He got rid of the serpents, in the countries through which he was to march, by turning basketfuls of ibises upon them. Tharbis, the daughter of the King of Ethiopia, fell in love with him, and induced her father to surrender to him; and he returned in triumph with her to Egypt as his wife, and founded the city of Hermopolis to celebrate his victory. We see here, that if Moses remained true to the teachings of his mother and sister, and the simple faith of Israel, it was not for want of the broadest culture the world afforded. Egypt was the cradle of arts and letters, and the learned men of Greece traveled there to study the mysteries which were concealed under her hieroglyphics. Moses was a priest of Egypt in virtue of being a prince of a royal house. According to the Egyptian tradition, although a priest of Heliopolis, he always performed his devotions outside the walls of the city, in the open air, turned towards the sunrising. According to the language of St. Paul, "he endured as seeing Him that is invisible."

In Wilkinson's "Egypt," we have some interesting suggestions as to the life and training of the Egyptian priest, which go far to show what manner of education must have been given to Moses. The utmost purity of person was enjoined. Daily and nightly bathing of the whole person, a dress of pure linen, great exactness as to food, with strict dietetic regulations, were also a part of the training. The Egyptians were the fountains of physiological and medical knowledge to the nations of antiquity, and undoubtedly these studies were a part of the "wisdom" of the priests. Moses must also have passed through the lesser and the greater initiation into the mysteries of Egypt; in which were taught the unity of God, the immortality of the soul, and the retributions of a future life. Thus he had an opportunity of comparing that portion of the Divine teaching and traditions which had descended through Egypt, with the pure stream which had flowed down through the patriarchal families.

It thus appears that the Divine Being, in choosing the teacher and lawgiver to form his chosen nation, did not disdain the existing wisdom of the world up to that time. Moses had before him the results of all the world's experience in thought and culture. Egypt was the best there was to know, and he knew Egypt thoroughly. While, however, he often took suggestions from the ritual and philosophy of the Egyptians, the general bent of his institutes in reference to them was jealous and antagonistic.

At the end of such a training and such varied experience, — as priest, as general, as conqueror, — Moses returns to Egypt and meets again his sister, in whose heart the prophetic fire is still burning; and the sight of the oppression and misery of his people leads him to seek to interpose for their deliverance. The first act is the simple, unadvised movement of indignation at injustice; he sees a Hebrew slave writhing under the lash of an Egyptian; he kills the tyrant and delivers the slave. He next tries to rouse a national spirit of union among his people, and separates two who are fighting, with the words, "Ye are brethren, and should not contend." St. Stephen further interprets the heart of Moses at this crisis: "For he supposed that his brethren would have understood how that God by his hand would deliver them: but they understood not. But he that did his neighbor wrong thrust him away, saying, Who made thee a ruler and a judge over us? Wilt thou kill me as thou didst the Egyptian yesterday?" (Acts vii. 25, 27, 28.) According to Josephus, there were at this time envious and jealous plots hatching against Moses in the court of Pharaoh, and his life was threatened.

He fled to the land of Midian, where, with characteristic chivalry, his first act was to interfere for the protection of some women who were prevented by the brutality of the shepherd herdsmen from watering their flocks.

Still we see in him the protector of the weak and defenseless. In this case his interference procures for him the gratitude of the priest of the shepherd tribe, and the exiled Egyptian prince becomes a shepherd in the wilderness of Midian. He marries and settles down, apparently content with the life of a simple herdsman. This seems to have been one of those refluent tides to which natures of great sensibility are liable, after a short experience of the realities of life. At once ardent and tender, Moses had been ready to cast in his fortunes with his oppressed and suffering people; but he found them unwilling to listen to him, and unworthy of freedom. His heart sinks, — the grandeur of courts, military renown, the wisdom of Egypt, are all less in his eyes than even the reproach of a good cause; but he feels himself powerless and alone, rejected by the very people whom he came to serve. Like the Greater Prophet of whom he was the type, "He came unto his own, and his own received him not."

In sinking of heart and despair, the solitude of the wilderness, its loneliness and stern simplicity, are a refuge and rest to him. In the great calm of nature he draws near to Him who is invisible. What is most peculiar in the character of Moses, with all his advantages of beauty, rank, station, education, and military success, is a singular absence of self-esteem and self-reliance. When the God of his fathers appears in flaming fire and commissions him to go and lead forth his oppressed people, Moses shrinks from the position, and prays that it may be given to another. He is not eloquent; he says, he is of stammering speech and a slow tongue, and he prays the Lord to choose another. How often it happens that the work of the world is thus put upon men who shrink from it, — not from indolence, but from an exalted ideality, a high conception of the work to be done! Moses was dumb and stammering with low-minded, vulgar-natured men, as men who live high up in the radiant air of the nobler feelings often are. How bring his great thoughts and purer feelings down to their conceptions? He must have a spokesman, and evidently regards his brother Aaron as better fitted to take the lead than himself.

Aaron seems to be a specimen of that class of men — facile, sympathetic, easily moved, and with a ready gift of words — whom greater natures often admire for a facility and fluency which their very greatness denies to them. And yet it is this Aaron who, when Moses had been more than a month absent on the mount, was carried away by the demand of the people to make them a visible god; and who, if his brother had not cast himself down in agony of intercession, would have been swept away by the Divine anger.

In the great scene of the national deliverance, after the passage of the Red Sea, behold Moses and Miriam once more reunited in a grand act of national triumph! A solemn procession goes forth on the shores of the sea, and Moses leads the psalm of thanksgiving. "And Miriam the prophetess, the sister of Aaron, took a timbrel in her hand; and all the women went out after her with timbrels and with dances. And Miriam answered them, saying, Sing ye to the Lord, for he hath triumphed gloriously; the horse and his rider hath he thrown into the sea." The solemn union of man and woman in this great public act of worship and thanksgiving, which inaugurated a free nation, is indicative of the equality given to women by the Divine Being in all that pertains to the spiritual and immortal. "On your sons and *your daughters*," says the prophet Joel, "I will pour out of my spirit, and *they* shall prophesy"; and the same passage is quoted by St. Peter as expressive of the genius of the opening Christian dispensation. Thus we find at the opening of the Mosaic, as well as the Christian dispensation, this announcement of the equality of the sexes in their spiritual nature.

Many circumstances make it probable that as Moses and Miriam unitedly led the devotions of the people on this most solemn of national festivals, so they continued to be united in administrative station during that important period when the national code of laws and religious ritual were being crystallized and consolidated. We infer from a passage in the prophet Micah,* that it was not in mere brotherly fondness that Moses would have consulted this sister, who had been to him as a mother, but that she was understood to be one of the divinely appointed leaders of the people, and that he was thus justified in leaning upon her for counsel.

Moses was distinguished above all men we read of in history by a singular absence of egoism. He was like a mother in the midst of the great people whose sins, infirmities, and sorrows he bore upon his heart with scarcely a consciousness of

* Micah, who prophesied in the reign of Hezekiah, represents the Divine Being as thus addressing his people: "I brought thee up out of the land of Egypt; I sent before thee *Moses and Aaron and Miriam*" (Micah vi. 4). This is an indorsement more direct than any other prophetess ever received.

self. He had no personal interests. He was a man so lowly and gentle of demeanor that all his associates felt free to advise him. Thus his father-in-law, Jethro, visiting him in the wilderness, expresses himself with perfect freedom in regard to the excessive toil he is undergoing in the care of the people, and suggests the appointment of elders who should share the work of management. The eighteenth chapter of Exodus is a beautiful picture of the character and demeanor of Moses towards his father-in-law, and of his meek readiness to take advice. It appears that in all the long, laborious journey through the wilderness, Moses felt the burden and the responsibility altogether more than the honor, and there is a despairing freedom in the complaints he sometimes pours out to his God. Thus in one of the periods of national discontent, when the people were all "weeping and murmuring every man in his tent door," Moses says, "Wherefore hast thou afflicted thy servant? and why have I not found favor in thine eyes, that thou layest the burden of all this people upon me? Have I conceived all this people, — have I begotten them, that thou shouldst say, Carry them in thy bosom as a nursing father beareth the sucking child, unto the land which thou swarest unto their fathers? I am not able to bear all this people alone, because it is too heavy for me. And if thou deal thus with me, kill me, I pray thee, out of hand, if I have found favor in thy sight; and let me not see my wretchedness." The answer to this prayer is the appointment of seventy elders, under the care of God, to be sharers in the responsibilities of Moses. This division of responsibility seems to have relieved Moses, and he had not a thought of divided honor, though it at once occurred to others with regard to him. When the gift of prophecy descended upon some of these seventy elders, it seems to have been imagined by some that this honor would take from the dignity of Moses; and we are told (Num. xi. 28, 29), "Joshua, the son of Nun, the servant of Moses, one of his young men, answered and said, My lord Moses, forbid them. And Moses said unto him, Enviest thou for my sake? Would God that all the Lord's people were prophets!" If now we consider this singular meekness and unselfishness of Moses, we may easily see how it might be a temptation to an ambitious, self-asserting spirit to cross beyond the proper limit of advice and counsel into that of tyrannical dictation.

We have seen, in the few scenes where Miriam has appeared, that she had a peculiar, prompt self-assertion and ready positiveness which made leadership a necessity and a pleasure to her. She was a woman to court rather than shrink from responsibility, and to feel to the full all the personal dignity and glory which her rank and position gave her; and, accordingly, the sacred narrative, which conceals no fault, informs us how gradually these unwatched traits grew up into the very worst form of selfish ambition. After all the trials and sorrows of Moses, all the cabals and murmurings that wearied his soul and made him feel that life was a burden to him, we come at last to the severest trial of his life, when the sister and brother on whom he had leaned joined against him. The whole incident, recorded in Numbers xii., is most painful and most singular. "And Miriam and Aaron spake against Moses on account of an Ethiopian woman whom he had married." This is after the visit of his Midianite father-in-law, Jethro, who brought back to Moses his wife and two sons, from whom he had been long separated. It is supposed by some that this "woman of Cush" is the person referred to. If Moses had to this time been without a wife, he had been entirely devoted to his sister. Now another female influence comes in, — the wife of Moses may have felt disposed to assert her position among the women of Israel, and thus a broil may have arisen. One can easily imagine subjects of contention, and great vivacity of dissent, and the authority of Moses would naturally be referred to as the supreme one.

Miriam and Aaron join together to repudiate that authority, and set themselves up as equals. "And they said, Hath the Lord indeed spoken *only* by Moses? Hath he not spoken also by *us?* And the Lord heard it. And the Lord spake suddenly to Moses and Aaron and Miriam, Come out ye three unto the tabernacle of the congregation. And they three came out. And the Lord came down in the pillar of cloud, and stood in the door of the tabernacle, and called forth Moses and Aaron and Miriam, and he said: Hear now my words. If there be a prophet among you, I the Lord will make myself known unto him in a vision, and will speak unto him in a dream. My servant Moses is not so, who is faithful in all my house. With him I will speak mouth to mouth, even apparently, and not in dark speeches, and the similitude of the Lord shall he behold. Wherefore, then, were ye not afraid to speak against my servant Moses? And the anger of the Lord was kindled, and the Lord departed from them, and the cloud departed from the tabernacle; and behold Miriam became leprous, white as snow; and Aaron looked upon Miriam, and behold she was leprous. And Aaron said to Moses, Alas, my lord, lay not this sin upon us, wherein we have done foolishly and wherein we have sinned. Let her not be as one dead, of whom the flesh is half consumed when he cometh out of his mother's womb. And Moses cried unto the Lord, saying, Heal her now, O Lord, I beseech thee." The answer given to Moses draws a strong simile from the customs of those desert tribes where the father holds almost the sacred place of a god in the family. If her own father had expressed towards her the utmost extreme of mingled indignation and loathing at her conduct, would she not be ashamed for a while? And the command is given that she be shut out from the camp for seven days.

It is evidence of the high position held by this woman, that the whole camp of Israel waited during those seven days, while she was suffering under this terrible rebuke. The severity of the rebuke and punishment which fell upon Miriam seems at first sight excessive. But we shall notice, in the whole line of the traditions with respect to the prophetic office, the most complete unselfishness is absolutely required. To use the prophetic gift in any manner for personal ambition or aggrandizement, was sacrilege. The prophet must be totally, absolutely without self. His divine gifts must never be used for any personal and individual purpose, even for the relief of utmost want. Thus the great prophets, Elijah and Elisha, gifted with miraculous power, wandered hungry in the desert, and waited to be fed by God.

Thus Jesus, the Head of all the Prophets, when after wandering forty days he was an hungered, refused the suggestion to feed himself by his own miraculous power, and also the suggestion to glorify himself by a public display of that power.

Miriam, as we have seen, had naturally a great many of those personal traits which easily degenerate into selfish ambition. She was self-confident, energetic, and self-asserting by nature, and she had been associating with a brother whose peculiar unselfishness and disposition to prefer others in honor before himself had given full scope to her love of dictation. Undoubtedly, in most things her influence and her advice had been good, and there had been, in her leadership among the women of Israel, much that was valuable and admirable. But one of the most fearful possibilities in our human experience is the silent manner in which the divine essence exhales from our virtues and they become first faults and afterward sins. Sacred enthusiasms, solemn and awful trusts for noble purposes, may, before we know it, degenerate into mere sordid implements of personal ambition. In the solemn drama that has been represented in Scripture, the punishment that falls on the prophetess symbolizes this corruption. God departs from the selfish and self-seeking soul, and, with God, all spiritual life. The living, life-giving, inspired prophetess becomes a corrupt and corrupting leper. Such was the awful lesson spoken in this symbol of leprosy; and, while the gifted leader of Israel waited without the camp, the nation pondered it in silence.

One cannot but wonder at the apparent disproportion of the punishment upon Aaron. Yet, by careful observation, we shall find it to be a general fact in the Divine dealings, that the sins of weakness are less severely visited than the sins of strength. Aaron's was evidently one of those weak and yielding natures that are taken possession of by stronger ones, as absolutely as a child is by a grown man. His was one of those sympathetic organizations which cannot resist the force of stronger wills. All his sins are the sins of this kind of temperament. To suffer bitterly, and to repent deeply, is also essential to this nature; and in the punishment which fell on the sister who had tempted him, Aaron was more punished than in anything that could have befallen himself. There is utter anguish and misery in the cry which he utters when he sees his sister thus stricken.

There seems to have been a deep purpose in thus appointing to the priestly office a man peculiarly liable to the sins and errors of an excess of sympathy. The apostle says, that the proper idea of a priest was one "who could have compassion on the ignorant, and on them that are out of the way, for that he also is compassed with infirmity." Among men such humility is only acquired by bitter failures. At the same time a nature so soft and yielding could not be smitten like a stronger one without being utterly destroyed. Aaron appears to have been so really crushed and humbled by the blow which struck his sister that he suffered all of which he was capable. The whole office of the priest was one of confession and humiliation. In every symbol and every ceremony he expressed a sense of utmost unworthiness and need of a great expiation. It seems, therefore, in sympathy with the great and merciful design of such an office, that for its first incumbent should be chosen a man representing the infirmity rather than the strength of humanity. Our own experience in human nature is, that those who err from too sympathetic an organization, and a weak facility in receiving impressions from others, may yet have great hold on the affections of men, and be the most merciful counsellors of the sinful and tempted.

The great Leader of Israel, who proclaimed his name through Moses as forgiving iniquity, transgression, and sin, evidently fully forgave and restored both Miriam and Aaron, since he remained in the priestly office, and she is subsequently mentioned in Holy Writ as an ordained prophetess.

After this scene in the desert we lose sight of Miriam entirely, and are only reminded of her in one significant passage, where it is said to Israel, "Remember what the Lord thy God did to Miriam by the way, after ye were come forth from Egypt (Deut. xxiv. 9). Her death is recorded, Numbers xx. 1. Josephus gives an account of her funeral obsequies, which were celebrated in the most solemn manner for thirty days; the same honor was shown to a woman endowed with the prophetic commission that was given to her brothers; and not only so, but, as late as the time of St. Jerome, the tomb of Miriam was shown as an object of veneration.

One thing in respect to the sacred and prophetic women of the Jewish race is peculiar. They were uniformly, so far as appears, married women and mothers of families, and not like the vestal virgins of antiquity, set apart from the usual family duties of women. Josephus mentions familiarly the husband of Miriam as being Hur, the well-known companion and assistant of Moses on a certain public occasion. He also refers to Bezaleel, one of the architects who assisted in the erection of the tabernacle, as her grandson. We shall find, by subsequent examination of the lives of prophetic women who were called to be leaders in Israel, that they came from the bosom of the family, and were literally, as well as metaphorically, mothers in Israel. In the same year that Miriam died, Aaron, her brother, was also laid to rest, and, of the three, Moses remained alone.

It is remarkable that while Jewish tradition regarded Miriam with such veneration, while we see her spoken of in Holy Writ as a divinely appointed leader, yet there are none of her writings transmitted to us, as in the case of other and less revered prophetesses. The record of her fault and its punishment is given with the frankness with which the Bible narrates the failings of the very best; and, after that, nothing further is said. But it is evident that that one fault neither shook her brother's love nor the regard of the nation for her. Josephus expressly mentions that the solemn funeral honors which were shown her, and which held the nation as mourners for thirty days, were ordered and conducted by Moses, who thus expressed his love and veneration for the sister who watched his infancy and shared his labors. The national reverence for Miriam is shown in the Rabbinic tradition, that, on account of her courage and devotion in saving her brother's life at the Nile, a spring of living water, of which the people drank, always followed her footsteps through her wanderings in the wilderness. On her death the spring became dry. No more touching proof of a nation's affectionate memory can be given than a legend like this. Is it not in a measure true of every noble, motherly woman?

Yet, like many of her sex who have watched the cradle of great men, and been their guardians in infancy and their confidential counsellors in maturity, Miriam is known by *Moses* more than by herself.

As sunshine reappears in the forms of the plants and flowers it has stimulated into existence, so much of the power of noble women appears, not in themselves, but in the men who are gradually molded and modified by them. It was a worthy mission of a prophetess to form a lawgiver. We cannot but feel that from the motherly heart of this sister, associated with him in the prophetic office, Moses must have gained much of that peculiar knowledge of the needs and wants and feelings of women which in so many instances shaped his administration.

The law which protected the children of an unbeloved wife from a husband's partiality, the law which secured so much delicacy and consideration to a captive woman, the law which secured the marriage-rights of the purchased slave and forbade making merchandise of her, the law which gave to the newly married wife the whole of the first year of her husband's time and attention, are specimens of what we mean when we say that the influence of a noble-hearted woman passed into the laws of Moses. No man could be more chivalric or more ready to protect, but it required a woman's heart to show where protection was most needed, and we see in all these minute guardings of family life why the Divine Being speaks of a woman as being divinely associated with the great lawgiver: "I sent before you Moses and Aaron and Miriam."

Thus a noble womanly influence passed through Moses into permanent institutions. The nation identified her with the MAN who was their glory, and Miriam became immortal in Moses.

THE FINDING OF MOSES.

SLOW glides the Nile: amid the margin flags,
Closed in a bulrush ark, the babe is left, —
Left by a mother's hand. His sister waits
Far off; and pale, 'tween hope and fear, beholds
The royal maid, surrounded by her train,
Approach the river-bank, — approach the spot
Where sleeps the innocent. She sees them stoop
With meeting plumes; the rushy lid is oped,
And wakes the infant, smiling in his tears, —
As when along a little mountain lake
The summer south-wind breathes with gentle sigh,
And parts the reeds, unveiling, as they bend,
A water-lily floating on the wave.

James Grahame.

THE PASSAGE OF THE RED SEA.

O WELCOME came the morn, where Israel stood
In trustless wonder by the avenging flood!
O, welcome came the cheerful morn, to show
The drifted wreck of Zoan's pride below!
The mangled limbs of men — the broken car —
A few sad relics of a nation's war;
Alas, how few! Then, soft as Elim's well,
The precious tears of new-born freedom fell.
And he, whose hardened heart alike had borne
The house of bondage and the oppressor's scorn,
The stubborn slave, by hope's new beams subdued,
In faltering accents sobbed his gratitude,
Till kindling into warmer zeal, around
The virgin timbrel waked its silver sound;
And in fierce joy, no more by doubt suppress,
The struggling spirit throbbed in Miriam's breast.
She, with bare arms, and fixing on the sky
The dark transparence of her lucid eye,
Poured on the winds of heaven her wild, sweet harmony.
"Where now," she sang, "the tall Egyptian spear?
On's sunlike shield, and Zoan's chariot, where?
Above their ranks the whelming waters spread!
Shout, Israel, for the Lord hath triumphéd!"
And every pause between, as Miriam sang,
From tribe to tribe the martial thunder rang,
And loud and far their stormy chorus spread, —
"Shout, Israel, for the Lord hath triumphéd!"

Reginald Heber.

THE TRIUMPH OF ISRAEL.

YE daughters and soldiers of Israel, look back!
Where, where are the thousands who shadowed your track, —
The chariots that shook the deep earth as they rolled, —
The banners of silk, and the helmets of gold?

Where are they, — the vultures, whose beaks would have fed
On the tide of your hearts ere the pulses had fled?
Give glory to God, who in mercy arose,
And strewed 'mid the waters the strength of our foes!

When we traveled the waste of the desert by day,
With his banner-cloud's motion He marshaled our way;
When we saw the tired sun in his glory expire,
Before us He walked in a pillar of fire!

But this morn, and the Israelites' strength was a reed
That shook with the thunder of chariot and steed:
Where now are the swords and their far-flashing sweep?
Their lightnings are quenched in the depths of the deep!

O Thou who redeemest the weak one at length,
And scourgest the strong in the pride of their strength, —
Who holdest the earth and the sea in Thine hand,
And rulest Eternity's shadowy land, —

To Thee let our thoughts and our offerings tend,
Of virtue the Hope, and of sorrow the Friend;
Let the incense of prayer still ascend to Thy throne,
Omnipotent, — glorious, — eternal, — alone!

Anonymous.

MIRIAM'S SONG.

SOUND the loud timbrel o'er Egypt's dark sea!
Jehovah has triumphed! His people are free!
Sing, — for the pride of the tyrant is broken;
His chariots, his horsemen, all splendid and brave,
How vain was their boasting! the Lord hath but spoken,
And chariots and horsemen are sunk in the wave.
Sound the loud timbrel o'er Egypt's dark sea!
Jehovah has triumphed! His people are free!

Praise to the Conqueror, praise to the Lord,
His word was our arrow, His breath was our sword!
Who shall return to tell Egypt the story
Of those she sent forth in the hour of her pride?
For the Lord hath looked out from His pillar of glory,
And all her brave thousands are dashed in the tide.
Sound the loud timbrel o'er Egypt's dark sea!
Jehovah has triumphed! His people are free!

Thomas Moore.

DEBORAH THE PROPHETESS.

THE Book of Judges is the record of a period which may be called the Dark Ages of the Jewish Church, even as the mediæval days were called the Dark Ages of Christianity. In both cases, a new system of purity and righteousness, wholly in advance of anything the world had ever before known, had been inaugurated by the visible power of God, — the system of Moses, and the system of Christ. But these pure systems seem, in each case, to have been allowed to struggle their own way through the mass of human ignorance and sin. The ideal policy of Moses was that of an ultra-democratic community, so arranged that perforce there must be liberty, fraternity, and equality. There was no chance for overgrown riches or abject poverty. Landed property was equally divided in the outset, and a homestead allowed to each family. Real estate could not be alienated from a family for more than a generation; after that period, it returned again to its original possessor. The supreme law of the land was love. Love, first, to the God and Father, the invisible head of all; and secondly, towards the neighbor, whether a Jewish brother or a foreigner and stranger. The poor, the weak, the enslaved, the old, the deaf, the blind, were protected by solemn and specific enactments. The person of woman was hedged about by restraints and ordinances which raised her above the degradation of sensuality to the honored position of wife and mother. Motherhood was exalted into special honor, and named as equal with fatherhood in the eye of God. "Ye shall fear every man *his mother* and his father, and keep my Sabbaths: I am the Lord." (Lev. xix. 3.)

Refinement of feeling, personal cleanliness, self-restraint, order, and purity were taught by a system of ordinances and observances, which were intertwined through all the affairs of life, so that the Jew who lived up to his law must of necessity rise to a noble manhood. But this system, so ideally perfect, encountered an age of darkness. Like all beautiful ideals, the theocratic republic of Moses suffered under the handling of coarse human fingers. Without printed books or printing, or any of the thousand modern means of perpetuating ideas, the Jews were constantly tempted to lapse into the customs of the heathen tribes around. The question whether Jehovah or Baal were God was kept open for discussion, and sometimes, for long periods, idolatry prevailed. Then came the subjugation and the miseries of a foreign yoke, and the words of Moses were fulfilled: "Because thou servedst not the Lord thy God, with joyfulness, and with gladness of heart, for the abundance of all things, therefore shalt thou serve the enemy whom the Lord shall send against thee, in hunger and in thirst, and in nakedness, and in want of all things; and he shall put a yoke of iron on thy neck, till he have destroyed thee."

The history of the Jewish nation, in the Book of Judges, presents a succession of these periods of oppression, and of deliverance by a series of divinely inspired leaders, sent in answer to repentant prayers. It is entirely in keeping with the whole character of the Mosaic institutions, and the customs of the Jewish people, that one of these inspired deliverers should be a woman. We are not surprised at the familiar manner in which it is announced, as a thing quite in the natural order, that the chief magistrate of the Jewish nation, for the time being, was a woman divinely ordained and gifted. Thus the story is introduced:—

"And the children of Israel did evil in the sight of the Lord when Ehud was dead, and the Lord sold them into the hands of Jabin, King of Canaan, that reigned in Hasor, the captain of whose host was Sisera, which dwelt in Harosheth of the Gentiles. And the children of Israel cried unto the Lord; for he had nine hundred chariots of iron, and twenty years he mightily oppressed the children of Israel. And Deborah, the prophetess, the wife of Lapidoth, she judged Israel at that time. And she dwelt under the palm-tree of Deborah, between Ramah and Bethel, in

Mount Ephraim, and the children of Israel came up to her for judgment. And she sent and called Barak, the son of Abinoam, and said unto him: Hath not the Lord God of Israel said, Go draw towards Mount Tabor, and take with thee ten thousand men of the children of Zebulun and the children of Naphtali? And I will draw unto thee, at the river Kishon, Sisera, the captain of Jabin's army, with his chariots and his multitude, and I will deliver him into thy hands. And Barak said: If *thou* wilt go with me, I will go; but if thou wilt not go with me, I will not go. And she said: I will surely go with thee; notwithstanding, the journey that thou takest shall not be for thine honor, for the Lord shall sell Sisera into the hand of a woman."

In all this we have a picture of the reverence and confidence with which, in those days, the inspired woman was regarded. The palm-tree which shaded her house becomes a historical monument, and is spoken of as a well-known object. The warlike leader of the nation comes to her submissively, listens to her message as to a divine oracle, and obeys. He dares not go up to battle without her, but if she will go he will follow her. The prophetess is a wife, but her husband is known to posterity only through her. Deborah was the wife of Lapidoth, and therefore Lapidoth is had in remembrance even down to our nineteenth century.

This class of prophetic and inspired women appear to have been the poets of their time. They were, doubtless, possessed of that fine ethereal organization, fit to rise into the higher regions of ecstasy, wherein the most exalted impressions and enthusiasms spring, as birds under tropic sunshine. The Jewish woman was intensely patriotic. She was a living, breathing impersonation of the spirit of her nation; and the hymn of victory chanted by Deborah, after the issue of the conflict, is one of the most spirited specimens of antique poetry. In order to sympathize with it fully, we must think of the condition of woman in those days, when under the heel of the oppressor. The barriers and protections which the laws of Moses threw around the Jewish women inspired in them a sense of self-respect and personal dignity which rendered the brutal outrages inflicted upon captives yet more intolerable. The law of Moses commanded the Jewish warrior who took a captive woman to respect her person and her womanhood. If he desired her, it must be as a lawful wife; and even as a husband he must not force himself at once upon her. He must bring her to his house, and allow her a month to reconcile herself to her captivity, before he took her to himself. But among the nations around, woman was the prey of whoever could seize and appropriate her.

The killing of Sisera by Jael has been exclaimed over by modern sentimentalists as something very shocking. But let us remember how the civilized world felt when, not long since, the Austrian tyrant Heynau outraged noble Hungarian and Italian women, subjecting them to brutal stripes and indignities. When the civilized world heard that he had been lynched by the brewers of London, — cuffed, and pommeled, and rolled in the dust, — shouts of universal applause went up, and the verdict of society was, "Served him right." Deborah saw, in the tyrant thus overthrown, the ravisher and brutal tyrant of helpless women, and she extolled the spirit by which Jael had entrapped the ferocious beast, whom her woman's weakness could not otherwise have subdued.

There is a beautiful commentary on the song of Deborah in Herder's "Spirit of Hebrew Poetry." He gives a charming translation, to which we refer any one who wishes to study the oldest poem by a female author on record. The verse ascribed to Miriam seems to have been only the chorus of the song of Moses, and, for aught that appears, may have been composed by him; but this song of Deborah is of herself alone. It is one of the noblest expressions of devout patriotism in literature.

We subjoin a version of this poem, in which we have modified, in accordance with Herder, some passages of our ordinary translation.

"Praise ye Jehovah for the avenging of Israel,
When the people willingly offered themselves.
Hear, O ye kings; give ear, O ye princes.
I will sing praise to Jehovah;
I will praise Jehovah, God of Israel.

DEBORAH.

LANDELLE, *Pinx.* JEHENNE, *Lith.*

Jehovah, when thou wentest out from Seir,
When thou marchedst from Edom,
The earth trembled and the heavens dropped,
The clouds also poured down water."

The song now changes, to picture the miseries of an enslaved people, who were deprived of arms and weapons, and exposed at any hour and moment to the incursions of robbers and murderers: —

"In the days of Shamgar, the son of Anath,
In the days of Jael,
The highways were unoccupied,
And travelers walked through by-ways.
The inhabitants ceased from the villages,
Till I, Deborah, arose.
I arose a mother in Israel.
They went after strange gods;
Then came the war to their gates.
Was there then a shield or a spear
Among forty thousand in Israel?"

The theme then changes, to celebrate those whose patriotic bravery had redeemed their country: —

"My heart throbs to the governors of Israel
That offered themselves willingly among the people.
Bless ye Jehovah!
Speak, ye that ride on white asses,
Ye that sit in judgment, and ye that walk by the way,
They that are delivered from the noise of archers
In the place of drawing water,
There shall they rehearse the righteous acts of Jehovah,
His righteous acts towards the inhabitants of the villages.
Then shall the people go down to the gates.
Awake! awake! Deborah,
Awake! awake! utter a song!
Arise, Barak, and lead captivity captive,
Thou son of Abinoam!"

After this, another change: she reviews, with all a woman's fiery eloquence, the course which the tribes have taken in the contest, giving praise to the few courageous, self-sacrificing patriots, and casting arrows of satire and scorn on the cowardly and selfish. For then, as in our modern times, there were all sorts of men. There were those of the brave, imprudent, generous, "do-or-die" stamp, and there were the selfish conservatives, who only waited and talked. So she says: —

"It was but a small remnant that went forth against the mighty.
The people of Jehovah went with me against the mighty.
The march began with Ephraim,
The root of the army was from him;
With him didst thou come, Benjamin!
Out of Machir came down the leaders;
Out of Zebulun the marshals of forces;
And the princes of Issachar were with Deborah.
Issachar, the life-guard of Barak,
Sprang like a hind into the battle-field!"

It appears that the tribe of Reuben had only been roused so far as to *talk* about the matter. They had been brought up to the point of an animated discussion whether they should help or not. The poetess thus jeers at them: —

"By the brooks of Reuben there were great talkings and inquiries.
Why abodest thou in thy sheepfolds, Reuben?
Was it to hear the bleating of the flocks?
By the brooks of Reuben were great talks [but nothing more].
Gilead, too, abode beyond Jordan;
And why did Dan remain in his ships?
Asher stayed on the sea-shore and remained in his harbor.
Zebulun and Naphtali risked their lives unto the death
In the high places of the field of battle."

Now comes the description of the battle. It appears that a sudden and violent rain-storm and an inundation helped to rout the enemy and gain the victory; and the poetess breaks forth:—

"The kings came and fought;
The kings of Canaan in Taanach, by the waters of Megiddo;
They brought away no treasure.
They fought; from heaven the stars in their courses
They fought against Sisera.
The river Kishon swept them down,
That ancient river, Kishon.
O my soul! walk forth with strength!
Then was the rattling of hoofs of horses!
They rushed back, — the horses of the mighty."

And now the solemn sound of a prophetic curse: —

"Curse ye Meroz, saith the angel of Jehovah,
Curse ye bitterly the inhabitants thereof,

> Because they came not to the help of Jehovah,
> To the help of Jehovah against the mighty!"

Then follows a burst of blessing on the woman who had slain the oppressor; in which we must remember, it is a woman driven to the last extreme of indignation at outrages practiced on her sex that thus rejoices. When the tiger who has slain helpless women and children is tracked to his lair, snared, and caught, a shout of exultation goes up; and there are men so cruel and brutal that even humanity rejoices in their destruction. There is something repulsive in the thought of the artifice and treachery that beguiled and betrayed the brigand chief. But woman cannot meet her destroyer in open, hand-to-hand conflict. She is thrown perforce on the weapons of physical weakness; and Deborah exults in the success of the artifice with all the warmth of her indignant soul.

> "Blessed above women be Jael, the wife of Heber the Kenite!
> Blessed shall she be above women in the tent!
> He asked water and she gave him milk;
> She brought forth butter in a lordly dish.
> She put her hand to the nail,
> Her right hand to the workman's hammer.
> With the hammer she smote Sisera,
> She smote off his head.
> When she had stricken through his temple,
> At her feet he bowed, he fell, he lay prostrate.
> At her feet he bowed, he fell.
> Where he bowed, there he fell down dead!"

The outrages on wives, mothers, and little children, during twenty years of oppression, gives energy to this blessing on the woman who dared to deliver.

By an exquisite touch of the poetess, we are reminded what must have been the fate of all Judæan women except for this nail of Jael.

> "The mother of Sisera looked out at a window.
> She cried through the lattice,
> Why delay the wheels of his chariot?
> Why tarries the rattle of his horse-hoofs?
> Her wise ladies answered: yea, she spake herself.
> Have they not won? Have they not divided the prey?
> To every man a virgin or two;

> To Sisera a prey of divers colors, of divers colors and gold embroidery,
> Meet for the necks of them that take the spoil."

In the reckoning of this haughty princess, a noble Judæan lady, with her gold embroideries and raiment of needle-work, is only an ornament meet for the neck of the conqueror, — a toy, to be paraded in triumph. The song now rises with one grand, solemn swell, like the roll of waves on the sea-shore: —

> " So let all thine enemies perish, O Jehovah!
> But let them that love thee shine forth as the sun in his strength."

And as this song dies away, so passes all mention of Deborah. No other fragment of poetry or song from her has come down from her age to us. This one song, like a rare fragment of some deep-sea flower, broken off by a storm of waters, has floated up to tell of her. We shall see, as we follow down the line of history, that women of this lofty poetic inspiration were the natural product of the Jewish laws and institutions. They grew out of them, as certain flowers grow out of certain soils. To this class belonged Hannah, the mother of Samuel, and Huldah, the prophetess, and, in the fullness of time, Mary, the mother of Jesus, whose *Magnificat* was the earliest flower of the Christian era. Mary was prophetess and poet, the last and greatest of a long and noble line of women, in whom the finer feminine nature had been kindled into a divine medium of inspiration, and burst forth in poetry and song as in a natural language.

THE BATTLE OF JEZREEL.

ASS where of old the giant kings
Fought by Megiddo's water-springs,
And where the lords of Issachar
Came marching to the mountain war:
There now the quivered Ephraimite
O'er Tabor led his conquering might;
And, showering thick their shafts of flame,
Gilboa's sinewy archers came;
While, wearing each his regal crown,
Rode the great chiefs of Machir down,
Whose ancient patriarchal sway
The distant eastern hills obey.

Ah! why did Gilead then abide
Far off, by Jordan's peaceful side?
And wherefore seaward Asher lay
Supinely by his sheltered bay?
What power malign could Reuben hold,
To dwell the while by field and fold?
What from the war could him detain
Where shepherds roam the tented plain,
And, crowned with autumn's tawny leaf,
The sun-brown reaper binds the sheaf;
Where the herd's lordly monarch wades
Through Bashan's richly pastured glades,
Or stoops his shaggy brows to lave
In fords of Arnon's mountain wave?

. . . . .

But where is he, whose trumpet shrill
Shook the deep caves of Tabor's hill,—
To hail whose home-returning car,
E'en now Harosheth looks afar?
From many a tower and battlement
Far-off, unnumbered eyes are bent,

With eager joy and greed, to see
Those treasures of captivity,
Chained at his wheels, a weeping band,
Judæa's dark-eyed daughters stand.

Watchman, on yon turret high!
Saw you, down the tented sky,
O'er the length'ning file's array,
His victorious banners play?
Marked you, to the sunny beam
Burnished targe and helmet gleam,
And the snaffled steeds afar
Bearing the refulgent car?
Heard you yet the people's cry,
Or the cymbal's clash of joy?
Save him, blood-stained idols grim,
Ashtaroth and Baalim!

Alas! long through the latticed gate,
For him shall Syrian maidens wait;
For far away, their warrior bold
At Jael's feet lies stark and cold.
And Canaan's prancing hoofs in vain
Have tinted Taanach's thirsty plain:
Low sank to earth the bounding steed
That fed by Tigris' flowery mead;
Or, fleeter than the falcon's wing,
Scarce shook Orontes' crystal spring.
Beneath old Kishon's trampling waves,
Dark Hazor's archers found their graves.
Lift, Deborah, lift thy song, and cry,
"The Lord has triumphed gloriously!"

Rev. John Mitford (adapted).

DELILAH.

Baader, *Pinx.* Jehenne, *Lith.*

DELILAH THE DESTROYER.

THE pictures of womanhood in the Bible are not confined to subjects of the better class.

There is always a shadow to light; and shadows are deep, intense, in proportion as light is vivid. There is in bad women a terrible energy of evil which lies over against the angelic and prophetic power given to them, as Hell against Heaven.

In the long struggles of the Divine Lawgiver with the idolatrous tendencies of man, the evil as well as the good influence of woman is recognized. There are a few representations of loathsome vice and impurity left in the sacred records, to show how utterly and hopelessly corrupt the nations had become whom the Jews were commanded to exterminate. Incurable licentiousness and unnatural vice had destroyed the family state, transformed religious services into orgies of lust, and made woman a corrupter, instead of a saviour. The idolatrous temples and groves and high places against which the prophets continually thunder were scenes of abominable vice and demoralization.

No danger of the Jewish race is more insisted on in sacred history and literature than the bad power of bad women, and the weakness of men in their hands. Whenever idolatry is introduced among them it is always largely owing to the arts and devices of heathen women.

The story of Samson seems to have been specially arranged as a warning in this regard. It is a picture drawn in such exaggerated colors and proportions that it might strike the lowest mind and be understood by the dullest. As we have spoken of the period of the Judges as corresponding to the Dark Ages of Christianity, so the story of Samson corresponds in some points with the mediæval history of St. Christopher. In both is presented the idea of a rugged animal nature, the impersonation of physical strength, without much moral element, but seized on and used by a divine impulse for a beneficent purpose. Samson had strength, and he used it to keep alive this sacerdotal nation, this race from whom were to spring the future apostles and prophets and teachers of our Christianity.

Like some unknown plant of rare flower and fruit, cast out to struggle in ungenial soil, nipped, stunted, browsed down by cattle, trodden down by wild beasts, the Jewish race, in the times of the Book of Judges showed no capability of producing such men as Isaiah and Paul and John, much less Jesus. Yet, humanly speaking, in this stock, now struggling for bare national existence, and constantly in danger of being trampled out, was contained the capacity of unfolding, through Divine culture, such heavenly blossoms as Jesus and his apostles.

In fact, then, the Christian religion, with all its possibilities of hope and happiness for the human race, lay at this period germinant, in seed form, in a crushed and struggling race. Hence the history of Samson; hence the reason why he who possessed scarcely a moral element of character is spoken of as under the guidance of the Spirit of the Lord. A blind impulse inspired him to fight for the protection of his nation against the barbarous tribes that threatened their destruction, and with this impulse came rushing floods of preternatural strength. With the history of this inspired giant is entwined that of a woman whose name has come to stand as a generic term for a class, — Delilah! It is astonishing with what wonderful dramatic vigor a few verses create before us this woman so vividly and so perfectly that she has been recognized from age to age.

Delilah! not the frail sinner falling through too much love; not the weak, downtrodden woman, the prey of man's superior force; but the terrible creature, artful and powerful, who triumphs over man, and uses man's passions for her own ends, without an answering throb of passion. As the strength of Samson lies in his hair, so the strength of Delilah lies in her hardness of heart. If she could love, her power would depart from her. Love brings weakness and tears that make the hand tremble and the eye dim. But she who cannot love is guarded at all points; *her* hand never trembles, and no soft, fond weakness dims her eye so that she cannot see the exact spot where to strike. Delilah has her wants, — she wants money, she wants power, — and men are her instruments; she will make them her slaves to do her pleasure.

Samson, like the great class of men in whom physical strength predominates, appears to have been constitutionally good-natured and persuadable, with a heart particularly soft towards woman. He first falls in love with a Philistine woman whom he sees, surrendering almost without parley. His love is animal passion, with good-natured softness of temper; it is inconsiderate, insisting on immediate gratification. Though a Nazarite, vowed to the service of the Lord, yet happening to see this woman, he says forthwith: "I have seen a woman in Timnath, of the daughters of the Philistines; therefore get her for me for a wife. Then said his father and his mother, Is there never a woman of the daughters of thy people, that thou goest to take a Philistine woman to wife? But he said, Get her for me; for she pleaseth me well."

She is got; and then we find the strong man, through his passion for her, becoming the victim of the Philistines. He puts out a riddle for them to guess. "And they said to Samson's wife, Entice thy husband that he may declare unto us the riddle. And Samson's wife wept before him, and said, Thou dost but hate me, and lovest me not: thou hast put forth a riddle unto the children of my people and hast not told me. And she wept before him seven days, and on the seventh day he told her." A picture this of what has been done in kings' palaces and poor men's hovels ever since, — man's strength was overcome and made the tool of woman's weakness.

We have now a record of the way this wife was taken from him, and of the war he declared against the Philistines, and of exploits which caused him to be regarded as the champion of his nation by the Hebrews, and as a terror by his enemies. He holds them in check, and defends his people, through a course of years; and could he have ruled his own passions, he might have died victorious. The charms of a Philistine woman were stronger over the strong man than all the spears or swords of his enemies.

The rest of the story reads like an allegory, so exactly does it describe that unworthy subservience of man to his own passions, wherein bad women in all ages have fastened poisonous roots of power. The man is deceived and betrayed, with his eyes open, by a woman whom he does not respect, and who he can see is betraying him. The story is for all time. The temptress says: "How canst thou say, I love thee, when thy heart is not with me? Thou hast mocked me these three times, and hast not told me wherein thy great strength lieth. And it came to pass when she pressed him daily with her words, and urged him so that his soul was vexed to death, that he told her all his heart." Then Delilah runs at once to her employers. "She sent and called the lords of the Philistines, saying, Come up this once, he hath told me all his heart. And she made him sleep upon her knees; and called for a man, and bade him shave off the seven locks, and his strength went from him. And she said, The Philistines be upon thee, Samson, and he awoke and said, I will go out and shake myself, as at other times, and he wist not that the Lord was departed from him. But the Philistines took him, and put on him fetters of brass, and he did grind in their prison house."

Thus ignobly ends the career of a deliverer whose birth was promised to his parents by an angel, who was vowed to God, and had the gift of strength to redeem a nation. Under the wiles of an evil woman he lost all, and sunk lower than any slave into irredeemable servitude.

The legends of ancient history have their parallels. Hercules, the deliverer, made the scoff and slave of Omphale, and Antony, become the tool and scorn of Cleopatra, are but repetitions of the same story. Samson victorious, all-powerful, carrying the gates of Gaza on his back, the hope of his countrymen and the terror of his enemies; and Samson shorn, degraded, bound, eyeless, grinding in the prison-house of those he might have subdued, — such was the lesson given to the Jews of the power of the evil woman. And the story which has repeated itself from age to age, is repeating itself to-day. There are women on whose knees men sleep, to awaken shorn of manliness, to be seized, bound, blinded, and made to grind in unmanly servitude forever.

> "She hath cast down many wounded,
> Yea, many strong men hath she slain;
> Her house is the way to Hell,
> Going down to the chambers of Death."

SAMSON IN THE PHILISTINE PRISON.

[SAMSON, blind and in chains, sits, with an Attendant, in the open air. Enter MANOAH, his aged father.]

MANOAH.

O MISERABLE change! is this the man,
That invincible Samson, far renowned,
The dread of Israel's foes, who with a strength
Equivalent to angels walked their streets,
None offering fight; who single combatant
Dueled their armies ranked in proud array,
Himself an army, now unequal match
To save himself against a coward armed
At one spear's length? O ever-failing trust
In mortal strength! and O, what not in man
Deceivable and vain? Nay, what thing good
Prayed for, but often proves our woe, our bane?
I prayed for children, and thought barrenness
In wedlock a reproach; I gained a son,
And such a son as all men hailed me happy;
Who would be now a father in my stead?
O wherefore did God grant me my request,
And as a blessing with such pomp adorned?
Why are his gifts desirable, to tempt
Our earnest prayers, then, given with solemn hand
As graces, draw a scorpion's tail behind?
For this, did the angel twice descend?
For this ordained thy nurture holy, as of a plant
Select, and sacred, glorious for a while,
The miracle of men; then in an hour
Ensnared, assaulted, overcome, led bound,
Thy foe's derision, captive, poor, and blind,
Into a dungeon thrust, to work with slaves?

SAMSON IN THE PHILISTINE PRISON.

SAMSON.

Nothing of all these evils hath befallen me
But justly; I myself have brought them on,
Sole author I, sole cause; if aught seem vile,
As vile hath been my folly, who have profaned
The mystery of God given me under pledge
Of vow, and have betrayed it to a woman,
A Canaanite, my faithless enemy.

O indignity, O blot
To honor and religion! servile mind
Rewarded well with servile punishment!
The base degree to which I now am fallen,
These rags, this grinding, is not yet so base
As was my former servitude ignoble,
Unmanly, ignominious, infamous,
True slavery; and that blindness worse than this,
That saw not how degenerately I served.

MANOAH.*

But who is this? what thing of sea or land?
Female of sex it seems,
That so bedecked, ornate, and gay,
Comes this way sailing,
Like a stately ship
Of Tarsus, bound for the isles
Of Javan or Gadire,
With all her bravery on, and tackle trim,
Sails filled, and streamers waving,
Courted by all the winds, that hold them play,
An amber scent of odorous perfume
Her harbinger, a damsel train behind!
Some rich Philistian matron she may seem;
And now at nearer view, no other certain
Than Dalila thy wife.

SAMSON.

My wife! my traitress! let her not come near me!

* In the original poem, this and the next following speech of Manoah belong to the CHORUS of Samson's friends.

MANOAH.

Yet on she moves, now stands and eyes thee fixed,
About to have spoke; but now, with head declined,
Like a fair flower surcharged with dew, she weeps,
And words addressed seem into tears dissolved,
Wetting the borders of her silken veil:
But now again she makes address to speak.

Enter DALILA.*

DALILA.

With doubtful feet and wavering resolution
I came, still dreading thy displeasure, Samson,
Which to have merited, without excuse,
I cannot but acknowledge; yet, if tears
May expiate (though the fact more evil drew
In the perverse event than I foresaw),
My penance hath not slackened, though my pardon
No way assured. But conjugal affection,
Prevailing over fear and timorous doubt,
Hath led me on, desirous to behold
Once more thy face, and know of thy estate,
If aught in my ability may serve
To lighten what thou sufferest, and appease
Thy mind with what amends is in my power,
Though late, yet in some part to recompense
My rash, but more unfortunate misdeed.

SAMSON.

Out, out, hyena! these are thy wonted arts,
And arts of every woman false like thee,
To break all faith, all vows, deceive, betray,
Then as repentant to submit, beseech,

* Milton adopts the orthography of this name as given in the Greek of Josephus, *Dălila*, and the verse requires that it should be so pronounced.

"The Septuaginal version calls her *Dalida*. She is here regarded as the *wife* of Samson, a theory for several reasons improbable."

And reconcilement move with feigned remorse,
Confess, and promise wonders in her change;
Not truly penitent, but chief to try
Her husband, how far urged his patience bears,
His virtue or weakness which way to assail:
Then with more cautious and instructed skill
Again transgresses, and again submits.

DALILA.

And what if love, which thou interpretest hate,
The jealousy of love, powerful of sway
In human hearts, nor less in mine towards thee,
Caused what I did? I saw thee mutable
Of fancy, feared lest one day thou wouldst leave me
As her at Timna, sought by all means therefore
How to endure, and hold thee to me firmest:
No better way I saw than by impórtuning
To learn thy secrets, get into my power
Thy key of strength and safety. Thou wilt say,
Why then revealed? I was assured by those
Who tempted me, that nothing was designed
Against thee but safe custody and hold:
That made for me; I knew that liberty
Would draw thee forth to perilous enterprises,
While I at home sat full of cares and fears,
Wailing thy absence in my widowed bed;
Here I should still enjoy thee, day and night,
Mine and love's prisoner, not the Philistines',
Whole to myself, unhazarded abroad,
Fearless at home of partners in my love.

SAMSON.

Weakness is thy excuse,
And I believe it; weakness to resist
Philistian gold: if weakness may excuse,
What murderer, what traitor, parricide,
Incestuous, sacrilegious, but may plead it?
All wickedness is weakness: that plea therefore
With God or man will gain thee no remission.
But love constrained thee; love seeks to have love;

My love how couldst thou hope, who tookest the way
To raise in me inexpiable hate,
Knowing, as needs I must, by thee betrayed?
In vain thou strivest to cover shame with shame,
Or by evasions thy crime uncoverest more.

DALILA.

Since thou determinest weakness for no plea
In man or woman, though to thy own condemning,
Hear what assaults I had, what snares besides,
What sieges girt me round, ere I consented;
Which might have awed the best-resolved of men,
The constantest, to have yielded without blame.
It was not gold, as to my charge thou layest,
That wrought with me: thou knowest the magistrates
And princes of my country came in person,
Solicited, commanded, threatened, urged,
Adjured by all the bonds of civil duty
And of religion, pressed how just it was,
How honorable, how glorious, to entrap
A common enemy, who had destroyed
Such numbers of our nation: and the priest
Was not behind, but ever at my ear
Preaching how meritorious with the gods
It would be to ensnare an irreligious
Dishonorer of Dagon: what had I
To oppose against such powerful arguments?
Only my love of thee held long debate,
And combated in silence all these reasons
With hard contést: at length that grounded maxim
So rife and celebrated in the mouths
Of wisest men, that to the public good
Private respects must yield, with grave authority,
Took full possession of me, and prevailed;
Virtue, as I thought, truth, duty, so enjoining.

SAMSON.

I thought where all thy circling wiles would end;
In feigned religion, smooth hypocrisy!
But had thy love, still odiously pretended,

Been, as it ought, sincere, it would have taught thee
Far other reasonings, brought forth other deeds.
I, before all the daughters of my tribe
And of my nation, chose thee from among
My enemies, loved thee, as too well thou knewest;
Too well; unbosomed all my secrets to thee,
Not out of levity, but overpowered
By thy request, who could deny thee nothing;
Yet now am judged an enemy. Why then
Didst thou at first receive me for thy husband,
Then, as since then, thy country's foe professed?
Being once a wife, for me thou wast to leave
Parents and country; nor was I their subject;
Nor under their protection, but my own,
Thou mine, not theirs: if aught against my life
Thy country sought of thee, it sought unjustly,
Against the law of nature, law of nations.
These false pretexts, and varnished colors, failing,
Bare in thy guilt, how foul must thou appear!

DALILA.

In argument with men a woman ever
Goes by the worse, whatever be her cause.

SAMSON.

For want of words, no doubt, or lack of breath;
Witness when I was worried with thy peals.

DALILA.

I was a fool, too rash, and quite mistaken
In what I thought would have succeeded best.
Let me obtain forgiveness of thee, Samson;
Afford me place to show what recompense
Towards thee I intend for what I have misdone,
Misguided; only what remains past cure
Bear not too sensibly, nor still insist
To afflict thyself in vain: though sight be lost,
Life yet hath many solaces, enjoyed
Where other senses want not their delights,

At home in leisure and domestic ease,
Exempt from many a care and chance, to which
Eyesight exposes daily men abroad.
I to the lords will intercede, not doubting
Their favorable ear, that I may fetch thee
From forth this loathsome prison-house to abide
With me, where my redoubled love and care
With nursing diligence, to me glad office,
May ever tend about thee to old age,
With all things grateful cheered, and so supplied,
That, what by me thou hast lost, thou least shalt miss.

SAMSON.

No, no; of my condition take no care;
It fits not; thou and I long since are twain:
Nor think me so unwary or accursed,
To bring my feet again into the snare
Where once I have been caught: I know thy trains,
Though dearly to my cost, thy gins, and toils;
Thy fair enchanted cup, and warbling charms,
No more on me have power; their force is nulled;
So much of adder's wisdom I have learned,
To fence my ear against thy sorceries.
If in my flower of youth and strength, when all men
Loved, honored, feared me, thou alone couldst hate me,
Thy husband, slight me, sell me, and forego me;
How wouldst thou use me now, blind and thereby
Deceivable, in most things as a child.
Helpless, thence easily contemned and scorned,
And last neglected! how wouldst thou insult
When I must live uxorious to thy will
In perfect thraldom! how again betray me,
Bearing my words and doings to the lords
To gloss upon, and, censuring, frown or smile!
This jail I count the house of liberty
To thine, whose doors my feet shall never enter.

DALILA.

Let me approach at least, and touch thy hand.

SAMSON.

Not for thy life, lest fierce remembrance wake
My sudden rage to tear thee joint by joint.
At distance I forgive thee; go with that;
Bewail thy falsehood, and the pious works
It hath brought forth to make thee memorable
Among illustrious women, faithful wives!
Cherish thy hastened widowhood with the gold
Of matrimonial treason! so farewell.

DALILA.

I see thou art implacable, more deaf
To prayers than winds and seas; yet winds to seas
Are reconciled at length, and sea to shore:
Thy anger, unappeasable, still rages,
Eternal tempest, never to be calmed.
Why do I humble thus myself, and, suing
For peace, reap nothing but repulse and hate;
Bid go with evil omen, and the brand
Of infamy upon my name denounced?
To mix with thy concernments I desist
Henceforth, nor too much disapprove my own.
Fame, if not double-faced, is double-mouthed,
And with contráry blast proclaims most deeds;
On both his wings, one black, the other white,
Bears greatest names in his wild aery flight.
My name perhaps among the circumcised
In Dan, in Judah, and the bordering tribes,
To all posterity may stand defamed,
With malediction mentioned, and the blot
Of falsehood most unconjugal traduced.
But in my country, where I most desire,
In Ecron, Gaza, Asdod, and in Gath,
I shall be named among the famousest
Of women, sung at solemn festivals,
Living and dead recorded, who, to save
Her country from a fierce destroyer, chose
Above the faith of wedlock-bands; my tomb
With odors visited and annual flowers;
Not less renowned than in mount Ephraim

Jael, who with inhospitable guile
Smote Sisera sleeping, through the temples nailed.
Nor shall I count it heinous to enjoy
The public marks of honor and reward
Conferred upon me, for the piety
Which to my country I was judged to have shown.
At this whoever envies or repines,
I leave him to his lot, and like my own. [*Exit.*

MANOAH.

She 's gone, a manifest serpent by her sting
Discovered in the end, till now concealed.

SAMSON.

So let her go; God sent her to debase me,
And aggravate my folly, who committed
To such a viper his most sacred trust
Of secrecy, my safety, and my life.

From Milton's "SAMSON AGONISTES" (*condensed*).

JEPHTHA'S DAUGHTER.

MERLE, *Pinx.* JEHENNE, *Lith.*

JEPHTHA'S DAUGHTER.

THIS story, which has furnished so many themes for the poet and artist, belongs, like that of Samson, to the stormy and unsettled period of Jewish history which is covered by the Book of Judges.

Jephtha, an illegitimate son, is cast out by his brethren, goes off into a kind of border-land, and becomes, in that turbulent period, a leader of a somewhat powerful tribe.

These times of the Judges remind us forcibly, in some respects, of the chivalric ages. There was the same opportunity for an individual to rise to power by personal valor, and become an organizer and leader in society. A brave man was a nucleus around whom gathered others less brave, seeking protection, and the individual in time became a chieftain. The bravery of Jephtha was so great, and his power and consideration became such, that when his native land was invaded by the Ammonites, he was sent for by a solemn assembly of his people, and appointed their chief. Jephtha appears, from the story, to have been a straightforward, brave, generous, God-fearing man.

The story of his vow is briefly told. "And Jephtha vowed a vow unto the Lord and said, If thou wilt without fail deliver the children of Ammon into my hands, then it shall be that whatsoever cometh first out of my door to meet me, when I return, shall be the Lord's, and I will offer it as a whole offering unto the Lord." The vow was recorded, a great victory was given, and the record says, "And Jephtha came to Mizpah, unto his house, and behold, his daughter came out to meet him with timbrels. She was his only child, and beside her he had neither son nor daughter. And it came to pass, when he saw her, that he rent his clothes, and said, Alas! my daughter, thou hast brought me very low; for I have opened my mouth to the Lord, and cannot go back. And she said, My father, if thou hast opened thy mouth to the Lord, do to me according to that which hath proceeded out of thy mouth; forasmuch as the Lord hath taken vengeance for thee of thine enemies, even the children of Ammon. And she said unto her father, Let this thing be done for me: Let me alone two months, that I may go up and down upon the mountains to bewail my virginity, I and my fellows. And he said, Go. And he sent her away for two months, and she went with her companions and bewailed her virginity upon the mountains. And it came to pass at the end of two months, that she returned to her father, who did with her according to his vow."

And what was that? The popular version generally has been that Jephtha killed his daughter, and offered her a burnt sacrifice. Josephus puts this interpretation upon it, saying that "he offered such an oblation as was neither conformable to the law nor acceptable to God; not weighing with himself what opinion the hearers would have of such a practice." A large and very learned and respectable body of commentators among the Jews, both ancient and modern, deny this interpretation, and, as appears to us, for the best of reasons.

Jephtha was a Jew, and human sacrifice was above all things abhorrent to the Jewish law and to the whole national feeling. There is full evidence, in other pictures of life and manners given in the Book of Judges, that in spite of the turbulence of the times, there were in the country many noble, God-fearing men and women who intelligently understood and practiced the wise and merciful system of Moses.

Granting that Jephtha, living in the heathen border-land, had mingled degrading superstitions with his faith, it seems improbable that such men as Boaz, the husband of Ruth, Elkanah, the husband of Hannah, Manoah and his wife, the parents of Samson, and the kind of people with whom they associated, could have accepted, as Judge of Israel, a man whom their laws would regard as guilty of such a crime. Besides, the Jewish law contained direct provisions for such vows. In three or four places in the Jewish law, it is expressly stated that where a human being comes into the position of a whole offering to God, the life of that human being is not to be taken; and a process of substitution and redemption is pointed out. Thus the first-born of all animals and the first-born of all men were alike commanded to be made whole offerings to the Lord: the animals were slain and burnt, but the human being was redeemed. No one can deny that all these considerations establish a strong probability.

Finally, when historians and commentators are divided as to a fact, we are never far out of the way in taking that solution which is most honorable to our common human nature, and the most in accordance with our natural wishes. We suppose, therefore, that the daughter of Jephtha was simply taken from the ordinary life of woman, and made an offering to the Lord. She could be no man's wife; and with the feelings which were had in those days as to marriage, such a lot was to be lamented as the cutting off of all earthly hopes. It put an end to the house of Jephtha, as besides her he had no son or daughter, and it accounts for the language with which the account closes, "She knew not a man," — a wholly unnecessary statement, if it be meant to say that she was killed. The more we reflect upon it, the more probable it seems that this is the right view of the matter.

The existence from early times among the Jews of an order of women who renounced the usual joys and privileges of the family state, to devote themselves to religious and charitable duties, is often asserted. Walter Scott, a learned authority as to antiquities, and one who seldom made a representation without examination, makes Rebecca, in Ivanhoe, declare to Rowena that from earliest times such an order of women had existed among her people, and to them she purposes to belong.

We cannot leave the subject without pausing to wonder at the exquisite manner in which the historian, whoever he was, has set before us a high and lovely ideal of womanhood in this Judæan girl. There is but a sentence, yet what calmness, what high-mindedness, what unselfish patriotism, are in the words! "My father, if thou hast opened thy mouth to the Lord, do to me according to thy promise, forasmuch as the Lord hath taken vengeance on thine enemies, the children of Ammon."

Whatever it was to which she so calmly acceded, it was to her the death of all earthly hope, calmly accepted in the very flush and morning tide of victory. How heroic the soul that could meet so sudden a reverse with so unmoved a spirit!

JEPHTHA'S DAUGHTER.

SHE stood before her father's gorgeous tent,
To listen for his coming. Her loose hair
Was resting on her shoulders, like a cloud
Floating around a statue, and the wind,
Just swaying her light robe, revealed a shape
Praxiteles might worship. She had clasped
Her hands upon her bosom, and had raised
Her beautiful, dark, Jewish eyes to heaven,
Till the long lashes lay upon her brow.
Her lip was slightly parted, like the cleft
Of a pomegranate blossom; and her neck,
Just where the cheek was melting to its curve
With the unearthly beauty sometimes there
Was shaded, as if light had fallen off,
Its surface was so polished. She was quelling
Her light, quick breath, to hear; and the white rose
Scarce moved upon her bosom, as it swelled,
Like nothing but a lovely dream of light,
To meet the arching of her queenly neck.
Her countenance was radiant with love —
She looked like one to die for it — a being
Whose whole existence was the pouring out
Of rich and deep affections. I have thought
A brother's and a sister's love was much;
I know a brother's is — for I have been
A sister's idol — and I know how full
The heart may be of tenderness to her!
But the affection of a delicate child
For a fond father, gushing, as it does,
With the sweet springs of life, and pouring on,
Through all earth's changes, like a river's course,
Chastened with reverence, and made more pure
By the world's discipline of light and shade, —
'T is deeper — holier.

The wind bore on
The leaden tramp of thousands. Clarion notes
Rang sharply on the ear at intervals;
And the low, mingled din of mighty hosts
Returning from the battle pour'd from far,
Like the deep murmur of a restless sea.
They came, as earthly conquerors always come,
With blood and splendor, revelry and woe.
The stately horse treads proudly, — he hath trod
The brow of death as well. The chariot-wheels
Of warriors roll magnificently on, —
Their weight hath crushed the fallen. *Man* is there —
Majestic, lordly man — with his sublime
And elevated brow and godlike frame;
Lifting his crest in triumph, — for his heel
Hath trod the dying like a wine-press down!

The mighty Jephtha led his warriors on
Through Mizpeh's streets. His helm was proudly set
And his stern lip curled slightly, as if praise
Were for the hero's scorn. His step was firm,
But free as India's leopard; and his mail,
Whose shekels none in Israel might bear,
Was like a cedar's tassel on his frame.
His crest was Judah's kingliest; and the look
Of his dark, lofty eye, and bended brow,
Might quell the lion. He led on; but thoughts
Seemed gathering round which troubled him. The veins
Grew visible upon his swarthy brow,
And his proud lip was pressed as if with pain.
He trod less firmly; and his restless eye
Glanced forward frequently, as if some ill
He dared not meet were there. His home was near;

. . . . .

He gazed intensely forward. The tall firs
Before his tent were motionless. The leaves
Of the sweet aloe, and the clustering vines
Which half concealed his threshold, met his eye,
Unchanged and beautiful; and one by one,
The balsam, with its sweet-distilling stems,
And the Circassian rose, and all the crowd
Of silent and familiar things, stole up,

Like the recovered passages of dreams.
He strode on rapidly. A moment more,
And he had reached his home; when, lo! there sprang
One with a bounding footstep, and a brow
Of light, to meet him. O, how beautiful! —
Her dark eye flashing like a sunlit gem, —
And her luxuriant hair! — 't was like the sweep
Of a swift wing in visions. He stood still,
As if the sight had withered him. She threw
Her arms about his neck, — he heeded not.
She called him "Father," — but he answered not.
She stood and gazed upon him. Was he wroth?
There was no anger in that bloodshot eye.
Had sickness seized him? She unclasped his helm,
And laid her white hand gently on his brow,
And the large veins felt stiff and hard, like cords.
The touch aroused him. He raised up his hands,
And spoke the name of God, in agony.
She knew that he was stricken, then; and rushed
Again into his arms; and, with a flood
Of tears she could not bridle, sobbed a prayer
That he would tell her of his wretchedness.
He told her, — and a momentary flush
Shot o'er her countenance; and then the soul
Of Jephtha's daughter wakened; and she stood
Calmly and nobly up, and said 't was well, —
And she would die. . . . . . .
The sun had wellnigh set.
The fire was on the altar; and the priest
Of the High God was there. A wasted man
Was stretching out his withered hands to Heaven,
As if he would have prayed, but had no words, —
And she who was to die, the calmest one
In Israel at that hour, stood up alone,
And waited for the sun to set. Her face
Was pale, but very beautiful, — her lip
Had a more delicate outline, and the tint
Was deeper; but her countenance was like
The majesty of angels.
The sun set, —
And she was dead, — but not by violence.

Nathaniel P. Willis.

SONG OF JEPHTHA'S DAUGHTER.

SINCE our country, our God, O my sire!
Demand that thy daughter expire;
Since thy triumph was bought by thy vow,
Strike the bosom that 's bared for thee now!

And the voice of my mourning is o'er,
And the mountains behold me no more;
If the hand that I love lay me low,
There cannot be pain in the blow!

And of this, O my father! be sure, —
That the blood of thy child is as pure
As the blessing I beg ere it flow,
And the last thought that soothes me below.

Though the virgins of Salem lament,
Be the judge and the hero unbent!
I have won the great battle for thee,
And my father and country are free!

When this blood of thy giving hath gushed,
When the voice that thou lovest is hushed,
Let my memory still be thy pride,
And forget not I smiled when I died.

Lord Byron.

LAMENT OF THE VIRGINS.

"And it was a custom in Israel, that the daughters of Israel went yearly to lament the daughter of Jephtha, the Gileadite, four days in a year."—JUDGES xi. 40.

OH, of dance and song the pride,
Jephtha's daughter, young and fair,
Never now the wreath of bride,
Ne'er the bridal veil shall wear!
Ne'er with cymbals light advancing,
Shall she greet her true love home,
Never in the valleys dancing,
Bound like ocean's purest foam.
Never shall she whisper,—never,
Vows that bind the Hebrew maid;
Hers from all the world to sever,
Hers the hermit cell and shade.

O, of song and dance the pride,
Jephtha's daughter, young and fair;
She should be a hero's bride,
She a hero son should bear.
But her fortune is another,
She shall ne'er love's worship know;
Ne'er a babe shall call her mother,
Nestled on her breast of snow.
She hath gone from spring and fountain;
She hath vanished from the rills;
Lone she wanders on the mountain,
And her home is on the hills.

O, of dance and song the pride,
Jephtha's daughter, young and fair,
In the mount she must abide,
And her virgin vestments wear.

LAMENT OF THE VIRGINS.

There her foot that bounded lightly,
  Faint with maiden step shall go;
And her dance that was so sprightly,
  To a pensive gliding grow.
She shall bend 'mid caverns praying,
  Like a flower that trembles there,
While anear the wild fox, baying,
  Breaks alone the silent air.

O, of song and dance the pride,
  Jephtha's daughter, young and fair;
Angels with her shall abide,
  Angels smile upon her prayer.
Angels there shall be her lovers,
  In such love as angels use;
While each wing that o'er her hovers,
  Sheds around celestial dews:
Angels there, that cheer her sighing,
  Shall her loneliness beguile,
And the wings that shade her dying
  Waft her to the happy isle.

O, of dance and song the pride,
  Jephtha's daughter, young and fair;
Weep for her that doth abide
  On the lonely mountain there.
Many flowers like her have perished
  Ere their scented buds could ope;
But no flower was e'er so cherished,
  Ne'er like her a hero's hope.
Many maids have gone to slaughter,
  But they ne'er so lovely were:
Weep, O, weep for Jephtha's daughter;
  Weep, ye lovely, weep for her!

Arthur Cleveland Coxe.

RUTH.

DEVEDEUX, *Pinx.* JEHENNE, *Lith.*

RUTH THE MOABITESS.

THE story of Ruth is a beautiful idyl of domestic life, opening to us in the barbarous period of the *Judges*. In reading some of the latter chapters of that book, one might almost think that the system of Moses had proved a failure, and that the nation was lapsing back into the savage state of the heathen world around them; just as, in reading the history of the raids and feuds of the Middle Ages, one might consider Christianity a failure. But in both cases there were nooks and dells embosomed in the wild roughness of unsettled society, where good and honest hearts put forth blossoms of immortal sweetness and perfume. This history of Ruth unveils to us pictures of the best people and the best sort of life that were formed by the laws and institutes of Moses, — a life pastoral, simple, sincere, reverential, and benevolent.

The story is on this wise: A famine took place in the land of Judah, and a man named Elimelech went with his wife and two sons to sojourn in the land of Moab. The sons took each of them a wife of the daughters of Moab, and they dwelt there about ten years. After that, the man and both the sons died, and the mother, with her two widowed young daughters, prepared to return to her kindred. Here the scene of the little drama opens.

The mother, Naomi, comes to our view, a kind-hearted, commonplace woman, without any strong religious faith or possibility of heroic exaltation, — just one of those women who see the hard, literal side of a trial, ungilded by any faith or hope. We can fancy her discouraged and mournful air, and hear the melancholy croak in her voice as she talks to her daughters, when they profess their devotion to her, and their purpose to share her fortunes and go with her to the land of Israel.

"Turn again, my daughters; why will ye go with me? Are there yet any more sons in my womb, that they may be your husbands? Turn again, my daughters, go your way, for I am too old to have an husband. If I should say that I have hope to-night that I should have an husband, and bear sons, would ye tarry for them till they were grown? Would ye stay from having husbands? Nay, my daughters, it grieveth me for your sake that the hand of the Lord hath gone out against me."

This pre-eminently literal view of the situation seemed to strike one of the daughters as not to be gainsaid; for we read: "And they lifted up their voices and wept again, and Orpah kissed her mother-in-law, but Ruth clave unto her."

All the world through, from that time to this, have been these two classes of friends. The one weep, and kiss, and leave us to our fate, and go to seek their own fortunes. There are plenty of that sort every day. But the other are one with us for life or death.

The literal-minded, sorrowful old woman has no thought of inspiring such devotion. Orpah, in her mind, has done the sensible and only thing in leaving her, and she says to Ruth: "Behold, thy sister has returned unto her people and unto her gods; return thou after thy sister-in-law."

We see in this verse how devoid of religious faith is the mother. In a matter-of-course tone she speaks of Orpah having gone back to her gods, and recommends Ruth to do the like. And now the fair, sweet Ruth breaks forth in an unconscious poetry of affection, which has been consecrated as the language of true love ever since: "Entreat me not to leave thee, or to return from following after thee; for whither thou goest I will go, and where thou lodgest I will lodge: thy people shall be my people, and thy God my God. Where thou diest I will die, and there will I be buried: the Lord do so to me, and more also, if aught but death part thee and me."

Troth-plight of fondest lovers, marriage-vows straitest and most devoted, can have no love-language beyond this; it is the very crystallized and diamond essence of constancy and devotion. It is thus that minds which have an unconscious power of enthusiasm surprise and dominate their literal fellow-pilgrims. It is as if some silent dun-colored bird had broken out into wondrous ecstasies of silver song. Naomi looked on her daughter, and the narrative says, "When she saw that she was steadfastly minded to go with her, then she left speaking to her." But Ruth is ignorant of the beauty of her own nature; for Love never knows herself or looks in a mirror to ask if she be fair; and though her superior moral and emotive strength prevail over the lower nature of the mother, it is with a sweet, unconscious, yielding obedience that she follows her.

When they came back to their kindred, the scene is touchingly described. In her youth the mother had been gay and radiant, as her name, Naomi, "pleasant," signifies. "And it came to pass that when they came in, all the village was moved about them, and they said: Is this Naomi? And she said: "Call me not Naomi, call me Marah [bitterness]; for the Almighty hath dealt very bitterly with me. I went out full, and the Lord hath brought me again empty. Why then call ye me Naomi, seeing the Lord hath testified against me, and the Almighty hath afflicted me?"

We see here a common phase of a low order of religion. Naomi does not rebel at the Divine decree. She thinks that she is bitterly dealt with, but that there is no use in complaining, because it is the *Almighty* that has done it. It does not even occur to her that in going away from the land of true religion, and encouraging her sons to form marriages in a heathen land, she had done anything to make this affliction needful; and yet the whole story shows that but for this stroke the whole family would have settled down contentedly among the Moabites, and given up country and religion and God. There are many nowadays to whom just such afflictions are as needful, and to whom they seem as bitter and inexplicable.

The next scene shows us the barley-field of the rich proprietor, — "a mighty man, a man of wealth," the narrative calls him. Young men and maidens, a goodly company, are reaping, binding, and gathering. In the shade are the parched corn and sour wine, and other provisions set forth for the noontide rest and repast.

The gracious proprietor, a noble-minded, gentle old man, now comes upon the scene. "And behold, Boaz came from Bethlehem, and said to the reapers, The Lord be with you; and they answered, The Lord bless thee." The religious spirit of the master spread itself through all his hands, and the blessing that he breathes upon them was returned to him. The sacred simplicity of the scene is beyond praise.

He inquires of his men the history of this fair one who modestly follows the reapers, and, finding who she is, says: "Hearest thou, my daughter, go not to glean in any other field, but abide here with my maidens. Let thine eyes be upon the field that they reap, and go after them: have I not charged the young men not to touch thee? and when thou art athirst, go to the vessels and drink of that that the young men have drawn." Then she bowed herself and said: "Why have I found grace in thine eyes, that thou shouldst take knowledge of me, seeing I am a stranger?" And he said: "It hath been fully shown unto me all that thou hast done to thy mother-in-law since the death of thy husband; how thou hast left thy father and thy mother, and the land of thy nativity, and art come to a people that thou knewest not heretofore. The Lord recompense thy work, and a full reward be given thee of the God of Israel, under whose wings thou art come to trust."

We have afterwards the picture of the young gleaner made at home at the noontide repast, where the rich proprietor sat with his servants in parental equality, — "And she sat beside the reapers, and he did reach her parched corn, and she did eat and was sufficed."

There is a delicacy in the feeling inspired by the timid, modest stranger, which is expressed in the orders given by Boaz to the young men. "And it came to pass when she rose to glean, that Boaz commanded his young men, saying:

Let her glean even among the sheaves, and reproach her not; and let fall also some handfuls of purpose for her, that she may glean them, and rebuke her not."

Gleaning, by the institutes of Moses, was one of the allotted privileges of the poor. It was a beautiful feature of that system that consideration for the poor was interwoven with all the acts of common life. The language of the laws of Moses reminded the rich that they were of one family with the poor. "Thou shalt not harden thy heart nor shut thy hand from thy *poor brother*. Thou shalt surely give to him, and thy heart shall not be grieved when thou givest, because for this the Lord thy God shall bless thee." "And when ye reap the harvest of your land thou shalt not wholly reap the corners of the field, neither shalt thou gather the gleanings of thy harvest; and thou shalt not glean thy vineyard, neither shalt thou gather every grape of thy vineyard; thou shalt leave them for the poor and the stranger. I am the Lord." This provision for the unfortunate operated both ways. It taught consideration and thoughtfulness to the rich, and industry and self-respect to the poor. They were not humbled as paupers. They were not to be beggars, but gleaners, and a fair field for self-respecting labor was opened to them. In the spirit of these generous laws the rich proprietor veils his patronage of the humble maid. Ruth was to be abundantly helped, as it were, by a series of fortunate accidents.

We see in the character of Boaz the high-minded, chivalrous gentleman, devout in his religion Godward, and considerately thoughtful of his neighbor; especially mindful of the weak and helpless and unprotected. It was the working out, in one happy instance, of the ideal of manhood the system of Moses was designed to create.

And now the little romance goes on to a happy termination. The fair gleaner returns home artlessly triumphant with the avails of her day's toil, and tells her mother of the kind patronage she has received. At once, on hearing the name, the prudent mother recognizes the near kinsman of the family, bound, by the law of Moses and the custom of the land, to become the husband and protector of her daughter. In the eye of Jewish law and Jewish custom Ruth already belonged to Boaz, and had a right to claim the position and protection of a wife. The system of Moses solved the problem of woman by allotting to every woman a man as a protector. A widow had her son to stand for her; but if a widow were left without a son, then the nearest kinsman of the former husband was bound to take her to wife. The manner in which Naomi directs the simple-minded and obedient daughter to throw herself on the protection of her rich kinsman is so far removed from all our modern ideas of propriety that it cannot be judged by them. She is directed to seek the threshing-floor at night, to lie down at his feet, and draw over her his mantle; thus, in the symbolic language of the times, asserting her humble right to the protection of a wife. Ruth is shown to us as one of those artless, confiding natures that see no evil in what is purely and rightly intended. It is enough for her, a stranger, to understand that her mother, an honored Judæan matron, would command nothing which was not considered decorous and proper among her people. She obeys without a question. In the same spirit of sacred simplicity in which the action was performed it was received. There is a tender dignity and a chivalrous delicacy in the manner in which the bold yet humble advance is accepted.

"And Boaz awoke, and, behold, a woman lay at his feet. And he said, Who art thou? And she said, I am Ruth, thy handmaid. Spread thy skirt over me, for thou art my near kinsman. And he said, Blessed art thou of the Lord, my daughter, for thou hast shown more kindness at the end than in the beginning, inasmuch as thou followedst not the young men, poor or rich. And now, my daughter, fear not; I will do for thee all that thou requirest, for all the city of my people doth know that thou art a virtuous woman."

The very crucial test of gentlemanly delicacy and honor is the manner in which it knows how to receive an ingenuous and simple-hearted act of confidence. As in the fields Boaz did not ostentatiously urge alms upon the timid maiden, but suffered her to have the pleasure of gleaning for herself, so now he treats this act by which she throws herself upon his protection as an honor done to him, for which he is bound to be grateful. He hastens to assure her that he is her debtor for the preference she shows him. That courtesy and chivalric feeling for woman which was so strong a feature in the character of Moses, and which is embodied in so many of his laws and institutes, comes out in this fine Hebrew gentleman as perfectly, but with more simplicity, than in the Sir Charles Grandison of the eighteenth century. And so, at last, the lovely stranger, Ruth the Moabitess, becomes the wife of the rich landed proprietor, with the universal consent of all the people. "And all the people that were in the gates and the elders said, We are witnesses. The Lord make this woman that is come into thy house like Rachel and like Leah, which two did build the house of Israel."

From this marriage of the chivalrous, pious old man with the devoted and loving Ruth the Moabitess, sprang an auspicious lineage. The house of David, the holy maiden of Judæa and her son, whom all nations call blessed, were the illustrious seed of this wedding. In the scene at the birth of the first son of Ruth, we have a fine picture of the manners of those days. "And the women said unto Naomi, Blessed be the Lord which hath not left thee this day without a kinsman, that his name may be famous in Israel. And he shall be unto thee a restorer of thy life and a nourisher of thy old age: for thy daughter-in-law, which loveth thee, and is better to thee than seven sons, hath borne him. And Naomi took the child and laid it in her bosom, and became nurse unto it. And the women her neighbors gave it a name, saying, There is a son born to Naomi, and they called his name Obed; he is the father of Jesse, the father of David."

In all this we see how strong is the impression which the *loving* nature of Ruth makes in the narrative. From the union of this woman so tender and true, and this man so gracious and noble and chivalric, comes the great heart-poet of the world. No other songs have been so dear to mankind, so cherished in the heart of high and low, rich and poor, in every nation and language, as these Psalms of David.

> "It is that music to whose tone
>   The common pulse of man keeps time,
> In cot or castle's mirth or moan,
>   In cold or fervid clime."

In the tender friendship of David for Jonathan, we see again the loving constancy of Ruth in a manly form, — the love between soul and soul, which was "wonderful, passing the love of women." In the ideal which we form of Mary, the mother of Jesus, lowly, modest, pious, constant, rich in the power of love and in a simple, trustful faith, we see the transmission of family traits through generations. Dante, in his "Paradise," places Ruth among the holy women who sit at the feet of the glorified Madonna. The Providence that called a Moabitish ancestress into that golden line whence should spring the Messiah was a sort of morning star of intimation that He should be of no limited nationality; that he was to be the Son of MAN, the Lord and brother of all mankind.

RUTH.

IN the land of Bethlehem-Judah
Let us linger, let us wander;
Ephrath's sorrow, Rachel's pillar,
Lieth in the valley yonder;
And the yellow barley harvest
Floods it with a golden glory.
Let us back into the old time,
Dreaming of her tender story,
Of her true heart's strong devotion,
From beyond the Dead Sea water,
From the heathen land of Moab, —
Mahlon's wife and Mara's daughter.

On the terebinth and fig tree
Suns of olden time are shining,
And the dark leaf of the olive
Scarcely shows its silver lining;
For still noon is on the thicket,
Where the blue-necked pigeons listen
To their own reproachful music,
And the red pomegranates glisten;
As a queen a golden circlet,
As a maid might wear a blossom,
So the valley wears the cornfields
Heaving on her fertile bosom;
And the wild gray hills stand o'er them,
All their terraced vineyards swelling,
Like the green waves of a forest,
Up to David's mountain dwelling.

Lo! the princely hearted Boaz
Moves among his reapers slowly;

And the widowed child of Moab
  Bends behind the gleaners lowly,
Gathering, gleaning, as she goeth
  Down the slopes and up the hollows;
While the love of old Naomi
  Like a guardian angel follows.
And he speaketh words of kindness,
  Words of kindness, calm and stately;
Till he breaks the springs of gladness
  That lay cold and frozen lately;
And the love-flowers that had faded
  Deep within her bosom lonely,
Slowly open as he questions,
  Soon for him to blossom only,
When that spring shall fill with music,
  Like an overflowing river,
All his homestead; and those flowers
  Bloom beside his hearth forever.
Mother of a line of princes,
  Wrought into that race's story,
Whom the Godhead breaking earthward
  Marked with an unearthly glory!
Still he walks among the reapers,
  And the day is nearly over,
And the lonely mountain partridge
  Seeks afar his scanty cover;
And the flocks of wild blue pigeons,
  That had gleaned behind the gleaner,
Find their shelter in the thicket;
  And the cloudless sky grows sheener
With a sudden flush of crimson,
  Steeping in a fiery luster
Every sheaf-top in the valley,
  On the hillside every cluster.

Slowly, slowly fade, fair picture,
  Yellow lights and purple shadows,
On the valley, on the mountain,
  And sweet Ruth among the meadows!
Stay awhile, true heart, and teach us,
  Pausing in thy matron beauty,

Care of elders, love of kindred,
  All unselfish thought and duty.
Linger, Boaz, noble-minded!
  Teach us, haughty and unsparing,
Tender care for lowlier station,
  Kindly speech and courteous bearing.
Still each softest, loveliest color,
  Shrine the form beloved and living;
Heroine of our heart's first poem,
  Through our childhood's dreamland moving,
When the great old Bible opened,
  And a pleasant pastoral measure,
As our mothers read the story,
  Filled our infant hearts with pleasure.

Dublin University Magazine.

THE FAITH OF RUTH.

THE plume-like swaying of the auburn corn,
  By soft winds to a dreamy motion fanned,
Still brings me back thine image, O forlorn,
  Yet not forsaken, Ruth! I see thee stand
  Lone, 'midst the gladness of the harvest band,—
Lone as a wood-bird on the ocean's foam,
  Fallen in its weariness. Thy fatherland
Smiles far away! yet to the sense of home,
  That finest, purest, which can recognize
  Home in affection's glance, forever true
Beats thy calm heart; and if thy gentle eyes
  Gleam tremulous through tears, 't is not to rue
Those words, immortal in their deep love's tone,
  "Thy people and thy God shall be mine own!"

Felicia Hemans.

RUTH.

SHE stood breast-high amid the corn,
Clasped by the golden light of morn,
Like the sweetheart of the sun,
Who many a glowing kiss had won.

On her cheek an autumn flush
Deeply ripened; — such a blush
In the midst of brown was born,
Like red poppies grown with corn.

Round her eyes her tresses fell, —
Which were blackest none could tell;
But long lashes veiled a light
That had else been all too bright.

And her hat, with shady brim,
Made her tressy forehead dim; —
Thus she stood among the stooks,
Praising God with sweetest looks.

Sure, I said, God did not mean
Where I reap thou shouldst but glean;
Lay thy sheaf adown and come,
Share my harvest and my home.

Thomas Hood.

HANNAH.

BROCHART, *Pinx.* JEHENNE, *Lith.*

HANNAH THE PRAYING MOTHER.

THE story of Hannah is a purely domestic one, and is most valuable in unveiling the intimate and trustful life of faith that existed between the Jehovah revealed in the Old Testament and each separate soul, however retired and humble. It is not God the Lawgiver and King, but, if we may so speak, God in his private and confidential relations to the individual. The story opens briefly, after the fashion of the Bible, whose brevity in words is such a contrast to the tediousness of most professed sacred books.

"There was a man," says the record, "named Elkanah, and he had two wives; and the name of the one was Hannah, and the name of the other Peninnah, and Peninnah had children, but Hannah had none." Hannah, from the story, appears to have had one of those intense natures, all nerve and sensibility, on which every trouble lies with double weight. The lack of children in an age when motherhood was considered the essential glory of woman, was to her the climax of anguish and mortification. Nor was there wanting the added burden of an unfriendly party to notice and to inflame the hidden wound by stinging commentaries; for we are told that "her adversary provoked her sore, to make her fret." And thus, year by year, as the family went up to the sacred feast at Shiloh, and other exultant mothers displayed their fair sons and daughters, the sacred feast was turned into gall for the unblest one, and we are told that Hannah "wept and did not eat." "Then said Elkanah unto her, Hannah, why weepest thou? and why eatest thou not? and why is thy heart grieved? Am I not better to thee than ten sons?"

Hannah was one of a class of women in whom genius and a poetic nature are struggling with a vague intensity, giving the keenest edge to desire and to disappointment. All Judæan women desire children, but Hannah had that vivid sense of nationality, that identification of self with the sublime future of her people, that made it bitter to be excluded from all share in those hopes and joys of motherhood from which the earth's deliverer was to spring. She desired a son, as poets desire song, as an expression of all that was heroic and unexpressed in herself, and as a tribute to the future glories of her people. A poet stricken with paralysis might suffer as she suffered. But it was a kind and degree of sorrow, the result of an exceptional nature, which few could comprehend. To some it would afford occasion only for vulgar jests. Even her husband, devoted as he was, wondered at rather than sympathised with it.

It appears that there rose at last one of those flood-tides of feeling when the soul cries out for relief, and *must* have a Helper; and Hannah bethought her of the words of Moses, "What nation is there that hath their God *so nigh* unto them as the Lord our God is unto us, for all that we call unto him for?" It is precisely for such sorrows — intimate, private, personal, and not to be comprehended fully by any earthly friend — that an All-seeing, loving Father is needed. And Hannah followed the teachings of her religion when she resolved to make a confidant of her God, and ask of him the blessing her soul fainted for. She chose the sacred feast at Shiloh for the interview with the gracious Helper; and, after the festival, remained alone in the holy place in an ecstasy of fervent prayer. The narrative says: "And she was in bitterness of soul and prayed unto the Lord and wept sore. And she vowed a vow and said, O Lord of Hosts, if thou wilt indeed look on the affliction of thine handmaid, and remember me, and not forget thine handmaid, but will give unto thine handmaid a man-child, then will I give him unto the Lord all the days of his life. And it came to pass as she continued praying before the Lord, that Eli marked her mouth. Now Hannah she spake in her heart, only her lips moved, but her voice was not heard; therefore Eli thought she had been drunken."

He — dear, kind-hearted, blundering old priest — reproved her with about as much tact as many similar, well-meaning, obtuse people use nowadays in the management of natures whose heights and depths they cannot comprehend. Hannah meekly answers: "No, my lord, I am a woman of a sorrowful spirit; I have drunk neither wine nor strong drink, but have poured out my soul before the Lord. Count not thy handmaid for a daughter of Belial, for out of the abundance of my complaint and grief have I spoken hitherto. Then Eli answered and said, Go in peace, the God of Israel grant thee thy petition thou hast asked of him. And she said, Let thine handmaid find grace in thy sight. So the woman went her way and did eat, and her countenance was no more sad."

This experience illustrates that kind of prevailing prayer that comes when the soul, roused to the full intensity of its being by the pressure of some anguish, pours itself out like a wave into the bosom of its God. The very outgush is a relief; there is healing in the very act of self-abandonment, as the whole soul casts itself on God. And though there be no present fulfillment, yet, in point of fact, peace and rest come to the spirit. Hannah had no voice of promise, no external sign, only the recorded promise of God to hear prayer; but the prayer brought relief. All the agony of desire passed away. Her countenance was no more sad. In due time, the visible answer came. Hannah was made the happy mother of a son, whom she called Samuel, or "Asked of God."

This year, when the family went up to Shiloh, Hannah remained with her infant; for she said to her husband, "I will not go up until the child be weaned; and then will I bring him that he may appear before the Lord, and there abide forever." The period of weaning was of a much later date among Jewish women than in modern times; and we may imagine the little Samuel three or four years old when his mother prepares, with all solemnity, to carry him and present him in the temple as her offering to God. "And when she had weaned him she took him up with her, with three bullocks, and one ephah of flour, and a bottle of wine, and brought him unto the house of the Lord in

Shiloh; and the child was young. And they slew a bullock, and brought the child to Eli. And she said, O my lord, as thy soul liveth, my lord, I am the woman that stood by thee here praying unto the Lord. For this child I prayed, and the Lord hath given me my petition which I asked of him. Therefore also have I lent him to the Lord; as long as he liveth he shall be lent to the Lord. And she worshiped the Lord there."

And now the depths of this silent woman's soul break forth into a song of praise and thanksgiving. Hannah rises before us as the inspired poetess, and her song bears a striking resemblance in theme and in cast of thought to that of Mary the mother of Jesus, years after. Indeed, there is in the whole history of this sacred and consecrated child, a foreshadowing of that more celestial flower of Nazareth that should yet arise from the Judæan stock. This idea of a future Messiah and King permeated every pious soul in the nation, and gave a solemn intensity to the usual rejoicings of motherhood; for who knew whether the auspicious child might not spring from her lineage! We see, in the last verse of this poem, that Hannah's thoughts in her hour of joy fix themselves on the glorious future of the coming King and Anointed One as the climax of her joy.

It will be interesting to compare this song of Hannah with that of Mary, and notice how completely the ideas of the earlier mother had melted and transfused themselves into the heart of Mary. Years after, when the gathering forces of the Church and State were beginning to muster themselves against Martin Luther, and he stood as one man against a world, he took refuge in this song of the happy woman; printed it as a tract, with pointed commentaries, and spread it all over Europe; and in thousands of hamlets hearts were beating to the heroic words of the Judæan mother: —

"My heart rejoiceth in Jehovah,
My horn is exalted in Jehovah;
My speech shall flow out over my enemies,
Because I rejoice in thy salvation.
There is none holy as Jehovah:
For there is none beside thee:
Neither is there any rock like our God.

Talk no more so exceeding proudly;
Let not arrogance come out of thy mouth:
For Jehovah is a God of knowledge,
By him are actions weighed.
The bows of mighty men are broken,
But the weak are girded with strength.
The rich have hired out for bread;
But the hungry cease from want.
The barren woman hath borne seven;
The fruitful one hath grown feeble.
Jehovah killeth and maketh alive;
He bringeth down to the grave and bringeth up.
Jehovah maketh poor and maketh rich;
He bringeth low, and lifteth up.
He raiseth the poor out of the dust,
He lifteth the beggar from the dunghill,
To set them among princes,
To make them inherit the throne of glory;
For the pillars of the earth are Jehovah's,
He hath set the world upon them.
He will keep the feet of his saints,
The wicked shall be silent in darkness;
For by strength no man shall prevail.
The adversaries of Jehovah shall be broken to pieces;
Out of heaven shall he thunder upon them.
Jehovah shall judge the ends of the earth;
He shall give strength unto his King,
And exalt the horn of his Anointed."

This song shows the fire, the depth, the fervency of the nature of this woman, capable of rising to the sublimest conceptions. It is the ecstasy of the triumph of conscious weakness in an omnipotent protector. Through her own experience, as it is with every true soul, she passes to the experience of universal humanity; in her Deliverer she sees the Deliverer and Helper of all the helpless and desolate; and thus, through the gate of personal experience, she comes to a wide sympathy with all who live. She loves her God, not mainly and only for what he is to her, but for what he is to all. How high and splendid were these conceptions and experiences that visited and hallowed the life of the simple and lowly Jewish woman in those rugged and unsettled periods, and what beautiful glimpses do we get of the good and honest-hearted people that lived at that time in Palestine, and went up yearly to worship at Shiloh!

After this we have a few more touches in this beautiful story. The little one remained in the temple; for it is said, "And Samuel ministered before the Lord, being a child, girded with a linen ephod. Moreover, his mother made him a little coat and brought it to him from year to year, when she came up with her husband to offer the yearly sacrifice." How the little one was cared for the story does not say. In some passages of the Bible, we have intimations of an order of consecrated women who devoted themselves to the ministries of the temple, like Anna the prophetess, "who departed not from the temple, but served God with fasting and prayer, night and day." Doubtless from the hands of such were motherly ministries. One rejoices to hear that the Gracious Giver blessed this mother abundantly more than she asked or thought; for we are told that a family of three sons and two daughters were given to her.

We cannot forbear to add to this story that of the sacred little one, who grew fair as the sheltered lily in the house of God. Child of prayer, born in the very ardor and ecstasy of a soul uplifted to God, his very nature seemed heavenly, and the benignant Father early revealed himself to him, choosing him as a medium for divine messages. One of the most thrilling and poetic passages in the Bible describes the first call of the Divine One to the consecrated child. The lamps burning in the holy place; the little one lying down to sleep; the mysterious voice calling him; his innocent wonder, and the slow perception of old Eli of the true significance of the event, — all these form a beautiful introduction to the life of the last and most favored of those prophetic magistrates who interpreted to the Jewish people the will of God. Samuel was the last of the Judges, — the strongest, the purest, and most blameless, — the worthy son of such a mother.

THE PRESENTATION OF SAMUEL.

THE rose was in rich bloom on Sharon's plain,
When a young mother, with her first-born, thence
Went up to Zion; for the boy was vowed
Unto the temple service. By the hand
She led him, and her silent soul, the while,
Oft as the dewy laughter of his eye
Met her sweet, serious glance, rejoiced to think
That aught so pure, so beautiful, was hers
To bring before her God. So passed they on
O'er Judah's hills; and wheresoe'er the leaves
Of the broad sycamore made sounds at noon
Like lulling rain-drops, or the olive-boughs,
With their cool dimness, crossed the sultry blue
Of Syria's heaven, she paused that he might rest;
Yet from her own meek eyelids chased the sleep
That weighed their dark fringe down, to sit and watch
The crimson deepening o'er his cheek's repose,
As at a red flower's heart. And where a fount
Lay like a twilight star 'midst palmy shades,
Making its banks green gems along the wild,
There too she lingered, from the diamond wave
Drawing bright water for his rosy lips,
And softly parting clusters of jet curls
To bathe his brow.
At last the Fane was reached,
The Earth's One Sanctuary, — and rapture hushed
Her bosom, as before her, through the day,
It rose, a mountain of white marble, steeped
In light like floating gold. But when that hour
Waned to the farewell moment, when the boy
Lifted through rainbow-gleaming tears his eye
Beseechingly to hers, and half in fear
Turned from the white-robed priest, and round her arm

Clung even as joy clings, — the deep springtide
Of nature then swelled high, and o'er her child
Bending, her soul broke forth, in mingled sounds
Of weeping and sad song. "Alas!" she cried,
"Alas! my boy, thy gentle grasp is on me;
The bright tears quiver in thy pleading eyes,
And now fond thoughts arise,
And silver cords again to earth have won me;
And like a vine thou claspest my full heart, —
How shall I hence depart? —

"How the lone paths retrace where thou wert playing
So late, along the mountains, at my side!
And I, in joyous pride,
By every place of flowers my course delaying,
Wove, e'en as pearls, the lilies round thy hair,
Beholding thee so fair?

"And, O, the home whence thy bright smile hath parted,
Will it not seem as if the sunny day
Turned from its door away?
While through its chambers wandering, weary-hearted,
I languish for thy voice, which past me still
Went like a singing rill?

"Under the palm-trees thou no more shalt meet me,
When from the fount at evening I return,
With the full water-urn;
Nor will thy sleep's low dove-like breathings greet me
As 'midst the silence of the stars I wake,
And watch for thy dear sake.

"And thou, will slumber's dewy cloud fall round thee,
Without thy mother's hand to smooth thy bed?
Wilt thou not vainly spread
Thine arms, when darkness as a veil hath wound thee,
To fold my neck, and lift up, in thy fear,
A cry which none shall hear?

"What have I said, my child? Will *He* not hear thee,
Who the young ravens heareth from their nest?
Shall He not guard thy rest,

And, in the hush of holy midnight near thee,
Breathe o'er thy soul, and fill its dreams with joy?—
    Thou shalt sleep soft, my boy.

"I give thee to thy God,—the God that gave thee,
A well-spring of deep gladness, to my heart!
    And, precious as thou art,
And pure as dew of Hermon, He shall have thee,
My own, my beautiful, my undefiled!
    And thou shalt be His child!

"Therefore, farewell!—I go; my soul may fail me,
As the hart panteth for the water-brooks,
    Yearning for thy sweet looks,
But thou, my first-born, droop not, nor bewail me;
Thou in the Shadow of the Rock shalt dwell,
    The Rock of Strength.—Farewell!"

Mrs. Felicia Hemans.

HANNAH AND SAMUEL.

HER prattling child she brings in white arrayed,
Sorrow and joy in her fond heart contending,
To heavenly service for his lifetime lending,
Far from her sight, the son for whom she prayed.
Each year "a little coat" her hands had made,
She brought to him within God's courts attending.
Each hour her loving heart sweet thoughts was sending
To that fair offering on God's altar laid.
But richly was her sacrifice rewarded,
When to her holy and illustrious son
The foremost place in Israel was accorded;
So let our children be to God devoted
In prayerful training from their birth begun,
And 'mid heaven's thrones, O, may their names be noted!

Rev. R. Wilton.

ABIGAIL.

BROCHART, *Pinx.* JEHENNE, *Lith.*

ABIGAIL, WIFE OF DAVID.

THE marriage of the lovely Moabitess, Ruth, with the noble Boaz, and her consequent adoption into the family of the faithful, bore in time auspicious fruits. The great-grandson of Ruth was David, — the minstrel, the poet, the prophet, the warrior and king of the Jewish nation, — the man after God's own heart, chosen to stand in poetic song as the type of the future Messiah and King of the whole earth.

And here we cannot do better, to answer the popular but superficial estimates which have been made of this great man, than to quote a sentence or two from Carlyle: —

"Who is called the man after God's own heart? David the King fell into sins enough, — blackest crimes. There was no want of sin, and therefore unbelievers sneer and ask, Is this your man after God's own heart? The sneer I must say seems to me but a shallow one. What are faults, what are the outer details of a life, if the inner secrets of it — the remorse, temptation, the often-baffled, never-ended struggle of it — be forgotten? David's life and history as written for us in these Psalms of his I consider to be the truest emblem ever given of a man's moral progress and warfare here below. All earnest souls will ever discern in it the faithful struggle of an earnest human soul towards what is good and best; struggle often baffled, — sore baffled, driven as into entire wreck, — yet a struggle never-ended, ever with tears, repentance, true unconquerable purpose, begun anew."

The history of Abigail brings us directly into this era of David, and the circumstances under which he wooed and won her to be his wife carry us back far into the unsettled and formative period of human society, when life was a state of warfare, and the arm of the warrior was the last appeal in every controversy. The name *David* means *well beloved*, or *darling*, given to him doubtless as the youngest of a large family; and through all his history nothing is more remarkable than that warm magnetic power which drew all hearts towards him in personal affection. He was the Loving and the Beloved, wherever he moved. When Saul conspired against his life, so that he had to flee like an outcast, the son of his oppressor followed him to the desert, with a love which David says "passed the love of women," and the daughter of Saul, given to David as wife, clung to him with unshaken constancy. Cast out and wandering, David's personal attraction, the fame of his military exploits, drew men to his standard, and he soon became a chieftain at the head of a little army.

The situation resembled that of a highland chief, or of a knight-errant of the days of chivalry; and David appears before us the gallant, generous leader, at once the minstrel and the captain of the little band that wandered through the mountain fastnesses of Israel.

They encamp in the mountain regions of Paran, near the high pasture-lands of Mount Carmel, where the elevated plains and ridges are covered with the flocks and herds of a rich landowner, Nabal.

So far from allowing any predatory liberties with these wandering flocks, the martial leader, remembering his own peaceful early shepherd life, seems to have established his little army as a guard and protection around the flocks, keeping off the attacks of wild animals and of hostile tribes, and thus fairly entitling himself to some return of courtesy.

The wealth of this opulent landholder is set forth in the story that follows:—

"There was a man in Manon whose possessions were in Carmel; and the man was very great, and he had three thousand sheep and a thousand goats, and he was shearing his sheep in Carmel. Now the name of the man was Nabal, and the name of his wife Abigail; and she was a woman of a good understanding and of a beautiful countenance, but the man was churlish and evil in his doings, and he was of the house of Caleb."

The shearing of the sheep in those countries was a festive time of liberality, and David took advantage of it to seek some courteous recognition of the services he had rendered.

He sent a party of young men with this message: "Go to Nabal, and greet him in my name, and thus shall ye say to him that liveth in prosperity: Peace be both to thee and to thy house, and peace to all that thou hast." Then comes a modest recital of their friendly services, and he adds, "Wherefore let my young men find favor in thine eyes, for we come in a good day. Give, I pray thee, whatsoever cometh to thy hand unto thy son David."

And Nabal answered: "Who is David, and who is the son of Jesse? there be many servants nowadays that break away from their masters. Shall I take my bread and my water, and my flesh that I have killed for my shearers, and give it unto men whom I know not whence they be?"

A strongly loving nature implies a strong power of wrath, just as bright light is correlated with deep shadow. The ungenerous, brutal insult roused the indignation of David, and he was proceeding after the manner of his times to take signal vengeance, when the courage and prudence of a woman turned the whole course of things, as is thus related: —

"But one of the young men ran and told Abigail, Nabal's wife, saying, Behold David sent messengers out of the wilderness to salute our master, and he railed on them. But now, these men were very good to us, and we were not hurt, neither missed we anything so long as we were with them in the fields. They were a wall unto us, both night and day, while we were keeping the sheep. Now, therefore, know and consider what thou wilt do, for evil is determined against our master and against all his household, for he is such a son of Belial that a man cannot speak to him."

This character of Nabal, sketched with a few broad strokes, is a typical one, — unhappily but too common. A noble-minded, warm-hearted, generous woman is often mated with a hard, close, surly, ungenerous man, whose ungracious words and actions bring enmity upon his household.

It is here that the fineness and ready tact of the womanly

nature find their most efficient use. What the wife of Nabal did is thus told: —

"Then Abigail made haste, and took two hundred loaves, and two bottles of wine, and five sheep ready dressed, and five measures of parched corn, and an hundred clusters of raisins, and two hundred cakes of figs, and laid them upon asses. And she said to her servants, Go on before me; and she told not her husband Nabal. And it was so as she rode upon the ass that she came down by the covert of the hill, and behold, David and his men came down against her, and she met them. And when Abigail saw David, she hasted and lighted off the ass, and fell before David, and bowed herself to the ground, and fell at his feet and said, Upon me, my lord, upon me let this iniquity be, and let thy handmaid, I pray thee, speak in thine audience, and hear the words of thy handmaid. Let not my lord, I pray thee, regard this man of Belial, even Nabal, for as his name is so is he, Nabal is his name, and folly is with him; but I, thine handmaid, saw not the young men of my lord whom thou didst send. Now therefore, my lord, as the Lord liveth, and as thy soul liveth, seeing the Lord hath withholden thee from coming to shed blood, and avenging thyself with thine own hand, now let thine enemies and they that seek evil to my lord be as Nabal. And now this present that I have brought, let it be given to the men that follow my lord. I pray thee, forgive the trespass of thine handmaid, and the Lord will certainly make my lord a sure house, because my lord fighteth the battles of the Lord, and evil hath not been found in thee all thy days. Yet a man is risen to pursue thee, and to seek thy soul; but the soul of my lord shall be bound in the bundle of life with the Lord thy God, and the souls of thine enemies them shall he sling out as out of the middle of a sling. And it shall come to pass, when the Lord shall have done to my lord according to all the good that he hath spoken concerning thee, and shall have appointed thee ruler over Israel, that this shall be no grief unto thee, nor offense of heart unto my lord, either that thou hast shed blood causeless, or that my lord hath avenged himself; but when the Lord shall have dealt well with my lord, then remember thine handmaid."

It would be difficult in any literature to find more dignity, sweetness, bravery, tact, and distinctively womanly nobility than are seen in this address; and when we consider that it was made to a man romantically generous, and impulsively alive to every noble sentiment, we are not surprised that it carried all before it.

In the heat of his first indignation at the meanness of Nabal, David had forgotten his better self, his higher ideal; but the voice of this beautiful woman restored him to spiritual sanity, and he promptly and ingenuously acknowledged his fault, and yielded to her sway: —

"And David said to Abigail, Blessed be the Lord God of Israel, which sent thee this day to meet me; and blessed be thy advice, and blessed be thou, which hast kept me this day from coming to shed blood, and from avenging myself with mine own hand."

The remainder of the story is soon told: —

"So David received of her hand that which she had brought him, and said unto her, Go up in peace to thine house; see, I have hearkened to thy voice, and have accepted thy person. And Abigail came to Nabal; and behold, he held a feast in his house like the feast of a king; and Nabal's heart was merry within him, for he was very drunken; wherefore she told him nothing, less or more, until the morning light. But it came to pass in the morning, when the wine was gone out of Nabal, and his wife had told him these things, that his heart died within him, and he became as a stone. And it came to pass about ten days after, that the Lord smote Nabal, that he died.

"And when David heard that Nabal was dead, he said, Blessed be the Lord, that hath pleaded the cause of my reproach from the hand of Nabal, and hath kept his servant from evil; for the Lord hath returned the wickedness of Nabal upon his own head. And David sent and communed with Abigail, to take her to him to wife. And when the servants of David were come to Abigail, to Carmel, they spake unto her, saying, David sent us unto thee, to take thee to him to wife. And she arose, and bowed herself on her face to the earth, and said, Behold, let thine handmaid be a servant to wash the feet of the servants of my lord.

And Abigail hasted, and arose, and rode upon an ass, with five damsels of hers that went after her; and she went after the messengers of David, and became his wife."

We see in this little story what is the truest, best power and glory of woman, — the power to control the stormy passions of man, and recall him to his higher and purer self, when he is swept away by sudden tides of temptation. We can easily believe that it was not the last time in the history of David when he said to Abigail what every husband might say to a true wife, — "Blessed be the Lord God of Israel, which sent *thee* to me; and blessed be thy advice, and blessed be thou!"

The era of David was the chivalric period of Jewish history. It was essentially poetic in its points of view, and can only be understood by throwing ourselves back into the atmosphere of those days of imperfect moral development. The same God who has willed that plants and animals should struggle up through ages into perfect growths, seems also to have meant that human virtue should struggle through the ages before reaching in Jesus its highest type-form.

In David the elements of humanity were large and strong, and only partially harmonized. Lord Bacon says that revenge is a kind of "wild justice"; it is certainly the plant which, under Divine gardening, may make the mighty oak of justice which is needed to fortify society. The loftier impulse of forgiving love has also its place, and in David's life we see the blessed struggle between the two. It is the record of man following with unequal and halting pace the footsteps of a God.

The Psalms contain in full measure those cries for vengeance that are the first undisciplined impulses even of the noblest nature in view of wrong. But they contain too the traces of that forgiving tenderness which existed in equal proportions. When the ungrateful king, who had hunted David's life and made him a weary outcast, was in his hands, helpless and asleep, twice he spared his life, and deprecated only with tender and reverential words the injustice done to him. In both cases, for a time the heart of Saul was melted by the magnanimous love of David. When Saul was slain, David mourned him with a generous sorrow; he wept for him as a lover for his beloved. So when the ungrateful son Absalom had turned against him, and driven him out of his kingdom, David's loving heart still clung to him: "Be very gentle to the young man, even Absalom," was his charge. And when the rebel was slain, he said, "Would God I had died for thee, O Absalom, my son!" His disposition to love and forgiveness of so bitter and dangerous an enemy moved the indignation of fiery old Joab, who was scandalized at this bitter mourning over an ungrateful usurper: "Thou hast shamed this day the faces of all thy servants, which this day have saved thy life, in that thou lovest thine enemies and hatest thy friends; for I perceive that if Absalom had lived this day, and all we had died, it had pleased thee well." Do we not see in all this how David had, in bursts and gushes, fragments of that divine love of enemies which it was left for his celestial descendant more perfectly to manifest?

The dull elements of the diamond gather and crystallize slowly through ages; so traits which in David were clouded and obscure by earthly defilement shone forth in the Son of David dazzling and unalloyed.

DAVID.

SUGGESTED BY A STATUE.

AY, this is he, — the bold and gentle boy
That in lone pastures by the mountain's side
Guarded his fold, and through the midnight sky
Saw on the blast the God of battles ride;
Beheld his bannered armies on the height,
And heard their clarion sound through all the stormy night.

The valiant boy that o'er the twilight wold
Tracked the dark lion and ensanguined bear;
Following their bloody footsteps from the fold
Far down the gorges to their lonely lair, —
This the stout heart that from the lion's jaw
Back o'er the shuddering waste the bleeding victim bore.

Though his fair locks lie all unshorn and bare
To the bold toying of the mountain wind,
A conscious glory haunts the o'ershadowing air,
And waits with glittering coil his brows to bind,
While his proud temples bend superbly down,
As if they felt e'en now the burden of a crown.

Though a stern sorrow slumbers in his eyes,
As if his prophet glance foresaw the day
When the dark waters o'er his soul should rise,
And friends and lovers wander far away, —
Yet the graced impress of that floral mouth
Breathes of love's golden dream, and the voluptuous South.

Peerless in beauty as the prophet star
That in the dewy trances of the dawn

DAVID.

Floats o'er the solitary hills afar,
  And brings sweet tidings of the lingering morn;
Or, weary at the day-god's loitering wane,
Strikes on the harp of light a soft prelusive strain.

So his wild harp, with psaltery and shawm,
  Awoke the nations in thick darkness furled,
While mystic winds from Gilead's groves of balm
  Wafted its sweet hosannas through the world,—
So, when the Dayspring from on high he sang,
With joy the ancient hills and lowly valleys rang.

Ay, this is he,—the minstrel, prophet, king,
  Before whose arm princes and warriors sank;
Who dwelt beneath Jehovah's mighty wing,
  And from the river of his pleasures drank;
Or through the rent pavilions of the storm
Beheld the cloud of fire that veiled his awful form.

And now he stands as when in Elah's vale,
  Where warriors set the battle in array,
He met the Titan in his ponderous mail,
  Whose haughty challenge many a summer's day
Rang through the border hills, while all the host
Of faithless Israel heard, and trembled at his boast;

Till the light stripling from the mountain fold
  Stood, all unarmed, amid their sounding shields,
And, in his youth's first bloom, devoutly bold,
  Dared the grim champion of a thousand fields:
So stands he now, as, in Jehovah's might
Glorying, he met the foe and won the immortal fight.

Mrs. Sarah H. Whitman.

THE CALL OF DAVID.

LATEST born of Jesse's race,
Wonder lights thy bashful face,
While the prophet's gifted oil
Seals thee for the path of toil.
We, thy Angels, circling round thee,
Ne'er shall find thee as we found thee,
When thy faith first brought us near
To quell the lion and the bear.
Go! and 'mid thy flocks awhile
At thy doom of greatness smile;
Bold to bear God's heaviest load,
Dimly guessing of the road, —
Rocky road, and scarce ascended,
Though thy foot be angel-tended.
Twofold praise thou shalt attain
In royal court and battle-plain;
Then comes heartache, care, distress,
Blighted hope, and loneliness;
Wounds from friend and gifts from foe,
Dizzied faith, and guilt, and woe;
Loftiest aims by earth defiled,
Gleams of wisdom sin-beguiled,
Sated power's tyrannic mood,
Counsels shared with men of blood,
Sad success, parental tears,
And a dreary gift of years.
Strange, that guileless face and form
To lavish on the scarring storm!
Yet we take thee in thy blindness,
And we buffet thee in kindness;
Little chary of thy fame, —
Dust unborn may bless or blame, —
But we mould thee for the root
Of man's promised healing Fruit,
And we mould thee hence to rise,
As our brother, to the skies.

J. H. Newman, D.D.

WITCH OF ENDOR.

BROCHART, *Pinx.* JEHENNE, *Lith.*

THE WITCH OF ENDOR.

HAT was a witch, according to the law of Moses, and why was witchcraft a capital offense? A witch was the dark shadow of a prophetess.

A prophetess was a holy woman drawing near to the spiritual world by means of faith and prayer, and thus inspired by God with a knowledge beyond the ordinary power of mortals. Her prophecies and her guidance were all from the only true source of knowledge; the spirits that attended her were true and heavenly spirits, and she became a medium by whom the will of God and the perplexed path of duty were made plain to others. A witch, on the contrary, was one who sought knowledge of the future, not from the one supreme God, but through all those magical charms, incantations, and ceremonies by which the spirits of the dead were sought for interference in the affairs of men. The guilt and the folly of seeking these consisted in the fact that there was another and a legitimate supply for that craving of the human heart.

Man is consciously weak, helpless, burdened with desires and fears which he knows not how to supply or allay. Moses distinctly stated to the Jews that their God was "*nigh* unto them for ALL they should call upon him for." The examples of holy men and women in sacred history show that, even for private and personal griefs, and intimate sorrows and perplexities, there was immediate access to the gracious Jehovah, there were direct answers to prayer. Had Hannah, in her childless longings and misery, sought a woman who had a familiar spirit, she would have broken the law of the land, and committed an act of rebellion against her King and Father. But she went directly to God, and became a joyful mother.

Besides the personal access of the individual by prayer, there were always holy mediums raised up from time to time in the nation, who were lawful and appointed sources of counsel and aid. There were always the prophet and prophetess, through whom there was even nearer access to the guardian God, and we repeatedly read of application made to these sources in case of sickness or sorrow or perplexity. The high-priest, by virtue of his office, was held to possess this power. Exactly what the Urim and Thummim were, the learned do not seem to agree; it is sufficient to know that they were in some way the instruments of a lawful mode appointed by God, through which questions asked of the high-priest might be answered, and guidance given in perplexing cases.

And now, on the other hand, as to the *witch*, and how her unlawful processes were carried on, we get more help from one vivid, graphic picture than by all the researches of archæologists. We therefore give entire the singular and poetic story in the First Book of Samuel.

"Now Samuel was dead, and all Israel had lamented him, and buried him in Ramah, even in his own city. And Saul had put away those that had familiar spirits, and the wizards, out of the land. And the Philistines gathered themselves together, and came and pitched in Shunem: and Saul gathered all Israel together, and they pitched in Gilboa. And when Saul saw the host of the Philistines, he was afraid, and his heart greatly trembled. And when Saul inquired of the Lord, the Lord answered him not, neither by dreams, nor by Urim, nor by prophets. Then said Saul unto his servants, Seek me a woman that hath a familiar spirit, that I may go to her, and inquire of her. And his servants said to him, Behold, there is a woman that hath a familiar spirit at Endor. And Saul disguised himself, and put on other raiment, and he went, and two men with him, and they came to the woman by night: and he said, I pray thee, divine unto me by the familiar spirit, and bring me him up whom I shall name unto thee. And the woman said unto him, Behold, thou knowest what Saul hath done, how he hath cut off those that have familiar spirits, and the wizards, out of the land: wherefore then layest thou a snare for my life, to cause me to die?

And Saul sware to her by the Lord, saying, As the Lord liveth, there shall no punishment happen to thee for this thing. Then said the woman, Whom shall I bring up unto thee? And he said, Bring me up Samuel. And when the woman saw Samuel, she cried with a loud voice: and the woman spake to Saul, saying, Why hast thou deceived me? for thou art Saul. And the king said unto her, Be not afraid; for what sawest thou? And the woman said unto Saul, I saw gods ascending out of the earth. And he said unto her, What form is he of? And she said, An old man cometh up; and he is covered with a mantle. And Saul perceived that it was Samuel, and he stooped with his face to the ground, and bowed himself. And Samuel said to Saul, Why hast thou disquieted me, to bring me up? And Saul answered, I am sore distressed; for the Philistines make war against me, and God is departed from me, and answereth me no more, neither by prophets, nor by dreams: therefore I have called thee, that thou mayest make known unto me what I shall do. Then said Samuel, Wherefore then dost thou ask of me, seeing the Lord is departed from thee, and is become thine enemy? And the Lord hath done to him, as he spake by me: for the Lord hath rent the kingdom out of thine hand, and given it to thy neighbor, even to David: Because thou obeyedst not the voice of the Lord, nor executedst his fierce wrath upon Amalek, therefore hath the Lord done this thing unto thee this day. Moreover the Lord will also deliver Israel with thee into the hand of the Philistines: and to-morrow shalt thou and thy sons be with me: the Lord also shall deliver the host of Israel into the hand of the Philistines. Then Saul fell straightway all along on the earth, and was sore afraid, because of the words of Samuel: and there was no strength in him; for he had eaten no bread all the day, nor all the night. And the woman came unto Saul, and saw that he was sore troubled, and said unto him, Behold, thine handmaid hath obeyed thy voice, and I have put my life in my hand, and have hearkened unto thy words which thou spakest unto me: now therefore, I pray thee, hearken thou also unto the voice of thine handmaid, and let me set a morsel of bread before thee; and eat, that thou mayest have strength, when thou goest on thy way. But he refused, and said,

I will not eat. But his servants, together with the woman, compelled him, and he hearkened unto their voice. So he arose from the earth, and sat upon the bed. And the woman had a fat calf in the house, and she hasted, and killed it, and took flour, and kneaded it, and did bake unleavened bread thereof. And she brought it before Saul, and before his servants; and they did eat. Then they rose up, and went away that night."

We do not need to inquire what a witch was, or why she was forbidden, further than this story shows. She is placed here as exactly the contrary alternative to God, in the wants and sorrows of life. The whole tenor of instruction to the Jews was, that there was no Divine anger that might not be appeased and turned away by deep, heartfelt repentance and amendment. In the GREAT NAME revealed to Moses, the Jehovah declares himself "merciful and gracious, slow to anger, of great kindness, forgiving iniquity, transgression, and sin," — there is but a single clause added on the side of admonitory terror, — "who will by no means clear the guilty." A favorite mode in which the guardian God is represented as speaking is that he "repenteth of the evil" he thought to do, in response to penitent prayer.

Saul had broken with his God on the score of an intense self-will, and he did not repent. The prophet Samuel had announced wrath, and threatened final rejection, but no humiliation and no penitence followed. In this mood of mind, when his fear came as desolation, all the avenues of knowledge or aid which belonged to God's children were closed upon him, and he voluntarily put himself in the hands of those powers which were his declared enemies.

The scene as given is so exactly like what is occurring in our day, like incidents that so many among us have the best reason for knowing to be objectively facts of daily occurrence, that there is no reason to encumber it with notes and comments as to the probability of the account. The woman was a medium who had the power of calling up the spirits of the dead at the desire of those who came to her. She is not represented at all as a witch after the Shakespearean style. There is no "eye of newt and toe of frog," no caldron or grimaces to appall. From all that appears, she was a soft-hearted, kindly, cowardly creature, turning a penny as she could, in a way forbidden by the laws of the land; quite ready to make up by artifice for any lack of reality; who cast her line into the infinite shadows, and was somewhat appalled by what it brought up.

There is a tone of reproof in the voice of the departed friend: "Why hast thou *disquieted* me, to bring me up?" And when Saul says, "God hath forsaken us, and will not answer," the reproving shade replies, "Wherefore come to *me*, seeing God hath become thine enemy?" In all this is the voice of the true and loyal prophet, who from a child had sought God, and God alone, in every emergency, and ever found him true and faithful.

This story has its parallel in our days. In our times there is a God and Father always nigh to those who diligently seek him. There is communion with spirits through Jesus, the great High-Priest. There are promises of guidance in difficulties and support under trials to all who come to God by Him.

In our days, too, there are those who propose, for the relief of human perplexities and the balm for human sorrows, a recourse to those who have familiar spirits, and profess to call back to us those who are at rest with God.

Now, while there is no objection to a strict philosophical investigation and analysis and record of these phenomena considered as psychological facts, while, in fact, such investigation is loudly called for as the best remedy for superstition, there is great danger to the mind and moral sense in *seeking them as guides in our perplexities or comforters in our sorrows.* And the danger is just this, that they take the place of that communion with God and that filial intercourse with him which is alone the true source of light and comfort. Most especially, to those whose souls are weakened by the anguish of some great bereavement, is the seeking of those that have familiar spirits to be dreaded. Who could bear to expose to the eye of a paid medium the sanctuary of our most sacred love and sorrow? and how fearful is the thought that some wandering spirit, in the voice and with the tone and manner of those dearest to us, may lead us astray to trust in those who are not God!

The most dangerous feature we know of in these professed spirit-messages is their constant tendency to place themselves before our minds as our refuge and confidence rather than God. "Seek US, trust US, believe in US, rely on US," — such is always the voice that comes from them.

In Isaiah viii. 19, the prophet describes a time of great affliction and sorrow coming upon the Jews, when they would be driven to seek supernatural aid. He says: "And when they shall say unto you, Seek unto them that have familiar spirits, and to wizards that peep and mutter; should not a nation seek unto their God? should the living seek unto the dead? To the law, and to the testimony; if they speak not according to this word, there is no light in them." The prophet goes on to say that those who thus turn from God to these sources of comfort "shall be hardly bestead and hungry, and shall fret themselves."

All our observation of those who have sought to these sources of comfort has been that they fall into just this restless hunger of mind, an appetite forever growing and never satisfied; and as their steps go farther and farther from the true source of all comfort, the hunger and thirst increase. How much more beautiful, safe, and sure that good old way of trust in God! The writer has had a somewhat large observation of the very best and most remarkable phenomena of that which is claimed to be spirit communion; she does not doubt the reality of many very remarkable appearances and occurrences; she has only respectful and tender sympathy for those whose heart-sorrows they have consoled. But when this way of guidance and consolation is put in the place of that direct filial access to God through Jesus which the Bible reveals, it must be looked upon as the most illusive and insidious of dangers. The phenomena, whatever they are, belong to forces too little understood, to laws too much unknown, that we should trust ourselves to them in the most delicate, critical, and sacred wants of our life.

Better than all is the way spoken of by Jesus when he, the Comforter, Guide, Teacher, Friend, will manifest himself to the faithful soul as he does not to the world: "If a man love me, he will keep my words, and my Father will love him, and we will come and make our abode with him."

SAUL AND THE WITCH OF ENDOR.

THOU, whose spell can raise the dead,
Bid the prophet's form appear:
"Samuel, raise thy buried head!
King, behold the phantom seer!"

Earth yawned; he stood the center of a cloud:
Light changed its hue, retiring from his shroud.
Death stood all glassy in his fixéd eye;
His hand was withered, and his veins were dry;
His foot in bony whiteness glittered there,
Shrunken, and sinewless, and ghastly bare:
From lips that moved not, and unbreathing frame,
Like caverned winds the hollow accents came.
Saul saw, and fell to earth, as falls the oak,
At once, and blasted by the thunder-stroke.

"Why is my sleep disquieted?
Who is he that calls the dead?
Is it thou, O king? Behold,
Bloodless are these limbs, and cold:
Such are mine; and such shall be
Thine to-morrow, when with me:
Ere the coming day is done,
Such shalt thou be, such thy son.
Fare thee well, but for a day,
Then we mix our mouldering clay.
Thou, thy race, lie pale and low,
Pierced by shafts of many a bow;
And the falchion by thy side
To thy heart thy hand shall guide:
Crownless, breathless, headless, fall
Son and sire, the house of Saul!"

Lord Byron.

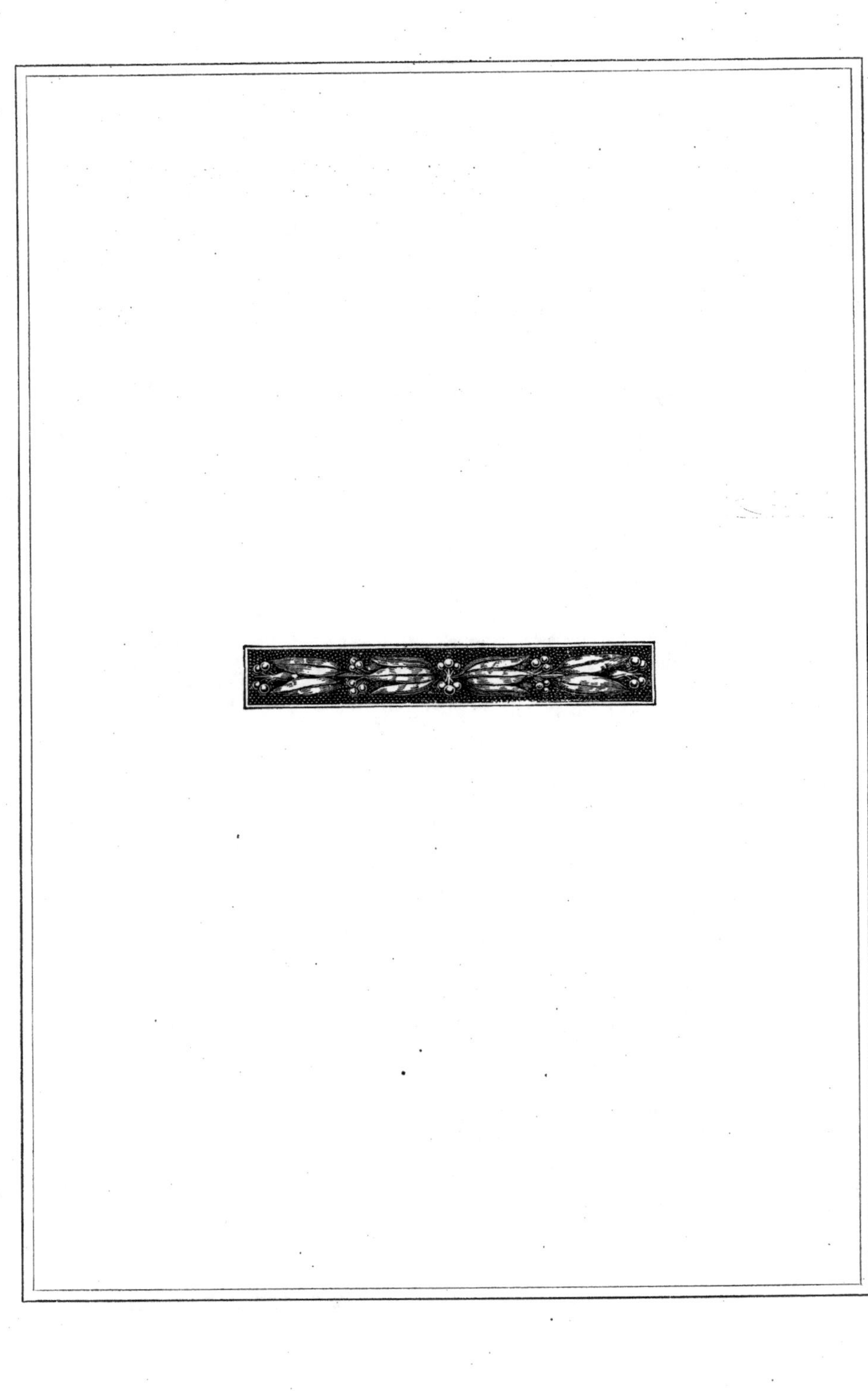

JEZEBEL.

BROCHART, *Pinx.* JEHENNE, *Lith.*

JEZEBEL, THE HEATHEN QUEEN.

IN direct contrast to the noble and beneficent power of good women in the sacred history, we have the most vigorous and impressive pictures of the dangerous side of female influence.

In fact, in the long struggle with idolatry through which the Jewish stock was gradually educated, and brought up to a steady and sublime spiritual conception of monotheism, the influence most seductive, and most dreaded and guarded against, was that of idolatrous women.

This carefulness was the more essential, as the idolatrous systems of the surrounding tribes of the Canaanites were founded upon the most unbridled licentiousness. The worship of Baal and Astarte, the god and goddess of the Phœnicians and Sidonians, as of the lesser Canaanite tribes, was characterized by rites of the most disgusting sensuality; and the influence of woman, as then employed, led to the utter dissolution of the family state, and the gradual extinction of the race.

This sheds light on what otherwise might seem the severe and even cruel decrees of extermination, which went forth against these tribes. It was a question between the existence of the Jewish race or their gradual extinction through the dissolving power of vice.

The philosophy of physical laws was then unknown. The Jewish race were to be kept from melting into the deadly corruption of sensualism that surrounded them, only by a constant and unsparing severity.

Intermarriages between the Jews and these foreign races was strictly forbidden, except in instances where the wife renounced her national religion and adopted that of her husband, as in the case of Ruth. But even the kings of Israel were often forward in their ambitious schemes to form these entangling alliances, and thus repeatedly was idolatry introduced under royal patronage.

Jezebel, the wife of Ahab, is the most striking instance of this kind. Her portrait, as sketched in the dramatic vigor of the Hebrew narrative, is as striking in its way as that of Lady Macbeth. There is the same haughty firmness, the same unflinching cruelty of determination, the same scorn of the remains of virtuous scruple in the mind of her husband.

But in one respect there is a difference: Lady Macbeth strikes us in the narrative as devoid of sensual passion, — a being whose sins are wholly of the intellect; Jezebel, on the contrary, appears as a sort of Lucretia Borgia, a union of fierceness and cruelty with seductive licentiousness.

Dean Stanley says of her: "She was a woman in whom with the reckless and licentious habits of an Oriental queen were united the sternest and fiercest qualities inherent in the Phœnician people. Her father, Ethbal, united with his royal office the priesthood of the goddess Astarte, and had come to the throne by the murder of his predecessor, Thelles."

She herself became the center of a propaganda of vices, — the patroness and example of a furious fanaticism of evil. The worship of her gods and the rites of her religion were not merely to be tolerated in Israel, — they were to reign. They were carried through the land at the point of the sword. The prophets of Jehovah were hunted as for their lives, and had to flee to the shelter of the mountain caves, while a gorgeous retinue of the priests of Baal filled the courts of the palace. It is supposed that no less than four hundred of the prophets of Baal, and an equal number of the prophets of Astarte, were nourished at the queen's table. To all human appearance, the worship of Jehovah was overthrown. Ahab, with what was left to him of conscience and fear of God, was but a puppet in the hands of this imperious, voluptuous, brilliant woman. Her name became a proverb for the fanaticism of licentiousness. Thus in the Book of Revelations the name Jezebel is given to a female teacher professing to be a prophetess, and teaching licentious doctrines: I have a few things against thee, because thou sufferest "that woman Jezebel, that calleth herself a prophetess, to teach and to cause my servants to commit fornication, and to eat things sacrificed to idols."

The whole history of the conflict of the Prophet Elijah with the evil force of this woman is one of the grandest stories of the Old Testament. A three years' drought reduced the nation to the extremity of distress. We have touching pictures in detail of what that distress of utter famine was. The poor widow, gathering two sticks to dress her last handful of meal, that she and her son might eat and die, is an image that sets the minutiæ of famine before us.

Ahab is represented as not hard-hearted, or devoid of conscience. He cannot stand up against his overbearing wife, and yet he is evidently convicted in his own conscience of the sin that has brought all this misery upon the land.

"And there was a sore famine in Samaria. And Ahab called Obadiah, which was the governor of his house. (Now Obadiah feared the Lord greatly: for it was so, when Jezebel cut off the prophets of the Lord, that Obadiah took an hundred prophets, and hid them by fifty in a cave, and fed them with bread and water.) And Ahab said unto Obadiah, Go into the land, unto all fountains of water, and unto all brooks; peradventure we may find grass to save the horses and mules alive, that we lose not all the beasts.

"So they divided the land between them, to pass throughout it: Ahab went one way by himself, and Obadiah went another way by himself."

It appears that Elijah as the representative of Jehovah is bitterly thought of by Ahab as the author of the miseries that have come upon the land. During his wanderings in the desert, Ahab has sent everywhere in vain to seek the prophet; but now, suddenly, dark and awful, Elijah stands before him.

"And it came to pass, when Ahab saw Elijah, that Ahab said unto him, Art thou he that troubleth Israel?

"And he answered, I have not troubled Israel; but thou, and thy father's house, in that ye have forsaken the commandments of the Lord, and thou hast followed Baalim. Now therefore send, and gather to me all Israel unto Mount Carmel, and the prophets of Baal four hundred and fifty, and the prophets of the groves four hundred, which eat at Jezebel's table.

"So Ahab sent unto all the children of Israel, and gathered the prophets together unto Mount Carmel. And Elijah came unto all the people, and said, How long halt ye between two opinions? if the Lord be God, follow him: but if Baal, then follow him. And the people answered him not a word. Then said Elijah unto the people, I, even I only, remain a prophet of the Lord; but Baal's prophets are four hundred and fifty men. Let them therefore give us two bullocks; and let them choose one bullock for themselves, and cut it in pieces, and lay it on wood, and put no fire under: and I will dress the other bullock, and lay it on wood, and put no fire under. And call ye on the name of your gods, and I will call on the name of the Lord; and the God that answereth by fire, let him be God. And all the people answered and said, It is well spoken."

It appears that the extremity of national distress had produced one of those reflex tides in which the nation was ready for any change that promised hope. It would seem also as if Jezebel, in her proud belief in her own faith, was scornfully willing to let the trial be made. Perhaps she deemed it the most sagacious way of diverting the rising popular tumult, to let the people have the amusement of a solemn pageant. After all, it was a pity if her eight hundred and fifty priests, with their robes of office, and their timbrels and music and pomp of ceremony, could not outface one plain stern man in a camel's-hair garment! Let him try his hand, she said, in haughty security.

We have now a most graphic picture of the worship of Baal. His altar is built, the offering laid thereon.

"And they took the bullock which was given them, and they dressed it, and called on the name of Baal from morning even until noon, saying, O Baal, hear us. But there was no voice, nor any that answered. And they leaped upon the altar which was made. And it came to pass at noon, that Elijah mocked them, and said, Cry aloud; for he is a god; either he is talking, or he is pursuing, or he is in a journey, or peradventure he sleepeth, and must be awaked. And they cried aloud, and cut themselves after their manner with knives and lancets, till the blood gushed out upon them.

"And it came to pass, when midday was past, and they prophesied until the time of the offering of the evening sacrifice, that there was neither voice, nor any to answer, nor any that regarded."

And now the one lone man who stands for the forsaken Jehovah speaks to the people: "Come near unto me"; and at once they all flock to his side and stand around him. Then, with twelve stones for the twelve tribes of Israel, he proceeds to build again the long-forsaken altar of the Lord. It was the altar of the God of their fathers and mothers; the altar of Him who had brought Israel out of Egypt, who had led them through the wilderness by cloud and fire and fed them with manna, who had nourished and brought them up as children. In that company were probably the seven thousand whom the all-seeing eye had marked, that had never bowed the knee to Baal; and with a throbbing, solemn impulse they gather round the prophet and aid the holy work. The altar is so constructed that there can be no deception; it is repeatedly so drenched with water that nothing but a divine fire from above can possibly consume the sacrifice.

And now came on the hallowed hour, once more remembered, when the evening sacrifice was wont to ascend to Jehovah from his temple; and the solitary prophet, the one representative of the forsaken religion, approached the altar and said, "Lord God of Abraham, and Isaac, and Jacob, let it be known this day that thou art a God in Israel, and that I am thy servant, and that I have done all these things at thy word. Hear me, O Lord, hear me, that this people may know that thou art the Lord God that hast turned their hearts back again." Then from heaven the fire of the Lord fell, and consumed the burnt sacrifice, and the wood, and the stones, and the dust, and licked up the water that was in the trench. And when all the people saw it, they fell on their faces and cried, "Jehovah—he is God! Jehovah is God!" And Elijah said, "Take the priests of Baal: let not one escape." And they took them to the brook Kishon and slew them there.

And now the long-delayed rain-clouds gather welcome blackness in the heavens, and Elijah sends the joyful news to Ahab: "Prepare thy chariot and get thee down, that the rain stop thee not. And it came to pass that the heaven was black with clouds, and there was a great rain. And Ahab rode and went to Jezreel; and the hand of the Lord was upon Elijah, and he girded up his loins and ran before his chariot to the entrance of Jezreel."

Overjoyed at the advent of rain and the prospect of returning plenty, Ahab recounts to Jezebel the result of the trial, and the overthrow of her prophets. For the moment, the Jew asserts himself, — he sympathizes with the victory of his father's religion.

But when Jezebel hears of the destruction of her prophets, she declares her dauntless nature. In a burst of rage, sharp and incisive as the lightning, she sends to Elijah the message, "So let the gods do to me, if I make not thy life as one of them by to-morrow." It is evident Ahab dare not protect him, and the prophet of Jehovah is once more an outcast fugitive. The record of his lonely wanderings, his discouragements and faintings, and angelic visitings and communings with God in the wilderness, are among the most touching of the lessons of ancient Scripture. As Elijah for the time vanishes from the scene, we have an incident which sets Jezebel before us in her most repulsive aspects.

A poor man owns a vineyard near the king's garden. The king fancies it and offers to buy it; but that love of the family homestead so peculiar to the Jews makes the owner averse to selling. The rest of the story can only be told as it stands in the text: —

"And Naboth said to Ahab, The Lord forbid it me, that I should give the inheritance of my fathers unto thee. And Ahab came into his house heavy and displeased. And he laid him down upon his bed, and turned away his face, and would eat no bread. But Jezebel his wife came to him, and said unto him, Why is thy spirit so sad, that thou eatest no bread? And he said unto her, Because I spake unto Naboth the Jezreelite, and said unto him, Give me thy vineyard for money; or else, if it please thee, I will give thee another vineyard for it; and he answered, I will not give thee my vineyard.

"And Jezebel his wife said unto him, Dost thou now govern the kingdom of Israel? arise, and eat bread, and let thine heart be merry; I will give thee the vineyard of Naboth the Jezreelite."

So said — so done. She takes the king's signet-ring, and goes to work. Even with her despotic education she must so far conform to Jewish custom that there must be the form of a trial for crime before the estate can be confiscated. But witnesses, judge, and jury are all alike puppets in the hands of the evil woman who governs Israel. It is easy to find false witnesses who testify to blasphemy, and obsequious judges to condemn, and ready executioners to execute. A few hours suffice, and Jezebel comes to Ahab. "Arise, and go and take possession of the vineyard of Naboth, which he refused to give thee for money; for Naboth is dead. And it came to pass, when Ahab heard that Naboth was dead, that Ahab rose up to go down to the vineyard of Naboth the Jezreelite, to take possession of it.

"And the word of the Lord came to Elijah the Tishbite, saying, Arise, go down to meet Ahab king of Israel, which is in Samaria; behold, he is in the vineyard of Naboth, whither he is gone down to possess it. And thou shalt speak unto him, saying, Thus saith the Lord, Hast thou killed, and also taken possession? And thou shalt speak unto him, saying, Thus saith the Lord, In the place where dogs licked the blood of Naboth shall dogs lick thy blood, even thine.

"And Ahab said to Elijah, Hast thou found me, O mine enemy? And he answered, I have found thee; because thou hast sold thyself to work evil in the sight of the Lord."

And of Jezebel the Lord said, "The dogs shall eat Jezebel by the wall of Jezreel. Him that dieth of Ahab in the city the dogs shall eat; and him that dieth in the field shall the fowls of the air eat."

And now one scene more, fearfully dramatic, closes the career of Jezebel. The awful mills grind slowly, but they grind without ceasing, — her hour comes at last.

Let us imagine the city of Jezreel with the terraces and kiosks and turrets of the royal palace overtopping the wall, and commanding the view of the surrounding plain. There the proud, wicked woman still reigns in her pride and voluptuousness. The doom of her weak husband has been fulfilled. The dogs have licked his blood where the blood of Naboth was shed. Elijah, the prophet, has gone to the bosom of that God for whom he suffered so much, but the sure word of his prophecy does not fail.

The Prophet Elisha receives a command to go and anoint the avenger, who shall hasten the punishment of the doomed house. While Jehu is sitting at meat, a prophet calls him to private interview, which is thus told:—

"So the young man, even the young man the prophet, went to Ramoth-gilead. And when he came, behold, the captains of the host were sitting; and he said, I have an errand to thee, O captain. And Jehu said, Unto which of all us? And he said, To thee, O captain. And he arose, and went into the house; and he poured the oil on his head, and said unto him, Thus said the Lord God of Israel, I have anointed thee king over the people of the Lord, even over Israel. And thou shalt smite the house of Ahab thy master, that I may avenge the blood of my servants the prophets, and the blood of all the servants of the Lord, at the hand of Jezebel. For the whole house of Ahab shall perish; and I will make the house of Ahab like the house of Jeroboam the son of Nebat, and like the house of Baasha the son of Ahijah; and the dogs shall eat Jezebel in the portion of Jezreel, and there shall be none to bury her. And he opened the door and fled."

And now, anointed to a mission of wrath, Jehu drives forth with his train, and meets first Joram the son of Ahab.

"And it came to pass when Joram saw him, he said, Is it peace, Jehu? And Jehu said, What peace, so long as the whoredoms and witchcrafts of thy mother Jezebel are so many? And Jehu drew a bow with his full strength, and smote Joram, and the arrow went out at his heart, and he sunk down in his chariot. Then said Jehu to his chief captain, Take him up and cast him on the portion of Naboth the Jezreelite!"

And now the avenging train sweeps on to Jezreel, and from the window of a lofty overhanging kiosk Jezebel sees the victor coming. Evidently swift forerunners had told of the slaughter of her son, but she is unappalled. The matchless word-painting of the history shall be left to tell the end of the story.

"And when Jehu was come to Jezreel, Jezebel heard of it, and she painted her face, and tired her head, and looked out at a window. And as Jehu entered in at the gate, she said, Had Zimri peace, who slew his master? And he lifted up his face to the window, and said, Who is on my side? who? And there looked out to him two or three eunuchs. And he said, Throw her down. So they threw her down; and some of her blood was sprinkled on the wall, and on the horses; and he trode her under foot. And when he was come in, he did eat and drink, and said, Go, see now this cursed woman, and bury her; for she is a king's daughter. And they went to bury her; but they found no more of her than the scull, and the feet, and the palms of her hands. Wherefore they came again, and told him. And he said, This is the word of the Lord, which he spake by his servant Elijah the Tishbite, saying, In the portion of Jezreel shall dogs eat the flesh of Jezebel; and the carcass of Jezebel shall be as dung upon the face of the field in the portion of Jezreel; so that they shall not say, This is Jezebel."

THE END FORETOLD.

Scene. — *The garden of the palace at Jezreel.* Time. — *After the murder of Naboth.*

Ahab *and* Jezebel.

Ahab.

ES, that will do. A road can softly bend
Round yonder swell, and so approach the house.
The ground, I hear, takes kindly to all sorts
Of useful herbs, far kindlier than that
Which thus we rescue, leaving free the space
Beneath our palace windows for the sweep
Of one pure curve in undulation fine,
Tree leading tree, sward brightening into flowers,
Flowers melting modestly again to green,
In placid breadth of beauty. Not till now
Did I dare hope that all the high-toned joy
Which the eye, educated to a sense of form
And hue in landscape, woos into the soul,
Could glad me, looking from my palace white
O'er the sweet hills and plains of Jezreel.

Jezebel.

Ay, and to whom does Ahab owe all this?
Not only that she flung the froward slave
Who barred his path, like carrion 'neath his wheel,
But that in princely Sidon, long ago,
She showed him what was beauty? Say, my lord,
When Argive kings and chiefs desire to send
A present unto one they honor most
Or dearliest love, whether a woven robe,
Of colors blended like the rose and snow
Of morning's earliest blush, or goodly vase
Of silver, lipped with gold, and of a form
Compared with which, in beauty's pricelessness,
The silver and the gold were nothing worth,
Where do they seek it?

Ahab.

O, I know! but now
This Jezreel will be Sidon; will it not,

Mine irresistible? Hush! look you there,—
A cold pang thrills me through from head to heel,—
It is Elijah.

ELIJAH.

King of Israel,
Give ear unto my words. Thus saith the Lord:
Hast thou done murder, and so speedily
Taken possession? Doth the innocent blood
Not speak to me against thee from the ground?
I will bring evil on thee and thy house.
Thy branch shall wither. Him of Ahab's name
That dieth in the city dogs shall eat,
And him that falleth in the field the fowls
Shall tear; and in the place where Naboth fell
The dogs shall dip their tongues in Ahab's blood.

JEZEBEL.

Thou haggard, rude, and frenzy-tainted man,
How dar'st thou thus insult thy lord, the king?

ELIJAH.

I have a message, Jezebel, for thee.

JEZEBEL.

For me?—I do defy thee and thy Jah:
Begone, or slaves shall whip thee from the place,—
A public scorn.

ELIJAH.

Cease raging, Jezebel;
I see the quivering of thy livid lip
And thy cowed eye; the Light that speaks from mine
Hath quelled thee.

JEZEBEL.

Nay, presume not then too far;
But—for I see the king is moved—I will
Consent to reason with thee. Tell me, then,
Why, from the first, when I was young and came
From mine own people and my land to be
The Queen of Israel, cherishing the wish,
Dear as an infant growing 'neath my heart,
That my adopted country should rejoice
And prosper in my reign, thou didst assay

To do me wrong, to thwart me, to o'erthrow
The gods I worship?

ELIJAH.

Because, from the first,
Thou, Queen of Israel, madest it thine aim
To quench the nation's vital spark, to kill
That which is Israel's soul, inbreathed from heaven;
To change the Hebrew worshiper of One,
A Spirit, infinite, invisible,
Into a heathen bowing reckless down
To many things called gods.

JEZEBEL.

Thou knowest well
In the beginning we allowed the rite
Of Israel's God, demanding nothing more
Than that great Baal and radiant Ashtoreth
Should be supremely honored.

ELIJAH.

To consent
To this on part of any Israelite
Had been the deadliest treason.

. . . . .

JEZEBEL.

. . . . .

Is arrogance a virtue? Hast thou heard
That there is sin in pride? Why, then, do ye,
The Hebrews, sole among the nations spread
Upon the equal breast of mother earth,
Exclude all gods except your own? deny
That other gods exist? refuse to share
The general harmony, and to extend
That courteous tolerance to neighbor gods
Which neighbor peoples do not grudge to yours?

ELIJAH.

A nation shall be true unto itself:
An alien life means falsity and death.
No place, no name, no right to land or life,
Hath Israel, save as chosen by the Lord
To testify for him; to set the fact

Of his existence, oneness, sovereignty,
Massively visible before the world.

. . . . .

O Jezebel, hadst thou but known thy day,
Hadst thou but heard the voice that called to thee,
When thou, still young, from Sidon's coast did come
To reign in Israel; hadst thou loved the light,
And turned from idols to the living God;
Hadst thou been wedded truly to the land,
An Israelite indeed, in faith, hope, love;
O, how serene with Heaven's best blessedness,
How richly dowered in joy of doing good,
How full of love and peace thy life had been!
A Ruth in crowned and radiant graciousness,
A Deborah in regal strength of soul;
Around thee, as we learned to love thee well,
The air would all have rung with welcoming;
Thy voice and that of Ahab would have been
A rallying sound to bring again to one
Our Ephraim and Judah's scattered flock;
And glory brighter than of David's throne
Had beamed from Dan even to Beersheba.
And now thy day is past; thy night draws near.

JEZEBEL.

I will no longer speak with thee: begone!

ELIJAH.

But I must speak, and thou shalt hear, thy doom.
Ere many moons had seen thee Israel's queen,
With impious cruelty thou dipp'dst thy hand
In blood of God's own prophets. Far away
In Gilead, where I dwelt in peacefulness,
The mighty wail of Israel reached mine ears
Over the prophets fallen. Since that day,
With cruel wile, with steadfast subtlety,
With dark satanic sorcery, thou hast striven
To make this people unclean as thyself;
And last and worst, because a poor, brave man,
True to himself, his land, his God, was bold
To face the king as free man ought to face,
And to deny his covetous request,
Thou hast most basely murdered him.

JEZEBEL.

Nay, this
Is all too much. My lord, my husband, what!
Dost thou stand by and hear me thus reviled?
This fellow is a rebel, and would raise
Commotion in the land, and bid the folk
Forget their duty unto thee and me.

ELIJAH.

Woman, when such as thou is on the throne,
It is not sacrifice of lamb or kid,
It is not prayer at morn or eventide,
That is a people's service worthiest
Of God's acceptance. No. It is to leave
The babe in crib, the lamb within the fold,
The priest beside the altar, and to draw
The sword of vengeanee, spread the flag, and preach
God's message of revolt. Hush! Hear me still.
. . . . . Thus saith the Lord:
From that same tower where thou so oft has planned
Thy sacrilegious murders, plotted oft
Against the God of Israel, reveled wild
In guilt adulterous, thou shalt be hurled
Down headlong, shrieking in thy mad despair.
Horse-hoofs shall trample on thy crashing bones.
Dogs licked the blood of Naboth; but his limbs
Were stiff and cold before they came to him.
Whilst thou art quivering in the pangs of death,
While ear still hears and flesh still feels, the dogs
Shall rush upon thee, rend thee, tear thy flesh,
And drink thy blood.

JEZEBEL.

Inhuman savage, peace!

She draws a dagger from her girdle and flies at him, attempting to stab him. He disappears.

Where is he? Gone! O that this biting steel
Had pierced his heart!
Well? good my lord the king,
Your knees still knock together? Prithee look
A little like a man. How I despise thee!

Abridged from "THE DAYS OF JEZEBEL," *by Peter Bayne.*

THE CAPTIVE MAID.

LANDELLE, *Pinx.* JEHENNE, *Lith.*

THE LITTLE MAID OF ISRAEL.

THE Old Testament history has here and there glimpses of romantic narrative, which open like flowery valleys among Alpine ranges. One of the prettiest of these is the record of a little captive Judæan girl, who had been taken and carried into slavery by a guerilla party of Syrians. The story is so brightly and dramatically given in the Bible, that it is a living picture of those far-off ages.

In it we see, first, how the characteristic energy, brightness, and vigor of the Jewish female character come out even in this nameless captive child. Her quickness and ready wit had apparently gained for her a confidential position near the wife of the highest lord of the Syrian court, and, like the child Miriam before the princess of Egypt, she is forward, prompt, and busy with suggestion and advice.

The great man to whose household she belonged, the prime minister and chief counselor of the king, was afflicted with the worst form of incurable leprosy. So the text says:—

"And the Syrians had gone out by companies, and had brought away captive out of the land of Israel a little maid; and she waited on Naaman's wife. And she said unto her mistress, Would God my lord were with the prophet that is in Samaria! for he would recover him of his leprosy. And one went in and told this lord, saying, Thus and thus saith the maid that is of the land of Israel."

We can see in this story that the maid is an indulged pet in the establishment, free to speak her own little mind, and that she speaks in a way that attracts attention and wins respect. The whole power and flavor of a mighty oak is in every acorn, and this little seed of the Judæan stock carried the whole national dignity in her heart. *Her* people, she remembered, had a refuge in such troubles, — the power of Almighty God to heal and save was always vested in some mighty prophet, — and O, would to God that her master were with the Prophet in Samaria!

The reported words are caught up with the eagerness with which the drowning catch at straws. Leprosy to all ancient medicinal means was incurable; it was a way to death, slow, agonizing, and certain. The reputation of the Jews for miraculous wonders was current among surrounding nations, and the thing applicated to one of these prophets is deemed worth a trial.

The King of Syria now appears in the foreground. Israel is his conquered tributary province, and if there is any healing to be had there he will order it up for his favorite. A splendid caravan is mustered, and with ten talents of silver, and six thousand pieces of gold, and ten changes of raiment, and a letter from the King of Syria to his vassal the King of Israel, the great lord journeys forth. The letter of the king is brief and to the point: "Behold I have herewith sent Naaman my servant unto thee that thou mayest recover him of his leprosy."

Ahab, King of Israel, was a timorous, cowardly man, consciously out of favor with the God of his people, and with the Prophet who represented him at this time; so he rent his clothes and said, "Am I God, to kill and to make alive, that this man doth send unto me to recover a man from his leprosy? See, how he seeketh a quarrel against me!"

And when Elisha, the man of God, heard that he had rent his clothes, he sent to the king, saying, "Wherefore hast thou rent thy clothes? Let him come now to me, and he shall know that there is a Prophet in Israel."

Next, we have the scene where the prince, with his splendid caravan, is drawn up before the house of the Prophet.

Without even coming to the door, the Prophet simply sends the message: "Go and wash in Jordan seven times, and thy flesh shall come again to thee, and thou shalt be clean."

The lordly negligence of the message roused the indignation of the prince, — "I thought he would come out to me, and stand and call on the name of Jehovah his God, and strike his hand over the place and recover the leper. Are not Abana and Pharpar, rivers of Damascus, better than all the waters of Israel? may I not wash in them and be clean?" So he turned and went away in a rage.

We have a beautiful specimen of the domestic character of Oriental servitude in the language of his servant to the great man on this occasion: —

"My father, if the prophet had bid thee do some great thing, wouldst thou not have done it? how much rather then, when he saith unto thee, Wash and be clean!"

The good sense and fidelity of this rebuke is silently acknowledged, the Prophet's command obeyed, and in all the glow of restored life and health, the grateful prince comes back once more to the door of the Prophet. He comes with gifts, offerings of boundless gratitude; but the Prophet will take nothing. The grace of God is to be given, but can never be bought. For a prophet of Jehovah to accept a reward for the mercy dispensed through him was sacrilege; and though the prince urged with the passionate enthusiasm of gratitude, the Prophet was inflexible.

The story now gives us a glimpse of the ignoble side of the Jewish character, the selfish trading shrewdness which has made the name of the Jew a proverb. Gehazi, the servant of the Prophet, however, will find his types in many a Yankee village, —a man without moral delicacy, incapable of seeing that there is anything too sacred to become a matter of trade and barter. His master, in his view, has let slip an opportunity, but there is no reason why *he* should not turn an honest penny!

He pursues the grateful chief, and with a feigned tale of the sudden arrival of guests to his master, proposes to accept some of the offered wealth, and, having drawn largely on the generosity of the prince, he returns quietly with his ill-gotten spoils to his master's presence. The rest of the story is a most thrilling picture of what manner of man a Judæan prophet was: —

He went in and stood before his master. And Elisha said to him, "Whence comest thou, Gehazi?" And he said, "Thy servant went no whither." And he said unto him, "Went not my heart with thee, when the man turned again from his chariot to meet thee?" Then, in view of the oppressed and humbled condition of Israel, he adds, "Is it a time to receive money, and to receive garments, and olive-yards, and vineyards, and sheep, and oxen, and menservants, and maidservants? The leprosy, therefore, of Naaman shall cleave unto thee, and to thy seed forever."

And he went out from his presence a leper as white as snow.

Such was the Divine estimate of the guilt of turning the sacred prophetic office into a matter of gain.

This story bears such evident moral application, there are in it such similitudes to certain crises in every human history, that it might almost be taken for a sacred allegory or myth, — the graceful dress of a universal truth. As such it has always been used in the Church.

The soul seeking relief from the deep, unappeasable anguish of conscious moral degradation, weakness, and corruption, comes to the Prophet of the Lord. When the refuge and the remedy are pointed out, how often does the very simplicity of the process prove a stumbling-block! "To give the soul up with the faith of a little child to the cleansing love of Christ." How apparently simple, and yet how many shrink back from it! Rites, ceremony, rituals, sacraments, penances, — all the "rivers of Damascus" seem better than this one simple Jordan of faith. They will do some *great* thing, but this simple internal act of self-surrender they cannot bring themselves to.

The hero of this story was a heathen lord, who at first, certainly, regarded the Jehovah of Israel only as one of the many gods that divided the earth. There are not wanting those in our day who have gone back to the old heathen stand-point: the living God revealed in the Bible is only one of the many gods of antiquity, the patron of the old Hebrews; the Jordan is no more than any other little muddy rivulet. But when the soul comes in its thirst and its fever and its restlessness, and demands peace and joy and hope, and assurance of eternal life, how is it to be given? Does any book but the Bible, any God but the living Jehovah, promise *peace* that passeth understanding? And can anything short of this be health and soundness?

What became of the little daughter of Zion who figures so happily in this narrative, we hear not. That the Prince became a grateful worshiper of Jehovah is apparent from the story; and it is not too much to suppose that around this little maiden might have gathered a cluster of converts to the faith which had wrought such wonders for her master.

NAAMAN'S SERVANT.

"WHO for the like of me will care?"
  So whispers many a mournful heart,
When in the weary, languid air,
  For grief or scorn we pine apart.

So haply mused yon little maid,
  From Israel's breezy mountain borne,
No more to rest in Sabbath shade,
  Watching the free and waving corn.

A captive now, and sold and bought,
  In the proud Syrian's hall she waits,
Forgotten, — such her moody thought, —
  Even as the worm beneath the gates.

But One who ne'er forgets is here:
  He hath a word for thee to speak;
O serve him yet in duteous fear,
  And to thy Gentile lord be meek!

So shall the healing Name be known
  By thee on many a heathen shore,
And Naaman on his chariot throne
  Wait humbly by Elisha's door.

By thee desponding lepers know
  The sacred water's seven-fold might;
Then wherefore sink in listless woe?
  Christ's poor and needy claim your right;

Your heavenly right to do and bear
  All for his sake; nor yield one sigh
To pining doubt; nor ask, "What care
  In the wide world for such as I?"

John Keble.

THE SYRIAN CAPTAIN.

O wash in Jordan's limpid stream,"
Of old the holy prophet said;
"Its waves with healing virtue teem,
And health and purity they spread."

The Syrian captain vainly thought
The streams his native land supplied
Might yield the benefit he sought,
And rival Israel's fairest tide.

Too little for his courtly gait
The simple rule Elisha gave,
Nothing to suit his sumptuous state
He saw in Jordan's flowing wave.

Incensed, he turned his steps aside,
"And is this all?" disdainful said, —
"Some greater thing he might have tried,
And on the place his hand have laid.

"Abana's, — Pharpar's rivers flow,
With health and healing influence filled;
In them I 'll bathe my limbs, and show
The powerful virtue which they yield."

His humble menials wiselier deem,
Urge him to prove the small command;
And now emerging from the stream,
In fairest health they see him stand.

The Syrian captain's case is ours: —
We scorn to wash in Jordan's wave,
And fancy our own boasted powers
From woe and from disease will save.

WOMAN IN SACRED HISTORY.

Let us inquire, in humble faith,
  What waters may effectual be
To save us from the power of death,
  From sickness and from sorrow free.

Let all who hail the gospel light
  Our greater Prophet hear and live,
No substituted splendid rite
  Can holy absolution give.

Rivers of oil, or wine, poured forth,
  Shall fail to wash the soul from sin;
Rich sacrifice is nothing worth
  To heal the wound the heart within.

The Captain of our hope and faith
  Obeyed the Father's will and died;
He died an ignominious death,
  Was persecuted, crucified!

His followers now his cross must wear,
  Must tread the suffering path he trod;
If rough the road, and full of care,
  The end is safe, — it leads to God.

Anon.

חסד
ליהודים

QUEEN ESTHER.

BOULANGER, *Pinx.* JEHENNE. *Lith.*

QUEEN ESTHER.

THE story of Esther belongs to that dark period in Jewish history when the national institutions were to all human view destroyed. The Jews were scattered up and down through the provinces captives and slaves, with no rights but what their conquerors might choose to give them. Without a temple, without an altar, without a priesthood, they could only cling to their religion as a memory of the past, and with some dim hopes for the future. In this depressed state, there was a conspiracy, armed by the regal power, to exterminate the whole race, and this terrible danger was averted by the beauty and grace, the courage and prudence, of one woman. The portrait of this heroine comes to us in a flush of Oriental splendor. Her story reads like a romance, yet her memory, in our very prosaic days, is embalmed as a reality, by a yearly festival devoted to it. Every year the festival of Purim in every land and country whither the Jews are scattered, reminds the world that the romance has been a reality, and the woman whose beauty and fascination were the moving power in it was no creation of fancy.

The style of the book of Esther is peculiar. It has been held by learned Jews to be a compilation made by Mordecai from the Persian annals. The name of Jehovah nowhere occurs in it, although frequent mention is made of fasting and prayer. The king Ahasuerus is supposed by the best informed to be the Xerxes of Herodotus, and the time of the story previous to the celebrated expedition of that monarch against Greece. The hundred and twenty-seven provinces over which he reigned are picturesquely set forth by Herodotus in his celebrated description of the marshaling of this great army. The vanity, ostentation, childish passionateness, and disregard of human life ascribed to the king in this story are strikingly like other incidents related by Herodotus.

When a father came to him imploring that he would spare one of his sons from going to the war, Xerxes immediately commanded the young man to be slain and divided, and the wretched father was obliged to march between the mangled remains. This was to illustrate forcibly that no human being had any rights but the king, and that it was presumptuous even to wish to retain anything from his service.

The armies of Xerxes were not *led* to battle by leaders in front, but driven from behind with whips like cattle. When the king's bridge of boats across the Hellespont was destroyed by a storm, he fell into a fury, and ordered the sea to be chastised with stripes, and fetters to be thrown into it, with the admonition, "O thou salt and bitter water, it is thus that thy master chastises thy insolence!" We have the picture, in Herodotus, of the king seated at ease on his royal throne, on an eminence, beholding the various ranks of his army as they were driven like so many bullocks into battle. When the battle went against him, he would leap from his throne in furies of impotent rage.

It is at the court of this monarch, proud, vain, passionate, and ostentatious, that the story opens, with a sort of dazzle of Eastern splendor. "Now it came to pass, in the days of Ahasuerus, which reigned from India even unto Ethiopia, over an hundred and twenty and seven provinces, that in those days, when King Ahasuerus sat on the throne of his kingdom, which was in Shushan the palace, in the third year of his reign, he made a feast unto all his princes and his servants; the powers of Persia and Media, the nobles and princes of the provinces, being before him: when he showed them the riches of his glorious kingdom and the honor of his excellent majesty."

On the last seven days of the feast the royal palace is thrown open to the populace of Shushan. The writer goes on to amplify and give particulars: In the courts of the king's garden were couches of gold and silver, on a pavement of colored marbles, with hangings of white, green, and blue, fastened by cords of purple and fine linen to silver rings in marble pillars.

There was wine poured forth in costly goblets of very quaint and rare device. Vashti, the queen, at the same time made a feast to all the women in the royal house which belonged to the king. In the year 1819 Sir Robert Ker Porter visited and explored the ruins of this city of Shushan. His travels were printed for private circulation, and are rare and costly. They contain elegant drawings and restorations of the palace at Persepolis which would well illustrate this story, and give an idea of the architectural splendor of the scenery of the drama here presented.

Of Shushan itself, — otherwise Susa, — he gives only one or two drawings of fragmentary ruins. The "satyrs have long danced and the bitterns cried" in these halls then so gay and glorious, though little did the king then dream of that.

At the close of the long revel, when the king was inflated to the very ultimatum of ostentatious vanity, he resolves, as a last glorification of self, to exhibit the unveiled beauty of his Queen Vashti to all the princes and lords of his empire.

Now, if we consider the abject condition of all *men* in that day before the king, we shall stand amazed that there was a woman found at the head of the Persian empire that dared to disobey the command even of a drunken monarch. It is true that the thing required was, according to Oriental customs, an indecency as great as if a modern husband should propose to his wife to exhibit her naked person. Vashti was reduced to the place where a woman deliberately chooses death before dishonor. The *naïve* account of the counsel of the king and princes about this first stand for woman's rights — their fear that the example might infect other wives with a like spirit, and weaken the authority of husbands — is certainly a most delightful specimen of ancient simplicity. It shows us that the male sex, with all their force of physical mastery, hold everywhere, even in the undeveloped states of civilization, an almost even-handed conflict with those subtler and more ethereal forces which are ever at the disposal of women. It appears that the chief councilors and mighty men of Persia could scarcely hold their own with their wives, and felt as if the least toleration would set them all out into open rebellion. So Vashti is deposed, *nem. con.*, by the concurrent voice of all the princes of the Medes and Persians.

Then comes the account of the steps taken to secure another queen. All the beautiful virgins through all the hundred and twenty-seven provinces are caught, caged, and sent traveling towards Shushan, and delivered over to the keeping of the chief eunuch, like so many birds and butterflies, waiting their turn to be sent in to the king. Among them all a Jewish maiden, of an enslaved, oppressed race, is the favored one. Before all the beauties of the provinces Esther is preferred, and the crown royal is set upon her head. What charmed about Esther was, perhaps, the reflection of a soul from her beautiful face. Every one of the best class of Jewish women felt secretly exalted by her conception of the dignity of her nation as chosen by the one true God, and destined to bring into the world the great prince and Messiah who should reign over the earth. These religious ideas inspired in them a lofty and heroic cast of mind that even captivity could not subdue. At all events there was something about Esther that gave her a power to charm and fix the passions of this voluptuous and ostentatious monarch. Esther is the adopted daughter of her kinsman Mordecai, and the narrative says that "Esther did the commandment of Mordecai, like as when she was brought up with him." At his command she forbears to declare her nationality and lineage, and Mordecai refrains from any connection with her that would compromise her as related to an obscure captive, though the story says he walked every day before the court of the woman's house to know how Esther did, and what should become of her.

In these walks around the palace he overhears a conspiracy of two chamberlains to murder the king, and acquaints Esther of the danger. The conspirators are executed, and the record passes into the Persian annals with the name of Mordecai the Jew, but no particular honor or reward is accorded to him at that time. Meanwhile, a foreign adventurer named Haman rises suddenly to influence and power, and becomes prime minister to the king. This story is a sort of door, opening into the interior of a despotic court, showing the strange and sudden reverses of fortune which attended that phase of human existence. Haman, inflated with self-consequence, as upstart adventurers generally are, is enraged at Mordecai for neglecting to prostrate himself before him as the other hangers-on of the court do. Safe in his near relationship to the queen, Mordecai appears to have felt himself free to indulge in the expensive and dangerous luxury of quiet contempt for the all-powerful favorite of the king.

It is most astounding next to read how Haman, having resolved to take vengeance on Mordecai by exterminating his whole nation, thus glibly and easily wins over the king to his scheme. "There is a nation," he says, "scattered abroad throughout all the provinces of the king's kingdom, and their laws are diverse from all people, neither keep they the king's laws, therefore it is not for the king's profit to suffer them." "If it please the king let it be written that they may be destroyed, and I will pay ten thousand talents of silver to the hands of them that have the charge of the business, to bring it into the king's treasury."

It is fashionable in our times to speak of the contempt and disregard shown to women in this period of the world among Oriental races, but this one incident shows that women were held no cheaper than men. *Human beings* were cheap. The massacre of hundreds of thousands was negotiated in an easy, off-hand way, just as a gardener ordains exterminating sulphur for the green bugs on his plants. The king answered to Haman, "The silver is given thee, and the people also, to do as seemeth to thee good."

Then, says the story, "the king's scribes were called on the thirteenth day of the first month, and there was written according to all that Haman had commanded, and the letters were sent by post into all the provinces, to destroy and to kill and cause to perish all Jews, both old and young, little children and women, in one day, of the twelfth month, which is the month Adar, to take the spoil of them for a prey. The posts went out, being hastened by the king's commandment, *and the king and Haman sat down to drink, but the city of Shushan was perplexed.*" And when Mordecai heard this he rent his clothes and put on sackcloth with ashes, and went into the midst of the city, and came even before the king's gate, for none might enter into the king's gate clothed in sackcloth. The Oriental monarch was supposed to dwell in eternal bliss and joyfulness: no sight or sound of human suffering or weakness or pain must disturb the tranquility of his court; he must not even suspect the existence of such a thing as sorrow.

Far in the luxurious repose of the women's apartments, sunk upon embroidered cushions, listening to the warbling of birds and the plash of fountains, Esther the queen knew nothing of the decree that had gone forth against her people. The report was brought her by her chamberlain that her kinsman was in sackcloth, and she sent to take it away and clothe him with costly garments, but he refused the attention and persisted in his mourning. Then the queen sent her chief chamberlain to inquire what was the cause of his distress, and Mordecai sent a copy of the decree, with a full account of how and by whom it had been obtained, and charging her to go and make supplication to the king for her people. Esther returned answer: "All the king's servants do know that whosoever, man or woman, shall come in to the king in the inner court, who is not called, there is one law to put them to death, except those to whom the king shall hold out the golden scepter that he may live, but I have not been called to appear before the king for thirty days."

We have here the first thoughts of a woman naturally humble and timid, knowing herself one of the outlawed race, and fearing, from the long silence of the king, that his heart may have been set against her by the enemies of her people. Mordecai sent in reply to this a sterner message; "Think not with thyself that thou shalt escape in the king's house more than all the Jews. For if thou altogether holdest thy peace at this time, then shall there enlargement and deliverance arise to the Jews from another quarter, but thou and thy father's house shall be cut off; and who knoweth whether thou art come to the kingdom for such a time as this?" And Esther sends this reply: "Go, gather together all the Jews that are in Shushan, and fast ye for me; neither eat nor drink for three days, night or day; and I and my maidens will fast likewise. And so I will go in unto the king, which is not according to law; and if I perish, I perish."

There are certain apochryphal additions to the book of Esther, which are supposed to be the efforts of some romancer in enlarging upon a historic theme. In it is given at length a prayer of Mordecai in this distress, and a detailed account of the visit of Esther to the king. The writer says, that, though she carried a smiling face, "her heart was in anguish for fear," and she fell fainting upon the shoulder of her maid. Our own account is briefer, and relates simply how the king saw Esther the queen standing in the court, and she obtained favor in his eyes, and he held out the golden scepter, and said to her, "What wilt thou, Queen Esther, what is thy request? and it shall be given thee, even to half of the kingdom." Too prudent to enter at once into a discussion of the grand subject, Esther seeks an occasion to study the king and Haman together more nearly, and her request is only that the king and Haman would come that day to a private banquet in the queen's apartments. It was done, and the king and Haman both came.

At the banquet her fascinations again draw from the king the permission to make known any request of her heart, and it shall be given, even to half of his kingdom. Still delaying the final issue, Esther asks that both the king and his minister may come to a second banquet on the morrow. Haman appears to have been excessively flattered at this attention from the queen, of whose nationality he was profoundly ignorant; but as he passed by and saw Mordecai in his old seat in the king's gate, "that he stood not up neither moved for him," he was full of indignation. He goes home to his domestic circle, and amplifies the account of his court successes and glories, and that even the queen has distinguished him with an invitation which was shared by no one but the king. Yet, he says, in the end, all this availeth me nothing, so long as I see Mordecai the Jew sitting in the king's gate. His wife is fruitful in resources. "Erect a gibbet," she says, "and to-morrow speak to the king, and have Mordecai hanged, and go thou merrily to the banquet." And the thing pleased Haman, and he caused the gallows to be made.

On that night the king could not sleep, and calls an attendant, by way of opiate, to read the prosy and verbose records of his kingdom, — probably having often found this a sovereign expedient for inducing drowsiness. Then, by accident, his ear catches the account of the conspiracy which had been averted by Mordecai. "What honor hath been shown this man?" he inquires; and his servants answered, There is nothing done for him. The king's mind runs upon the subject, and early in the morning, perceiving Haman standing as an applicant in the outer court, he calls to have him admitted. Haman came, with his mind full of the gallows and Mordecai. The king's mind was full, also, of Mordecai, and he had the advantage of the right of speaking first. In the enigmatic style sometimes employed by Oriental monarchs, he inquires, "What shall be done with the man whom the king delighteth to honor?" Haman, thinking this the preface to some new honor to himself, proposes a scheme. The man whom the king delights to honor shall be clothed in the king's royal robes, wear the king's crown, be mounted on the king's horse, and thus be led through the streets by one of the king's chief councilors, proclaiming, "This is the man whom the king delighteth to honor." "Then said the king: Make haste, and do even so as thou hast said unto Mordecai the Jew that sitteth in the king's gate. Let nothing fail of all that thou hast spoken." And Haman, without daring to remonstrate, goes forth and fulfills the king's command, with what grace and willingness may be imagined.

It is evident from the narrative that the king had not even taken the trouble to inquire the name of the people he had given up to extermination any more than he had troubled himself to reward the man who had saved his life. In both cases he goes on blindly, and is indebted to mere chance for his discoveries. We see in all this the same passionate, childish nature that is recorded of Xerxes by Herodotus when he scourged the sea for destroying his bridge of boats. When Haman comes back to his house after his humiliating public exposure, his wife comforts him after a fashion that has not passed out of use with her. "If that Mordecai," she says, "is of the seed of the Jews before whom thou hast begun to fall, thou shalt not prevail against him, but shall surely fall before him."

And now Haman and the king and Esther are once more in a

secluded apartment, banqueting together. Again the king says to her, "What is thy request, Esther?" The hour of full discovery is now come. Esther answers: "If I have found favor in thy sight, O king, and if it please the king, let *my life* be given me at my petition, and my people at my request. For we are sold, I and my people, to be slain and to perish. If we had only been sold to slavery, I had held my tongue." Then the king breaks forth, "Who is he, and where is he that durst presume in his heart to do so?" And Esther answered, "The adversary and enemy *is this wicked Haman!*" Then Haman was afraid before the king and queen, and he had the best reason to be so. The king, like an angry lion, rose up in a fury and rushed out into the gardens. Probably at this moment he perceived the net into which he had been drawn by his favorite. He has sent orders for the destruction of this people, to whom his wife belongs, and for whom she intercedes. Of course he never thinks of blaming himself. The use of prime ministers was as well understood in those days as now, and Haman must take the consequences as soon as the king can get voice to speak it. Haman, white with abject terror, falls fainting at the feet of Esther upon the couch where she rests, and as the king comes raging back from the gardens he sees him there. "What! will he force our queen also in our very presence?" he says. And as the word went out of the king's mouth, they covered Haman's face. All is over with him, and an alert attendant says: "Behold the gallows, fifty cubits high, that he made to hang Mordecai, the saviour of the king's life." Then said the king, "Hang him thereon."

Thus dramatically comes the story to a crisis. Mordecai becomes prime minister. The message of the king goes everywhere, empowering the Jews to stand for their life, and all the governors of provinces to protect them. And so it ends in leaving the nation powerful in all lands, under the protection of a queen and prime minister of their own nation.

The book of Esther was forthwith written and sent to the Jews in all countries of the earth, as a means of establishing a yearly commemorative festival called Purim, from the word "Pur," or "The lot." The festival was appointed, we are told, by the joint authority of Mordecai the Jew and Esther the queen. And to this day we Gentiles in New York or Boston, at the time of Purim, may go into the synagogue and hear this book of Esther chanted in the Hebrew, and hear the hearty curses which are heaped, with thumps of hammers and of fists, upon the heads of Haman and his sons whenever their names occur in the story,— a strange fragment of ancient tradition floated down to our modern times. The palace of Shushan, with its hangings of green and blue and purple, its silver couches, its stir and hum of busy life, is now a moldering ruin; but the fair woman that once trod its halls is remembered and honored in a nation's heart. It is a curious fact that the romantic history of Esther has twice had its parallel since the Christian era, as the following incident, from Schudt's "Memorabilia of the Jews,"* witnesses. In this rare and curious work — 4th book, 13th chapter — he says: "Casimir the Great, of Poland, in 1431, fell in love with a beautiful Jewess named Esther, whom he married and raised to the throne of Poland. He had by her two sons and several daughters. His love for her was so great that he allowed the daughters to be brought up in their mother's religion." Also it is related that Alphonso VIII., king of Spain, took to himself a beautiful Jewess as a wife. On account of her he gave such privileges to the Jews that she became an object of jealousy to the nobles, and was assassinated

The book of Esther fills an important place in the sacred canon, as showing the Divine care and protection extended over the sacred race in the period of their deepest depression. The beauty and grace of a woman were the means of preserving the seed from which the great Son of Man and desire of all nations should come. Esther held in her fair hand the golden chain at the end of which we see the Mother of Jesus. The "Prayer of Esther" is a composition ascribed to her, and still in honored use among the solemn services of the synagogue.

* Jüdische Merkwürdigkeiten. Frankfort and Leipsic, 1714.

ESTHER.

QUEEN ESTHER weighed the message well;
Her dark eyes seemed dark thoughts to tell,
As, fixed upon the kneeling slave,
Mute answer to his words they gave,
The while her pale lips, murmuring dim,
Spake to herself, and not to him.

"It is indeed a dreadful task
My cousin Mordecai doth ask.
'T was he who cheered my orphan grief
With visions of some great relief,
And, reading in the Holy Book,
Prophetic promise found and took,
Crowning a maiden all unknown
With glory from the Persian throne.
How oft he whispered, well I ween,
'My child, thou shalt be Persia's queen!'
And when through all the realm made haste
The news, 'Proud Vashti is disgraced!'
How thrilled his voice our quiet home,
'Hadassah, rise; thine hour is come!'
Amazed, the simple Hebrew maid
His summons heard, his word obeyed,
The appointed year in Shushan passed,
And with the king found grace at last.
The virgin of a lineage scorned
With royal purple was adorned,
And mistress of all lands confessed,
From India to the Ethiop west.

"Ah, cousin, 't were less hard before,
The dream of splendor to give o'er,

Forego the untouched crown, than now
To lose it from a sovereign brow, —
Resign the power already known,
Forsake the palace and the throne,
Transgress alike as queen and wife,
And forfeit rashly love with life!
The bird that erst was urged to flight,
Once gliding up the airy height,
No longer heeds the keeper's call
That bids it tamely pause or fall;
Would thou hadst never let me fly,
Or ne'er recalled me, Mordecai!

"The king loved Vashti once, they tell,
(Albeit, he swears me, not so well!)
Yet all his love to anger burned
At one proud answer she returned.
Kings must be loved with reverence;
Their royalty wears this defense;
And bidden queens must swiftly come,
And queens unbidden bide at home.
These thirty days I wait the word
That gives me audience with my lord;
Nor I, nor any, dare intrude
Unasked upon his solitude, —
Rash crime, that on the offender draws
Death, by the changeless Median laws!"

"O heart, that beats so loud within,
O traitor heart, that whispers sin!
Hast thou forgot thy Hebrew blood,
Thy race of kings before the Flood,
Thy people, patient to the end,
Thy God, almighty to defend?"

"Ah, Mordecai, thou sayest well,
Their fate is mine. And who can tell,
But I am come to power and state
To conquer Israel's evil fate?
Alas! I tremble while I think
How deep the abyss, how near the brink.

Jehovah! hear thine handmaid's prayer;
Make wise to plan, make bold to dare,
And in her life or death make known
Thy people's glory and thine own!

"Go, Hatach, bear to Mordecai
Hadassah's — nay, the queen's — reply:
Let all my Hebrew brethren fast
Until three days and nights are past;
For on the third day I will go
And face the King. It may be so
(Since he has said he loves me much)
That he will deign the pardoning touch, —
Yea, with the golden scepter give
Once more the right to love and live.
But if — Enough; tell Mordecai
I go, and if I die, I die!
He knows me; tell him thou hast heard
The queen's — his child Hadassah's — word,
His Hebrew sister on the throne:
Now haste, — and God defend his own!"

R. W. R.

THE LAST RESOLVE.

Esther iv. 16.

COME, trembling sinner, in whose breast
A thousand thoughts revolve, —
Come, with your guilt and fear oppressed,
And make this last resolve :

"I 'll go to Jesus though my sin
Hath like a mountain rose ;
I know his courts, I 'll enter in
Whatever may oppose.

"Prostrate I 'll lie before his throne
And there my guilt confess ;
I 'll tell him I 'm a wretch undone
Without his Sovereign grace.

"I 'll to the gracious King approach
Whose scepter pardon gives ;
Perhaps he may command my touch,
And then the suppliant lives.

"Perhaps he will admit my plea,
Perhaps will hear my prayer ;
But if I perish, I will pray,
And perish only there.

THE LAST RESOLVE.

"I can but perish if I go, —
  I am resolved to try;
For if I stay away, I know
  I must forever die."

Rev. Edmund Jones.

JUDITH THE DELIVERER.

NO female type of character has given more brilliant inspiration to the artist or been made more glowingly alive on canvas than Judith. Her story, however, is set down by competent scholars as a work of fiction. The incidents recorded in it have so many anachronisms as to time and place, the historical characters introduced are in combinations and relations so interfering with authentic history, that such authorities as Professor Winer,* of Leipsic, and others, do not hesitate to assign it to the realm of romance. This Apocryphal book is, in fact, one of the few sparse blossoms of æsthetic literature among the Jewish nation. It is a story ages before the time of the tales of the *Decameron*, but as purely a romance. Considered in this light, it is nobly done and of remarkable beauty. The character of Judith is a striking and picturesque creation, of which any modern artist might be proud. It illustrates quite as powerfully as a true story the lofty and heroic type of womanhood which was the result of the Mosaic institutions, and the reverence in which such women were held by the highest authorities of the nation.

The author begins with the account of a destructive and terrible war which is being waged on the Jewish nation for refusing to serve in the armies of one Nabuchodonosor, king of Assyria, in an attack on the king of the Medes and Persians. All the names of this so-called war, and all the events as narrated, are out of joint with received history, and clearly as much creations of the writer's fancy as the Arabian Nights. It is stated that the Jews had just returned from the Babylonian captivity, and brought back their sacred vessels, and restored their temple

* Winer's Bible Dictionary, art. *Judith.*

worship after the long defilement of heathen servitude. But it is a matter of undisputed history that Nabuchodonosor was the king who carried the nation into captivity, and no other monarch of the name is known to history who performed deeds at all like those here narrated.

The story goes on to state how, to punish the Jews for not becoming his soldiers in the war, this king sent his chief commander, Holofernes, to carry destruction over their country. The mighty army of this general, and its ravages over the surrounding country, are set forth with an Oriental luxury of amplification. They come at last and straitly besiege the city of Bethulia. Whether this is a fictitious name for a real city, or whether it is a supposititious city, the creation of the author's imagination, critics are not fully decided; the story is just as pretty on one hypothesis as the other. The water being cut off, the people, suffering and dying of thirst, beset the chief-priests and elders to surrender the city to save their lives. Ozias, the chief ruler, temporizes, recommends five days of prayer; if before that time the God of Israel does not interpose, he promises to surrender.

And now the romance puts its heroine on the stage. After tracing her family and descent, it introduces her in these quaint words: "Now Judith was a widow in her house three years and four months. And she made her tent on the top of the house, put on sackcloth, and wore her widow's apparel; and she fasted all the days of her widowhood, save the eves of the Sabbaths, the Sabbaths, and the new moons and solemn feast-days of Israel. She was also of goodly countenance, and beautiful to behold, and her husband, Manasses, had left her gold and silver, and man-servants and maid-servants, and cattle, and lands; and she remained upon them. And there was none gave her an ill word, for she feared God greatly."

It is a striking exemplification of the elevated position which women held in the Jewish nation that a romance writer should introduce the incident that follows. Judith, hearing of the promise of the chief-ruler to surrender the city, sends her maid to call the governor and the chief men of the city, and they came unto her. And she said: "Hear now, O ye governors of the inhabitants of Bethulia, for the words that you have spoken are not right touching this oath, that you have promised to deliver the city to our enemies, unless within these days the Lord turn and help you. And now, who are ye that have tempted God this day, to stand in the stead of God to the children of men?"

She goes on to tell them that they have no right to say that unless God interfere for them before a certain time they will give up a sacred charge which has been entrusted to them to maintain; but it is rather their duty to stand at their posts and defend their city, without making conditions with him as to when or how he should help them. She says to them: "And now, try the Lord Almighty, and ye shall never know anything. For ye cannot find the depth of the heart of a man, neither can ye perceive what he thinketh; how, then, can ye search out God, that hath made all things, and comprehend his purposes? Nay, my brethren, provoke not the Lord our God to anger; for if he will not help within five days, he hath power to help us when he will, even every day. Do not bind the counsel of the Lord, for God is not a man that he may be threatened. Therefore, let us wait for salvation from him, and call upon him, and he will hear, if it please him."

She then shows them the disgrace and dishonor which will come upon them if they betray their trust, and they allow the sacred inheritance to be defiled and destroyed, and ends with a heroic exhortation: "Now, therefore, O brethren, let us show an example to our brethren, because their hearts depend on us, and the sanctuary and the house and the altar rest on us."

The governor and elders receive this message with respectful deference, apologize for yielding to the urgency of the people, who were mad with the sufferings of thirst, and compelled them to make this promise, and adds: "Therefore, pray thou for us, for thou art a goodly woman, and the Lord will send us rain, and fill our cisterns that we thirst no more." At this moment Judith receives a sudden flash of heroic inspiration, and announces to them, that, if they will send her forth without the city that night, the Lord will visit Israel by her hand. She adds that they must not inquire further of her purpose, until the design she has in view be finished. The magistrates, confiding implicitly in her, agree to forward her plan blindly.

The story now introduces us to the private oratory, where Judith pours out her heart before God. So says the narrative: "Then Judith fell on her face, and put ashes on her head, and uncovered the sackcloth wherewith she was clothed, and about the time that the incense of that evening was offered in Jerusalem in the house of the Lord, Judith cried with a loud voice to the Lord."

The prayer of Judith is eloquent in its fervent simplicity, and breathes that intense confidence in God as the refuge of the helpless, which is characteristic of Jewish literature. "Behold," she says, "the Assyrians are multiplied in their power, and are exalted with horse and man; they glory in the strength of their footmen; they trust in shield and spear and bow, and know not that thou art the Lord that breakest battles. The Lord is thy name. Throw down their strength in thy power, and bring down their force in thy wrath, for they have purposed to defile thy sanctuary, and to pollute the tabernacle where thy glorious name resteth, and to cast down with sword the home of thy altar. Behold their pride. Send thy wrath upon their heads, and give unto me, which am a widow, the power that I have conceived. For thy power standeth not in multitude, nor thy might in strong men; for thou art the God of the afflicted, thou art an helper of the oppressed, an upholder of the weak, a protector of the forlorn, a saviour of them that are without hope. I pray thee, I pray thee, O God of my father, King of every creature! hear my prayer, and make my speech and deceit to be their wound and stripe, who have purposed cruel things against thy covenant, and thy hallowed house, and against the house of the possession of thy children."

When she had thus prayed, the story goes on to say, she called her maid, and, laying aside the garments of her widowhood, dressed herself in the utmost splendor, adorning herself with jewels, and practicing every art of the toilet to set off her beauty. Thus attired, she with her maid went forth from the

JUDITH.

Horace Vernet, *Pinx.* Jehenne, *Lith.*

city towards the Assyrian army, meaning to be taken prisoner. As she designed, she was met by the outguards of the army, and carried at once to the tent of their general, professing that she had come to show him a way whereby he could go in and win all the hill country without loss of a man. The sensation produced by her entrance into the camp is well given: "Then there was a concourse through all the camp, for her coming was noised among the tents, and they came about her as she stood waiting without the tent of Holofernes; and they wondered at her beauty, and admired the children of Israel because of her, and every one said to his neighbors, Who would despise this people that have among them such women?"

The story next gives the scene where Holofernes, dazzled by her beauty and enchanted by her manners, becomes entirely subject to her will, receives and entertains her as a sovereign princess. She easily persuades him to believe the story she tells him. This people, she says, are under the protection of their God so long as they do not violate the rules of their religion, but, under the pressure of famine, they are about to eat of forbidden articles and to consume the sacred offerings due to the temple. Then their God will turn against them and deliver them into his hands. She will remain with him, and go forth from time to time; and when the sacrilege is accomplished, she will let him know that the hour to fall upon them is come.

So Judith is installed in state and all honor near the court of the commander, and enjoys to the full the right to exercise the rites of her national religion, — nay, the infatuated Holofernes goes so far as to promise her that, in the event of her succeeding in her promises, he will himself adopt the God of Israel for his God. After a day or two spent in this way, in which she goes forth every night for prayer and ablutions at the fountain, there comes the attempt to draw her into the harem of the general. Holofernes, in conference with Bagoas, the chief of his eunuchs, seems to think that the beautiful Judæan woman would laugh him to scorn if he suffered such an opportunity to pass unimproved. Accordingly a private banquet is arranged, and the chief of the eunuchs carries the invitation in true Oriental style, as follows: "Let not this fair damsel fear to come unto my lord, and to be honored in his presence, and to drink wine and be merry, and to be made this day as one of the Assyrians that serve in the house of Nabuchodonosor." Judith graciously accepts the invitation, decks herself with all her jewelry, and comes to the banquet and ravishes the heart of the commandant with her smiles. Excited and flattered, he drinks, it is said, more wine than ever he drunk before; so that, at the close of the feast, when the servants departed and Judith was left alone in the tent with him, he was lying dead drunk with wine on the cushions of his divan.

The rest is told in the story: "Then all went out and there was none left in the bedchamber, neither little nor great. Then Judith, standing by the bed, said in her heart, O Lord God of all power, look, at this present, on the work of my hands for the exaltation of Jerusalem. For now is the time to help thy inheritance and to execute my enterprise to the destruction of the enemies that are risen up against us. Then came she to the pillow of the couch, and took down the fauchion from thence, and approached his bed, and took hold of the hair of his head, and said, Strengthen me, O Lord God of Israel, this day, and she smote twice upon his neck with all her might, and she took away his head from him and went forth."

She returns to the city in the dim gray of the morning, bearing her trophy and the canopy and hangings of the bed whereon the enemy lay: "Then called Judith afar off to the watchmen, Open now the gates, for God, even our God, is with us to show his power yet in Israel and his strength against the enemy." A hasty midnight summons brings together the elders of the city. A fire is kindled, and they gather round her, as, radiant with triumphant excitement, she breaks forth in triumph: "Praise, praise, praise God, praise God, I say, for he has not taken away his mercy from the house of Israel, but hath destroyed the enemy by my hand this night." And she took the head out of the bag and showed it to them, and said: "Behold the head of Holofernes, the chief captain of the army of Assur, and behold the canopy where he did lie in his drunkenness, and the Lord hath smitten him by the hand of a woman. As the Lord liveth, who hath kept me in my way that I went, my countenance hath deceived him to his destruction, yet he hath not committed sin with me to defile and shame me."

Then Ozias said, "O daughter, blessed art thou among all the women of the earth, and blessed be the Lord God which created the heavens and the earth, which hath directed thee to the cutting off of the head of our chief enemy. For this thy confidence shall not depart from the hearts of men which remember the power of God forever. And God turn these things for a perpetual praise, because thou hast not spared thy life for the affliction of our nation, but hast avenged our ruin, walking in a straight way before our God. And all the people said, Amen, so be it."

The sequel of the story is, that the inspired prophetess directs her citizens to rush down upon the army in the first confusion of the loss of its general; and, this advice being followed, a general panic and rout of the hostile army follows, and the whole camp is taken and spoiled.

The story ends with a solemn procession of thanksgiving and worship, the men wreathed with flowers around their armor, and headed by Judith crowned with a garland of olive leaves, and leading forth a solemn rhythmic dance while she sings a hymn of victory. This song of Judith, evidently modeled on the victorious anthem of Deborah under the same circumstances, is less vigorous and fiery, but more polished and finished. Had it stood *alone*, it had been thought an unrivalled composition of its kind. The animus of it is, in some respects, the same with that of the song of Hannah, — it exults in the might of God as the protector of the weak and helpless. There is an intensely feminine exultation in the consciousness that she, though weak as a woman, has been made the means of overcoming this strength: —

"Assur came from the mountains of the north,
He came with ten thousands of armies.
The multitudes thereof stopped the torrents.
Their horsemen covered the hills.
He bragged that he would burn up my border,

That he would kill my young men with the sword,
That he would dash the sucking children against the ground,
And make the children a prey and the virgins a spoil;
But the Almighty Lord hath disappointed him by the hand of a woman!
The mighty one did not fall by young men,
Neither did the sons of Titans set upon him,
Nor did high giants set upon him;
But Judith, the daughter of Merari, weakened him with her beauty.
For the exaltation of the oppressed in Israel
She put off her garments of widowhood,
She anointed herself with ointment,
She bound her hair with a fillet,
She took a linen garment to deceive him;
Her sandals ravished his eyes,
Her beauty took his mind prisoner,
So the fauchion passed through his neck.
I will sing unto my God a new song:
O Lord, thou art great and glorious,
Wonderful in strength and invincible.
Let all creatures praise thee,
For thou speakest and they were made,
Thou sentest thy spirit and created them.
There is none can resist thy voice;
The mountains shall be moved from their foundations,
The rocks shall melt like wax at thy presence,
Yet art thou merciful to them that fear thee,
For all sacrifice is too little for a sweet savor unto thee,
All the fat is not enough for burnt-offerings;
But he that feareth the Lord is great at all times."

How magnificent is the conception of the woman here given! Lowly, devout, given up to loving memories of family life, yet capable in the hour of danger of rising to the highest inspirations of power. Poetess, prophetess, inspirer, leader, by the strength of that power by which the helpless hold the hand of Almighty God and triumph in his strength, she becomes the deliverer of her people.

JUDITH,

WITH THE HEAD OF HOLOFERNES.

SHE held the head all horrible with gore;
Nor of the woman in that act was seen
Aught save the alluring locks and beauteous mien:
"Hail, heroine, hail!" all voices cried before.

At the glad news, the damsels came with speed;
Some kissed her feet, and some her garment's hem,
None her right hand, for terrible to them
Was the remembrance of that fatal deed.

A hundred prophets sang the matron's fame;
"Fly round the world, thine everlasting name!
The sun through all his march shall tell thy story."
Great from that dread achievement though she rose,
Greater she stood at this triumphant close,
For she was humble in the height of glory.

From the Italian, by JAMES MONTGOMERY.

JEWISH BATTLE-SONG.

HO! Princes of Jacob! the strength and the stay
Of the daughter of Zion, — now up, and array!
Lo, the hunters have struck her, and bleeding alone,
Like a pard in the desert, she maketh her moan;
Up, with war-horse and banner, with spear and with sword,
On the spoiler go down in the might of the Lord!

She lay sleeping in beauty, more fair than the moon,
With her children about her, like stars in night's noon,
When they came to her covert, these spoilers of Rome,
And are trampling her children, and rifling her home;
O, up, noble chiefs! would you leave her forlorn
To be crushed by the Gentile, a mock and a scorn?

Their legions and cohorts are fair to behold,
With their iron-clad bosoms and helmets of gold;
But gorgeous and glorious in pride though they be,
Their avarice is broad as the grasp of the sea;
They talk not of pity; the mercies they feel
Are cruel and fierce as their death-doing steel.

Will they laugh at the hind they have struck to the earth,
When the bold stag of Naphtali bursts on their mirth?
Will they dare to deride and insult, when in wrath
The lion of Judah glares wild in their path?
O, say, will they mock us, when down on the plain
The hoofs of our steeds thunder over their slain?

They come with their plumes tossing haughty and free
And white as the crest of the old hoary sea;
Yet they float not so fierce as the wild lion's mane,
To whose lair ye have tracked him, whose whelps ye have slain;
But, dark mountain archer! your sinews to-day
Must be strong as the spear-shaft to drive in the prey.

And the tribes are all gathering; the valleys ring out
To the peal of the trumpet, the timbrel, the shout:
Lo, Zebulon comes; he remembers the day
When they periled their lives to the death in the fray;
And the riders of Naphtali burst from the hills
Like a swollen mountain-stream in the pride of its rills.

Like Sisera's rolls the foe's chariot-wheel,
And he comes, like the Philistine, girded in steel;
Like both shall he perish, if ye are but men,
If your javelins and hearts are as mighty as then;
He trusts in his buckler, his spear, and his sword;
His strength is but weakness; — we trust in the Lord!

George Lunt.

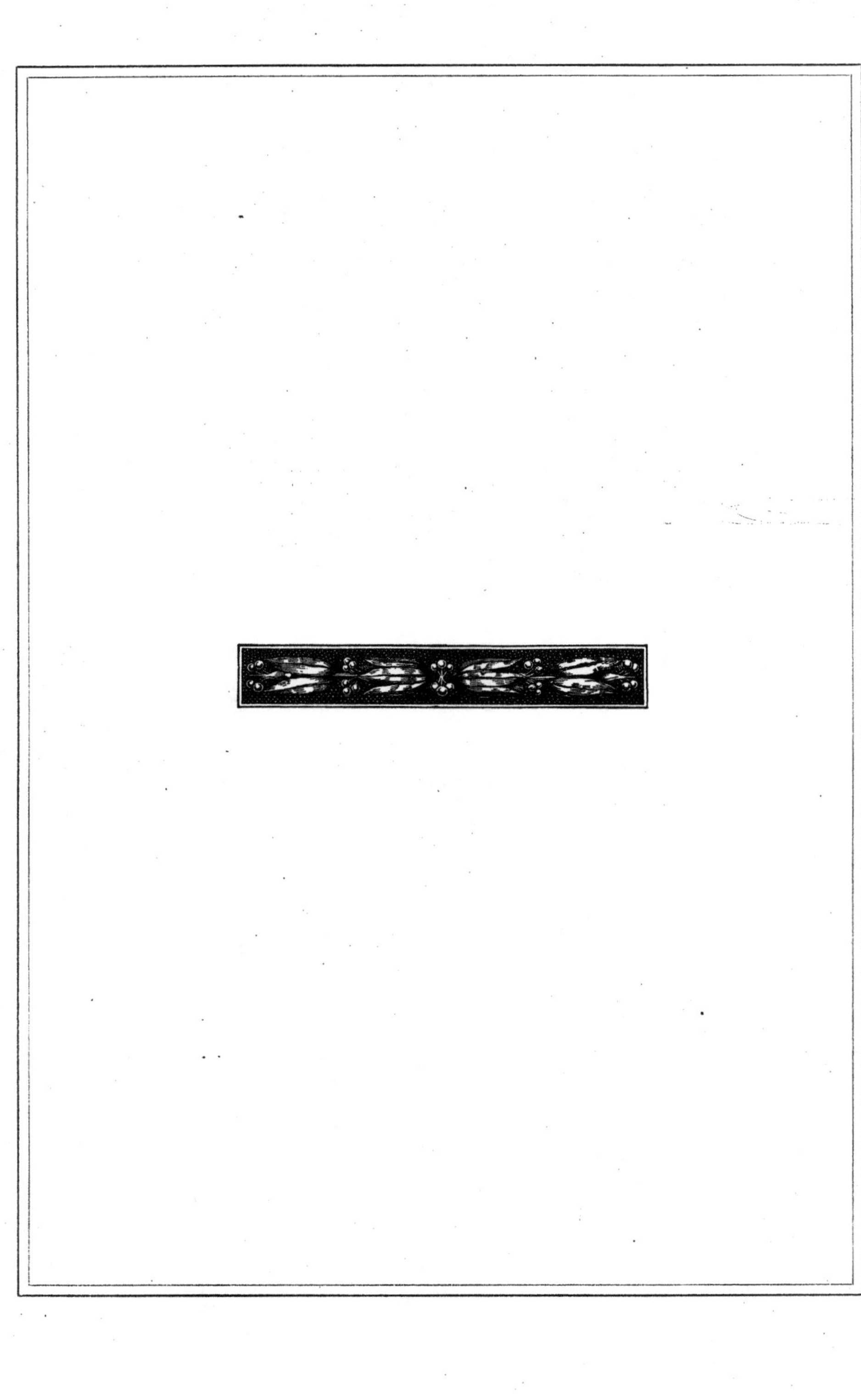

WOMEN OF THE CHRISTIAN ERA.

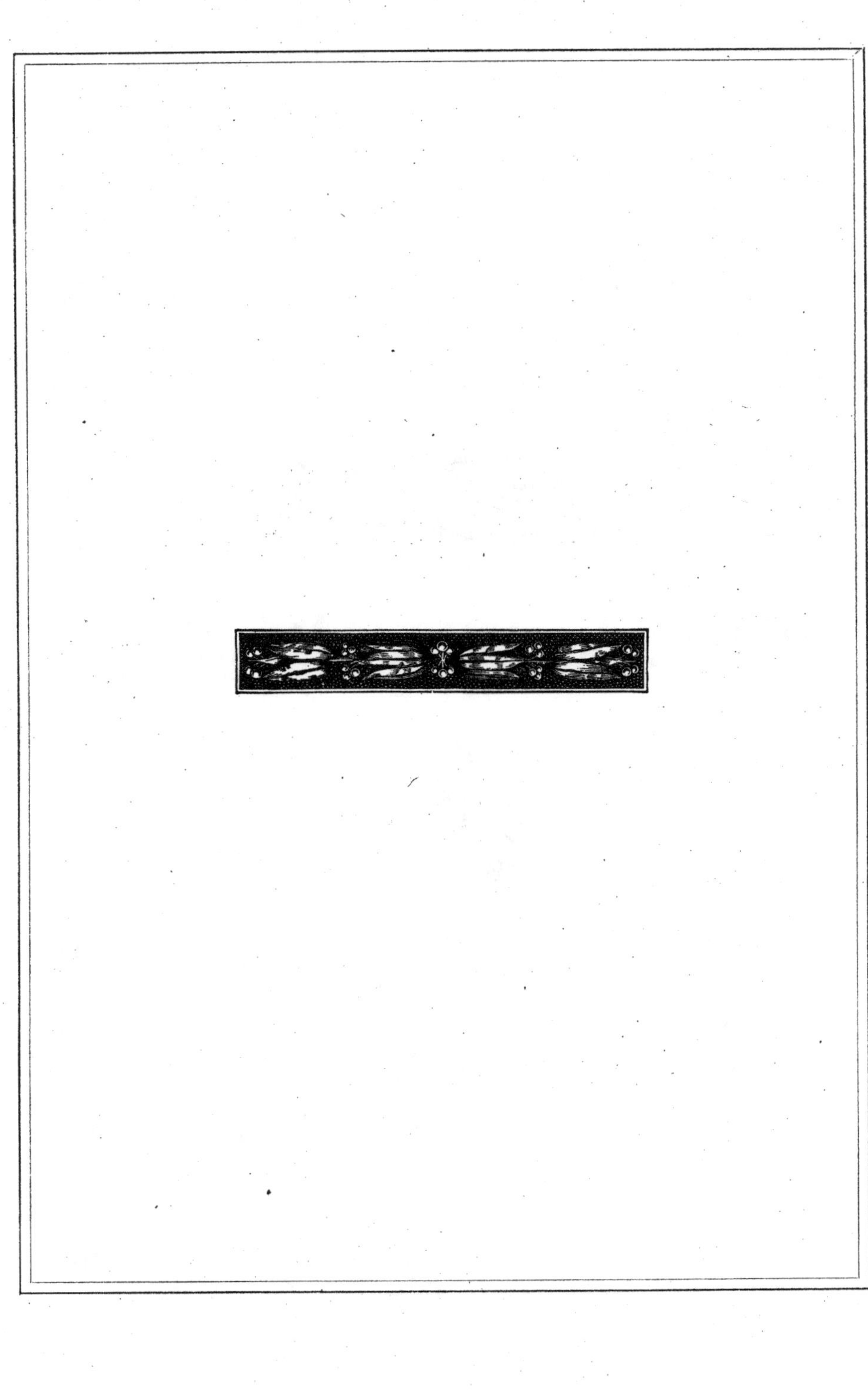

PALESTINE.

BLEST land of Judæa! thrice hallowed of song,
Where the holiest of memories pilgrim-like throng;
In the shade of thy palms, by the shores of thy sea,
On the hills of thy beauty, my heart is with thee.

With the eye of a spirit I look on that shore,
Where pilgrim and prophet have lingered before;
With the glide of a spirit I traverse the sod
Made bright by the steps of the angels of God.

Blue sea of the hills! in my spirit I hear
Thy waters, Gennesaret, chime on my ear;
Where the Lowly and Just with the people sat down,
And thy spray on the dust of His sandals was thrown.

Beyond are Bethulia's mountains of green,
And the desolate hills of the wild Gadarene;
And I pause on the goat-crags of Tabor to see
The gleam of thy waters, O dark Galilee!

Hark! a sound in the valley! where, swollen and strong,
Thy river, O Kishon, is sweeping along;
Where the Canaanite strove with JEHOVAH in vain,
And the torrent grew dark with the blood of the slain.

There down from his mountains stern Zebulon came,
And Naphtali's stag, with his eyeballs of flame,
And the chariots of Jabin rolled harmlessly on,
For the arm of the Lord was Abinoam's son.

There sleep the still rocks and the caverns which rang
To the song which the warrior-prophetess sang,
When the princes of Issachar stood by her side,
And the shout of a host in its triumph replied.

Lo! Bethlehem's hill-site before me is seen,
With the mountains around and the valleys between;
There rested the shepherds of Judah, and there
The song of the angels rose sweet in the air.

And Bethany's palm-trees in beauty still throw
Their shadows at noon on the ruins below;
But where are the sisters who hastened to greet
The lowly Redeemer, and sit at His feet?

I tread where the twelve in their wayfaring trod:
I stand where they stood with the chosen of God,—
Where His blessings were heard, and His lessons were taught,
Where the blind were restored, and the healing was wrought.

O, here with His flock the sad Wanderer came,—
These hills He toiled over in grief, are the same,—
The founts where He drank by the wayside still flow,
And the same airs are blowing which breathed on His brow.

And throned on her hills sits Jerusalem yet,
But the dust on her forehead, and chains on her feet;
For the crown of her pride to the mocker hath gone,
And the holy Shechinah is dark where it shone.

But wherefore this dream of the earthly abode
Of humanity clothed in the likeness of God?
Were my spirit but turned from the outward and dim,
It would gaze, even now, on the presence of Him!

Not in clouds and in terrors, but gentle as when,
In love and in meekness, He moved among men;
And the voice which breathed peace to the waves of the sea,
In the hush of my spirit would whisper to me!

PALESTINE.

And what if my feet may not tread where He stood,
Nor my ears hear the dashing of Galilee's flood,
Nor my eyes see the cross which He bowed Him to bear,
Nor my knees press Gethsemane's garden of prayer:

Yet, Loved of the Father, thy Spirit is near
To the meek, and the lowly, and penitent here;
And the voice of thy love is the same even now
As at Bethany's tomb, or on Olivet's brow.

O, the outward hath gone! — but, in glory and power,
The spirit surviveth the things of an hour;
Unchanged, undecaying, its Pentecost flame
On the heart's secret altar is burning the same!

John G. Whittier.

INVOCATION.

AND come, ye faithful! round Messiah seen,
With a soft harmony of tears and light
Streaming through all your spiritual mien,
As in calm clouds of pearly stillness bright,
Showers weave with sunshine, and transpierce their slight,
Ethereal cradle. From your heart subdued
All haughty dreams of power had winged their flight,
And left high place for martyr fortitude,
True faith, long-suffering love. Come to me, come!
And, as the seas beneath your Master's tread
Fell into crystal smoothness, round him spread
Like the clear pavement of his heavenly house;
So in your presence let the soul's great deep
Sink to the gentleness of infant sleep.

Felicia Hemans.

SONNETS.

I. THE ANNUNCIATION.

LOWLIEST of women, and most glorified!
In thy still beauty sitting calm and lone,
A brightness round thee grew, — and by thy side,
Kindling the air, a form ethereal shone,
Solemn, yet breathing gladness. From her throne
A queen had risen with more imperial eye,
A stately prophetess of victory
From her proud lyre had struck a tempest's tone,
For such high tidings unto *thee* were brought,
Chosen of Heaven! that hour: — but thou, O thou!
E'en as a flower with gracious rains o'erfraught,
Thy virgin head beneath its crown did bow,
And take to thy meek breast the all holy Word,
And own thyself *the handmaid of the Lord.*

II. THE SONG OF THE VIRGIN.

YET as a sun-burst flushing mountain snow
Fell the celestial touch of fire erelong
On the pale stillness of thy thoughtful brow,
And thy calm spirit lightened into song.
Unconsciously, perchance, yet free and strong
Flowed the majestic joy of tuneful words,
Which living harps the choirs of heaven among
Might well have linked with their divinest chords.
Full many a strain, borne far on glory's blast,
Shall leave, where once its haughty music passed,
No more to memory than a reed's faint sigh;
While thine, O childlike virgin! through all time
Shall send its fervent breath o'er every clime,
Being of God, and therefore not to die.

Felicia Hemans.

THE VIRGIN.

OTHER! whose virgin bosom was uncrost
With the least shade of thought to sin allied;
Woman! above all women glorified,
Our tainted nature's solitary boast;
Purer than foam on central ocean tost,
Brighter than eastern skies at daybreak strewn
With fancied roses, than the unblemished moon
Before her wane begins on heaven's blue coast;
Thy image falls to earth. Yet some, I ween,
Not unforgiven the suppliant knee might bend,
As to a visible Power, in which did blend
All that was mixed and reconciled in thee
Of mother's love with maiden purity,
Of high with low, celestial with terrene.

William Wordsworth.

THE SISTINE MADONNA.

RAPHAEL, *Pinx.* JEHENNE, *Lith.*

MARY THE MYTHICAL MADONNA.

NO woman that ever lived on the face of the earth has been an object of such wonder, admiration, and worship as Mary the mother of Jesus. Around her poetry, painting, and music have raised clouds of ever-shifting colors, splendid as those around the setting sun. Exalted above earth, she has been shown to us as a goddess, yet a goddess of a type wholly new. She is not Venus, not Minerva, not Ceres, nor Vesta. No goddess of classic antiquity or of any other mythology at all resembles that ideal being whom Christian art and poetry present to us in Mary. Neither is she like all of them united. She differs from them as Christian art differs from classical, wholly and entirely. Other goddesses have been worshiped for beauty, for grace, for power. Mary has been the Goddess of Poverty and Sorrow, of Pity and Mercy; and as suffering is about the only certain thing in human destiny, she has numbered her adorers in every land and climate and nation. In Mary, womanhood, in its highest and tenderest development of the MOTHER, has been the object of worship. Motherhood with large capacities of sorrow, with the memory of bitter sufferings, with sympathies large enough to embrace every anguish of humanity!—such an object of veneration has inconceivable power.

The art history that has gradually grown up around the personality of the Madonna is entirely mythical. It is a long poem, recorded in many a legend or tradition, and one which one may see represented, scene after scene, in many a shrine and church and monastery devoted to her honor.

According to these apocryphal accounts, the marvels begin before her birth. Her parents, Joachim and Anna, of the royal race of David, are childless, and bitterly grieved on this account. On a great festival-day, when Joachim brings a double offering to the Lord, he is rejected by the priest, saying, "It is not lawful for thee to bring thine offering, since thou hast not begotten issue in Israel." And Joachim was exceedingly sorrowful, and went away into the wilderness, and fasted forty days and forty nights, and said, "Until the Lord my God look upon mine affliction, my only meat shall be prayer." Then follows a long account of the affliction of Anna, and how she sat down under a laurel-tree in the garden, and bemoaned herself and prayed. "And behold, the angel of the Lord stood by her, and said, Anna, thy prayer is heard; thou shalt bring forth, and thy child shall be blessed through the whole world. See, also, thy husband Joachim is coming with his shepherds, for an angel hath comforted him also. And Anna went forth to meet her husband, and Joachim came from the pasture, and they met at the golden gate, and Anna ran and embraced her husband, and said, Now know I that the Lord hath blessed me."

Then comes the birth of the auspicious infant, with all manner of signs of good omen. "And when the child was three years old, Joachim said: Let us invite the daughters of Israel, that they may each take a taper and a lamp, and attend on her, that the child may not turn back from the temple of the Lord. And being come to the temple, they placed her on the first step, and she ascended all the steps to the altar, and the high-priest received her there, and kissed her and blessed her, saying, Mary, the Lord hath magnified thy name to all generations; in thee shall all nations of the earth be blessed."

A magnificent picture by Titian, in the Academy at Venice, represents this scene. Everything about it is in gorgeous style, except the little Mary, who is a very literal, earthly, chubby bit of flesh and blood, and not in the least celestial. In the Church of Santa Maria della Salute in Venice, however, the child Mary, going up the temple steps, is a perfect little angel with a cloud of golden hair. Then we have flocks of pictures representing the sacred girlhood of Mary. She is vowed to the temple service, and spins and weaves and embroiders the purple and fine linen for sacerdotal purposes. She is represented as looked upon with awe and veneration by all the holy women who remain in the courts of the Lord, especially by the prophetess Anna, who declares to her her high destiny. It is recorded that her life was sustained by the ministry of angels, who daily visited and brought to her the bread of Paradise and the water of the River of Life. It is the tradition of the Greek Church that Mary alone of all her sex was allowed to enter the Holy of Holies, and pray before the ark of the covenant.

In her fourteenth year the priest announced to her that it was time for her to be given in marriage, but she declared that she had vowed a life of virginity, and declined. But the high-priest told her that he had received a message from the Lord, and so she submitted. Then the high-priest inquired of the Lord, and was bid to order all the widowers of the people to come, each with his rod in his hand, that the Lord might choose one by a sign. And Joseph the carpenter came with the rest, and presented his rod, and lo! a white dove flew from it, and settled upon his head. According to St. Jerome, however, the tradition has another version. The rods of the candidates were placed in the temple over night, and lo! in the morning Joseph's rod had burst forth in leaves and flowers. The painting by Raphael, in the Brera at Milan, as fresh in color now as if but of yesterday, gives the mediæval conception of that wedding.

Then come pictures of the wonderful Annunciation, thick as lilies in a meadow. The angel rainbow-wings, bedropped with gold, drift noiselessly like a cloud into the oratory where the holy virgin is in prayer, and bring her the wonderful story. The visitation to her cousin Elizabeth, the birth of the infant Jesus, the visit of the shepherds, the adoration of the Magi, come to our minds with a confused and dazzling memory of all that human art can do, with splendor of colors and richness of fancy, to embellish the theme. The presentation in the temple, the flight into Egypt, the repose by the way, the home-life at Nazareth, each has its clusters of mythical stories that must be understood to read aright the paintings that tell them. We behold angels bending the branches of the trees to give the sacred wanderers fruit, — angels everywhere ministering about the simple offices of life, pouring water to wash the infant, holding the napkin, playing around him. Then come the darker scenes of the passion, the Via Dolorosa, the station by the cross, the sepulchers, in which all of pathos that human art can produce has been employed to celebrate the memory of that mother's sorrows.

There is a very ancient tradition spoken of by St. Ambrose, in the fourth century, as being then generally believed, that Christ, after his resurrection, appeared first to his mother, — she, who had his last cares for anything earthly, was first to welcome his victory over death. The story as given by Mrs. Jameson, in her "Legends of the Madonna," is, that Mary, when all was finished, retired to her solitude to pray, and wait for the promised resurrection; and while she prayed, with the open volume of the prophecies before her, a company of angels entered, waving their palms and singing, and then came Jesus, in white, having in his left hand the standard of the cross as one just returned from Hades, victorious over sin and death, and with him came patriarchs and prophets and holy saints of old. But the mother was not comforted till she heard the voice of her son. Then he raised his hand and blessed her, and said, "I salute thee, O my mother," and she fell upon his neck weeping tears of joy. Then he bade her be comforted, and weep no more, for the pain of death had passed away, and the gates of hell had not prevailed against him; and she thanked him, meekly, on her knees, that he had been pleased to bring redemption to man and make her the humble instrument of his mercy. This legend has something in it so grateful to human sympathies, that the heart involuntarily believes it. Though the sacred record is silent, we may believe that He, who loved his own unto the end, did not forget his mother in her hour of deepest anguish.

After the resurrection, the only mention made of Mary by the Evangelists is an incidental one in the first part of Acts.

She is spoken of as remaining in prayer with the small band of Christian disciples, waiting for the promised Spirit which descended upon the day of Pentecost. After this she fades from our view entirely. According to the mythical history, however, her career of wonder and glory is only begun. Imagination blossoms and runs wild in a tropical landscape of poetic glories.

Mary is now the mother of the Christian Church. Before departing on their divine missions, the apostles come and solicit her blessing. The apocryphal books detail, at length, the circumstances of her death and burial, and the ascension of her glorified body to heaven, commonly called the Assumption. We make a few extracts: "And on a certain day the heart of Mary was filled with an inexpressible longing to behold her divine son, and she wept abundantly; and, lo, an angel appeared before her, clothed in light as in a garment, and he saluted her, and said, Hail, O Mary! blessed be he that giveth salvation to Israel! I bring thee here a palm branch, gathered in Paradise; command that it be carried before thy bier on the day of thy death, for in three days thy soul shall leave thy body and thou shalt enter Paradise, where thy son awaits thy coming." Mary requested, in reply, three things,— the name of the angel; that she might once more see the apostles before her departure; and that on leaving the body no evil spirit should have power to affright her soul. The angel declared his name to be the Great and Wonderful, promised the reunion of the apostles around her dying bed, and assured her against the powers of darkness. "And having said these words, the angel departed into heaven; and, lo, the palm branch which he had left shed light in every leaf, and sparkled as the stars of the morning. Then Mary lighted the lamps and prepared her bed, and waited for the hour to come. And in the same instant John, who was preaching in Ephesus, and Peter, who was preaching at Antioch, and all the other apostles, who were dispersed in different parts of the world, were suddenly caught up by a miraculous power, and found themselves before the habitation of Mary. When Mary saw them all around her, she blessed and thanked the Lord, and placed in the hands of St. John the shining palm, and desired that he should bear it at the time of her burial."

It is then recorded that at the third hour of the night there came a sound as of a rushing mighty wind upon the house, and the chamber was filled with a heavenly odor, and Jesus himself appeared with a great train of patriarchs and prophets, who surrounded the dying bed, singing hymns of joy; and Jesus said to his mother, "Arise, my beloved, mine elect, come with me from Lebanon, mine espoused, and receive the crown prepared for thee." And Mary answered, "My heart is ready; in the book is it written of me, Lo, I come to do thy will." Then amid songs of angels, the soul of Mary left her body and passed to the arms of Jesus. A beautiful little picture by Fra Angelico represents this scene. The soul of Mary is seen as an infant in the arms of Jesus, who looks down on it with heavenly tenderness. The lifeless form, as it lies surrounded by the weeping apostles, has that sacred and touching beauty that so often seals with the seal of Heaven the face of the dead. It is a picture painted by the heart, and worthy to be remembered for a lifetime.

Then follows an account of the funeral, and where the body was laid; but, like that of Jesus, it was not destined to see corruption, and on the morning of the third day she rose in immortal youth and beauty, and ascended to heaven amid troops of angels, blowing their silver trumpets and singing as they rose, "Who is she that riseth fair as the moon, clear as the sun, terrible as an army with banners?" The legend goes on to say that Thomas was not present, and that when he arrived he refused to believe in her resurrection, and desired that her tomb should be opened; and when it was opened, it was found full of lilies and roses. Then Thomas, looking up to heaven, beheld her in glory, and she, for the assurance of his faith, threw down to him her girdle.

Thus far the legends.* One may stand in the Academy in

* The sources from which these are drawn are the apocryphal books of the New Testament.

Venice and see the scene of Mary's ascension in the great picture of Titian, which seems to lift one off one's feet, and fairly draw one upward in its glory of color and its ecstasy of triumphant joy. It is a charming feature in this picture that the holy mother is represented as borne up by myriads of lovely little children. Such a picture is a vivid rendering to the eye of the spirit of the age which produced it.

Once started, the current of enthusiasm for the Madonna passed all bounds, and absorbed into itself all that belonged to the Saviour of mankind. All the pity, the mercy, the sympathy, of Jesus were forgotten and overshadowed in the image of this divine mother. Christ, to the mind of the Middle Ages, was only the awful Judge, whom Michael Angelo painted in his terrific picture grasping thunderbolts, and dealing damnation on the lost, while his pitiful mother hides her eyes from the sight.

Dr. Pusey, in his "Eirenicon," traces the march of mariolatry through all the countries of the world. He shows how to Mary have been ascribed, one after another, all the divine attributes and offices. How she is represented commanding her son in heaven with the authority of a mother; and how he is held to owe to her submissive obedience. How she, being identified with him in all that he is and does, is received with him in the sacrament, and is manifest in the real presence. In short, how, by the enormous growth of an idea, there comes to be at last *no God but Mary.* Martin Luther describes, in his early experiences, how completely the idea of the true Redeemer was hidden from his mind by this style of representation; that in the ceremony of the mass he trembled, and his knees sunk under him for fear, on account of the presence of Christ the Judge of the earth. When we look back to the earlier ecclesiastical history, we find no trace of all this peculiar veneration. None of the Apocryphal Gospels have higher antiquity than the third or fourth century.

In Smith's Dictionary of the Bible, article *Mary*, this question is settled by a comprehensive statement.* "What," the writer says, "was the origin of this *cultus?* Certainly not the Bible.

* The article is by Rev. F. Meyrick, M. A., one of her Majesty's inspectors of schools, late fellow and tutor of Trinity College, Oxford.

There is not a word there from which it could be inferred, nor in the creeds, nor in the fathers of the first five centuries. We may trace every page they have left us, and we shall find nothing of the kind. There is nothing of the sort in the supposed works of Hermas and Barnabas, nor in the real works of Clement, Ignatius, and Polycarp; that is, the doctrine is not to be found in the first century. There is nothing in Justin Martyr, Tatian, Anathagoras, Theophilus, Clement of Alexandria, Tertullian; that is to say, nothing in the second century."

In the same manner he reviews the authors of the third, the fourth, the fifth century, and shows that there are no traces of this style of feeling. Moreover, he cites passages from the Christian fathers of the first three or four centuries, where Mary is as freely spoken of and criticised, and represented subject to sins of infirmity, as other Christians. Tertullian speaks of her "unbelief." Origen interprets the sword that should pierce through her heart as "unbelief"; and in the fourth century, St. Basil gives the same interpretation; in the fifth century, St. Chrysostom accuses her of excessive ambition and foolish arrogance and vainglory, in wishing to speak with Jesus while engaged in public ministries. Several others are quoted, commenting upon her in a manner that must be painful to the sensibility of even those who never cherished for her a superstitious veneration. No person of delicate appreciation of character can read the brief narrative of the New Testament and not feel that such comments do great injustice to the noblest and loveliest among women.

The character of Mary has suffered by reaction from the idolatrous and fulsome adoration which has been bestowed on her. In the height of the controversy between Protestants and the Romish church there has been a tendency to the side of unjust depreciation on the part of the former to make up for the unscriptural excesses of the latter. What, then, was the true character of Mary, highly favored, and blessed among women? It can only be *inferred* by the most delicate analysis of the little that the Scripture has given; this we reserve for another article.

ON A PICTURE OF THE VIRGIN MARY

BEARING DOVES TO SACRIFICE.

MY eyes climb slowly up, as by a stair,
To seek a picture on my chamber wall, —
A picture of the Mother of our Lord,
Hung where the latest twilight shadows fall.

My lifted eyes behold a childlike face,
Under a veil of woman's holiest thought,
O'ershadowed by the mystery of grace,
And mystery of mercy — God hath wrought.

Down through the dim old temple, moving slow,
Her drooping lids scarce lifted from the ground,
As if she faintly heard the distant flow
Of far-off seas of grief she could not sound.

I think archangels would not count it sin,
If, underneath the veil that hides her eyes,
They, seeing all things, saw the soul within
Held more of mother-love than sacrifice.

She walks erect, the Virgin undefiled;
Back from her throat the loose robe falls apart,
And e'en as she would clasp her royal Child,
She holds the dovelets to her tender heart.

No white wing trembles 'neath her pitying palm,
No feather flutters in this last warm nest,
And thus she bears them on, while solemn psalm
Wakes dim, prophetic stirrings in her breast.

WOMAN IN SACRED HISTORY.

Sweet Hebrew Mother! many a woman shares
  Thy crucifixion of her hopes and loves,
And in her arms to death unshrinking bears
  Her precious things, — even her turtle-doves.

But often, ere the temple's marble floor
  Has ceased the echo of her parting feet,
Her gifts prove worthless, — thine is evermore
  The gift of gifts, transcendent and complete.

We mothers, too, have treasures all our own,
  And, one by one, oft see them sacrificed:
Thou, Blessed among women, thou alone
  Hast held within thine arms the dear Child-Christ.

Therefore mine eyes mount up, as by a stair,
  To seek the picture on my chamber wall;
Therefore my soul climbs oft the steeps of prayer,
  To rest where shadows of thy Son's cross fall.

Catholic World.

THE ANNUNCIATION.

"And the angel came in unto her, and said, Hail, thou that art highly favored, the Lord is with thee : blessed art thou among women." — St. Luke i. 28.

THOU who deign'st to sympathize
With all our frail and fleshly ties,
Maker, yet Brother dear,
Forgive the too presumptuous thought,
If, calming wayward grief, I sought
To gaze on Thee too near.

Yet sure 't was not presumption, Lord,
'T was Thine own comfortable word
That made the lesson known :
Of all the dearest bonds we prove,
Thou countest sons' and mothers' love
Most sacred, most Thine own.

When wandering here a little span,
Thou took'st on Thee to rescue man,
Thou hadst no earthly sire :
That wedded love we prize so dear,
As if our heaven and home were here,
It lit in Thee no fire.

On no sweet sister's faithful breast
Wouldst Thou Thine aching forehead rest,
On no kind brother lean :
But who, O perfect filial heart,
Ere did like Thee a true son's part,
Endearing, firm, serene ?

Thou wept'st, meek maiden, mother mild,
Thou wept'st upon thy sinless Child,
Thy very heart was riven :

THE ANNUNCIATION.

And yet, what mourning matron here
Would deem thy sorrows bought too dear
By all on this side heaven?

A Son that never did amiss,
That never shamed His mother's kiss,
Nor crossed her fondest prayer:
Even from the tree he deigned to bow
For her His agonizéd brow,
Her, His sole earthly care.

Ave Maria! blessed maid!
Lily of Eden's fragrant shade,
Who can express the love
That nurtured thee so pure and sweet,
Making thy heart a shelter meet
For Jesus' holy Dove?

Ave Maria! mother blest,
To whom, caressing and caressed,
Clings the Eternal Child:
Favored beyond Archangels' dream,
When first on thee with tenderest gleam
Thy new-born Saviour smiled:—

Ave Maria! thou whose name
All but adoring love may claim,
Yet may we reach thy shrine;
For He, thy Son and Saviour, vows
To crown all lowly lofty brows
With love and joy like thine.

Blessed is the womb that bare Him,—blessed
The bosom where His lips were pressed,
But rather blessed are they
Who hear His word and keep it well,
The living homes where Christ shall dwell,
And never pass away.

Rev. John Keble.

STABAT MATER.*

"Now there stood by the cross of Jesus his mother." — St. John xix. 25.

T the cross her station keeping,
  Stood the mournful Mother weeping,
    Where He hung, the dying Lord;
For her soul, of joy bereavéd,
Bowed with anguish, deeply grievéd,
  Felt the sharp and piercing sword.

O, how sad and sore distresséd
Now was she, that mother blesséd
  Of the sole-begotten One;
Deep the woe of her affliction
When she saw the crucifixion
  Of her ever-glorious Son.

Who on Christ's dear mother gazing,
Pierced by anguish so amazing,
  Born of woman, would not weep?
Who on Christ's dear mother thinking,
Such a cup of sorrow drinking,
  Would not share her sorrows deep?

For His people's sins chastiséd,
She beheld her Son despiséd,
  Scourged and crowned with thorns entwined;
Saw Him then from judgment taken,
And in death by all forsaken,
  Till His spirit He resigned.

* It is but just to say that the following version of this celebrated hymn is not only much shorter than the original, but is altered from it in the important particular of the prayer in the last stanza, which, in Jacopone's lines, is addressed to the Virgin herself.

STABAT MATER.

Jesu, may such deep devotion
Stir in me the same emotion,
  Fount of Love, Redeemer kind!
That my heart, fresh ardor gaining,
And a purer love attaining,
  May with Thee acceptance find.

Abridged from the Latin of Fra Jacopone (*13th century*).

MARY THE MOTHER OF JESUS.

FROM out the cloudy ecstasies of poetry, painting, and religious romance, we grope our way back to the simple story of the New Testament, to find, if possible, by careful study, the lineaments of the real Mary the mother of our Lord. Who and what really was *the woman* highly favored over all on earth, chosen by God to be the mother of the Redeemer of the world? It is our impression that the true character will be found more sweet, more strong, more wonderful in its perfect naturalness and humanity, than the idealized, superangelic being which has been gradually created by poetry and art.

That the Divine Being, in choosing a woman to be the mother, the educator, and for thirty years the most intimate friend, of his son, should have selected one of rare and peculiar excellences seems only probable. It was from her that the holy child, who was to increase in wisdom and in stature, was to learn from day to day the constant and needed lessons of inexperienced infancy and childhood. Her lips taught him human language; her lessons taught him to read the sacred records of the law and the prophets, and the sacred poetry of the psalms; to her he was "subject," when the ardor of childhood expanding into youth led him to quit her side and spend his time in the temple at the feet of the Doctors of the Law; with her he lived in constant communion during those silent and hidden years of his youth that preceded his mission. A woman so near to Christ, so identified with him in the largest part of his life, cannot but be a subject of the deepest and most absorbing study to the Christian heart. And yet there is in regard to this most interesting subject an utter silence of any authentic tradition, so far as we have studied, of the first two or three centuries. There is nothing related by

St. John, with whom Mary lived as with a son after the Saviour's death, except the very brief notices in his Gospel. Upon this subject, as upon that other topic so exciting to the mere human heart, the personal appearance of Jesus, there is a reticence that impresses us like a divine decree of secrecy.

In all that concerns the peculiarly human relations of Jesus, the principle that animated his apostles after the descent of the Holy Spirit was, "Yea, though we have known Christ after the flesh, yet now, henceforth, know we him no more." His family life with his mother would doubtless have opened lovely pages; but it must remain sealed up among those many things spoken of by St. John, which, if they were recorded, the "world itself could not contain the books that should be written." All that we have, then, to build upon is the brief account given in the Gospels. The first two chapters of St. Matthew and the first two chapters of St. Luke are our only data, except one or two very brief notices in St. John, and one slight mention in the Acts.

In part, our conception of the character of Mary may receive light from her nationality. A fine human being is never the product of one generation, but rather the outcome of a growth of ages. Mary was the offspring and flower of a race selected, centuries before, from the finest physical stock of the world, watched over, trained, and cultured, by Divine oversight, in accordance with every physical and mental law for the production of sound and vigorous mental and bodily conditions. Her blood came to her in a channel of descent over which the laws of Moses had established a watchful care; a race where marriage had been made sacred, family life a vital point, and motherhood invested by Divine command with an especial sanctity. As Mary was in a certain sense a product of the institutes of Moses, so it is an interesting coincidence that she bore the name of his sister, the first and most honored of the line of Hebrew prophetesses, — Mary being the Latin version of the Hebrew Miriam. She had also, as we read, a sister, the wife of Cleopas, who bore the same name, — a custom not infrequent in Jewish families. It is suggested, that,

Miriam being a sacred name and held in high traditionary honor, mothers gave it to their daughters, as now in Spain they call them after the Madonna as a sign of good omen.

There is evidence that Mary had not only the sacred name of the first great prophetess, but that she inherited, in the line of descent, the poetic and prophetic temperament. She was of the royal line of David, and poetic visions and capabilities of high enthusiasm were in her very lineage. The traditions of the holy and noble women of her country's history were all open to her as sources of inspiration. Miriam, leading the song of national rejoicing on the shore of the Red Sea; Deborah, mother, judge, inspirer, leader, and poet of her nation; Hannah, the mother who won so noble a son of Heaven by prayer; the daughter of Jephtha, ready to sacrifice herself to her country; Huldah, the prophetess, the interpreter of God's will to kings; Queen Esther, risking her life for her people; and Judith, the beautiful and chaste deliverer of her nation, — these were the spiritual forerunners of Mary, the ideals with whom her youthful thoughts must have been familiar.

The one hymn of Mary's composition which has found place in the sacred records pictures in a striking manner the exalted and poetic side of her nature. It has been compared with the song of Hannah the mother of Samuel, and has been spoken of as taken from it. But there is only that resemblance which sympathy of temperament and a constant contemplation of the same class of religious ideas would produce. It was the exaltation of a noble nature expressing itself in the form and imagery supplied by the traditions and history of her nation. We are reminded that Mary was a daughter of David by certain tones in her magnificent hymn, which remind us of many of the Psalms of that great heart-poet.

Being of royal lineage, Mary undoubtedly cherished in her bosom the traditions of her house with that secret fervor which belongs to enthusiastic natures. We are to suppose her, like all Judæan women, intensely national in her feelings. She identified herself with her country's destiny, lived its life, suffered in its sufferings, and waited and prayed for its deliverance and glories. This was a time of her nation's deep humiliation. The throne and scepter had passed from Judah. Conquered, trodden down, and oppressed, the sacred land was under the rule of Pagan Rome; Herod, the appointed sovereign, was a blaspheming, brutal tyrant, using all his power to humiliate and oppress; and we may imagine Mary as one of the small company of silent mourners, like Simeon, and Anna the prophetess, who pondered the Scriptures and "looked for salvation in Israel." She was betrothed to her cousin Joseph, who was, like herself, of the royal lineage. He was a carpenter, in accordance with that excellent custom of the Jewish law which required every man to be taught a mechanical trade. They were in humble circumstances, and dwelt in a village proverbial for the meanness and poverty of its inhabitants. We can imagine them as *in*, but not *of*, the sordid and vulgar world of Nazareth, living their life of faith and prayer, of mournful memories of past national glory, and longing hopes for the future.

The account of the visitation of the angel to Mary is given by St. Luke, and by him alone. His Gospel was written later than those of Matthew and Mark, and designed for the Greek churches, and it seems but natural that in preparing himself to write upon this theme he should seek information from Mary herself, the fountain-head. Biblical critics discover traces of this communication in the different style of these first two chapters of St. Luke. While the rest of the book is written in pure classic Greek, this is full of Hebraisms, and has all the marks of being translated from the Syro-Chaldaic tongue, which was the popular dialect of Palestine, and in which Mary must have given her narrative.

Let us now look at the simple record. "And in the sixth month the angel Gabriel was sent from God unto a city of Galilee named Nazareth, to a virgin espoused to a man named Joseph, of the house of David, and the virgin's name was Mary. And the angel came in unto her and said, Hail, highly favored! the Lord is with thee; blessed art thou among women!

And when she saw him she was troubled at his saying, and cast in her mind what manner of salutation this should be."

All these incidents, in their very nature, could be known to Mary alone. She was in solitude, without a human witness; from her the whole detail must have come. It gives not only the interview, but the passing thoughts and emotions of her mind; she was agitated, and cast about what this should mean. We see in all this that serious, calm, and balanced nature which was characteristic of Mary. Habitually living in the contemplation of that spirit-world revealed in the Scriptures, it was no very startling thing to her to see an angel standing by, — her thoughts had walked among the angels too long for that; but his enthusiastic words of promise and blessing agitated her soul.

"And the angel said unto her, Fear not, Mary, for thou hast found favor with God, and behold thou shalt conceive in thy womb and bring forth a son and shalt call his name Jesus. He shall be great, and shall be called the Son of the Highest, and the Lord God shall give unto him the throne of his father* David, and he shall reign over the house of Jacob forever, and of his kingdom there shall be no end."

A weaker woman would have been dazzled and overcome by such a vision, — appealing to all her personal ambition, — and her pride of nation and her religious enthusiasm telling

* It is remarkable that in this interview the angel, in the same connection, informs Mary that her son shall have no human father, and that David shall be his ancestor. The inference is clear that Mary is herself of the house of David. Coincident with this we find a genealogy of Jesus in this Gospel of Luke differing entirely from the genealogy in Matthew. Very able critics have therefore contended that, as Luke evidently received his account from Mary, the genealogy he gives is that of *her* ancestry, and that the "*Heli*" who is mentioned in Luke as the ancestor of Jesus was his grandfather, the father of Mary. Very skillful and able Biblical critics have supported this view, among whom are Paulus, Spanheim, and Lightfoot. The latter goes the length of saying that there are no difficulties in these genealogies but what have been made by commentators. In Lightfoot, notes in Luke, third chapter, the argument is given at length, and he adds testimonies to show that Mary was called the daughter of Heli by the early Jewish Rabbins, who traduced her for her pretensions in reference to her son. He quotes three passages from different Rabbins in the Jerusalem Talmud, or "Chigagah," folio 77. 4, where this Mary, mother of Jesus, is denounced as the "daughter of *Heli* and mother of a pretender."

her that she had drawn the prize which had been the high ideal of every Jewish woman from the beginning of time. But Mary faces the great announcement with a countenance of calm inquiry. "Then said Mary to the angel, How shall this be, seeing I am yet a virgin?" And the angel answered and said unto her, "The Holy Ghost shall come upon thee; the power of the Highest shall overshadow thee; therefore, also, that holy progeny which shall be born of thee shall be called the Son of God; and behold, also, thy cousin Elisabeth, she also hath conceived a son in her old age; and this is the sixth month with her who was called barren. For with God nothing shall be impossible."

In this announcement a Jewish betrothed woman must have seen a future of danger to her reputation and her life; for who would believe a story of which there was no mortal witness? But Mary accepted the high destiny and the fearful danger with an entire surrender of herself into God's hands. Her reply is not one of exultation, but of submission. "Behold the handmaid of the Lord; be it unto me according to his word."

The next step taken by Mary is in accordance with the calmest practical good sense, and displays an energy and a control over other minds which must have been uncommon. She resolves to visit her cousin Elisabeth in the mountain country. The place is supposed to have been near Hebron, and involved a journey of some twenty miles through a rugged country. For a young maiden to find means of performing this journey, which involved attendance and protection, without telling the reason for which she resolved upon it, seems to show that Mary had that kind of character which inspires confidence, and leads those around her to feel that a thing is right and proper because she has determined it.

The scene of the visitation as given in St. Luke shows the height above common thought and emotion on which these holy women moved. Elisabeth, filled with inspired ardor, spoke out with a loud voice and said, "Blessed art thou among women, and blessed is the fruit of thy womb. And whence is this to me, that the mother of my Lord should come to me? And blessed be she that believed: for there shall be a performance of those things which have been promised of the Lord." Then the prophetic fire fell upon Mary, and she broke forth into the immortal psalm which the Church still cherishes as the first hymn of the new dispensation.

"My soul doth magnify the Lord;
My spirit hath rejoiced in God my Saviour,
For he hath regarded the low estate of his handmaid;
For, behold, henceforth all generations shall call me blessed!
For he that is mighty hath done great things to me,
And holy is his name,
And his mercy is on them that fear him
From generation to generation.
He hath showed strength with his arm;
He hath scattered the proud in the imagination of their hearts,
He hath put down the mighty from their seats
And exalted them of low degree,
He hath filled the hungry with good things
And the rich hath he sent empty away,
He hath holpen his servant Israel
In remembrance of his mercy,
As he spake to our fathers,
To Abraham and his seed forever."

In these words we see, as in the song of Hannah, the exaltation of a purely unselfish spirit, whose personal experiences merge themselves in those of universal humanity. One line alone expresses her intense sense of the honor done her, and all the rest is exultation in her God as the helper of the poor, the neglected, the despised and forgotten, and the Saviour of her oppressed country. No legend of angel ministrations or myths of miracle can so glorify Mary in our eyes as this simple picture of her pure and lofty unselfishness of spirit.

We are told that this sacred visit lasted three months. A mythical legend speaks of a large garden, pertaining to the priests' house, where Mary was wont to walk for meditation and prayer, and that, bending one day over a flower, beautiful, but devoid of fragrance, she touched it and thenceforth it became endowed with a sweet perfume. The myth is a lovely allegory of the best power of a true and noble Christian woman.

On returning to Nazareth, Mary confronted the danger which beset her situation with the peculiar, silent steadfastness which characterized her. From the brief narrative of Matthew, which mainly respects the feelings of Joseph, we infer that Mary made no effort at self-justification, but calmly resigned herself to the vindication of God in his own time and way. As the private feelings of Mary are recorded only by Luke, and the private experiences of Joseph by Matthew, it is to be supposed that the narrative is derived from these two sources.

We have no other characteristic incident of Mary's conduct; nothing that she said or did during the next eventful scenes of her life. The journey to Bethlehem, the birth of Jesus, the visit of the shepherds and of the magi, full of the loveliest poetic suggestion, are all silent shrines so far as utterance or action of hers is given to us. That she was peculiarly a silent woman is inferred from the only mention of her, in particular, by St. Luke when recording these wonderful scenes. When the shepherds, sent by angelic visitors, came to Bethlehem, we are told, "And they came with haste, and found Joseph and Mary, and the babe lying in a manger; and when they had seen it they made known abroad the saying which was told them concerning this child. And all that heard it wondered. *But Mary kept all these things and pondered them in her heart.*" She is one of those women who are remarkable for the things they do *not* say.

We next find her at Jerusalem, going with her husband to present her first-born son in the Temple, and to offer the humble sacrifice appointed for the poor. A modern English painting represents her as sheltering in her bosom the two innocent white doves destined to bloody death, emblems of the fate of the holy child whom she presented. Here the sacred story gives an interesting incident.

We catch a glimpse at one of the last of the Hebrew prophetesses in the form of Anna, of whom the narrative says, "She was of great age, and had lived with an husband seven years from her virginity, and she was a widow of about fourscore and four years, which departed not from the Temple, but served God with fasting and prayer day and night." She came in and welcomed the holy child. We are introduced also to the last of the prophets. "And behold there was a man in Jerusalem named Simeon, and the same was just and devout, waiting for the consolation of Israel, and the Holy Ghost was upon him, and it was revealed unto him by the Holy Ghost that he should not see death before he had seen the Lord's Messiah. And he came by the Spirit into the Temple; and when the parents brought in the child Jesus, to do for him according to the custom of the law, then took he him up in his arms and blessed God and said:—

> "Lord, now lettest thou thy servant depart in peace,
> For mine eyes have seen thy salvation
> Which thou hast prepared before the face of all people,
> A light to lighten the Gentiles and the glory of thy people Israel."

And Joseph and his mother marveled at the things which were spoken of him. The contrast between the helpless babe and the magnificence of his promised destiny kept them in a state of constant astonishment. And Simeon blessed them, and said unto Mary his mother, "Behold this child is set for the fall and the rising again of many in Israel, and for a sign that shall be spoken against. Yea, a sword shall pierce through thine own soul also, that the thoughts of many hearts may be revealed."

This prophecy must have been a strange enigma to Mary. According to the prediction of the angel, her son was to be a triumphant king, to reign on the throne of his father David, to restore the old national prestige, and to make his people rulers over the whole earth. The great truth that the kingdom was not of this world, and the dominion a moral victory; that it was to be won through rejection, betrayal, denial, torture, and shameful death; that the Jewish nation were to be finally uprooted and scattered,—all this was as much hidden from the eyes of Mary as from those of the whole nation. The gradual unveiling of this mystery was to test every character connected with it by the severest wrench of trial. The latent worldliness and pride of many, seemingly good, would be disclosed, and even the pure mother would be pierced to the very heart with the anguish of disappointed hopes. Such was the prophecy of which the life of Mary was a long fulfillment. The slow perplexity of finding an entirely different destiny for her son from the brilliant one foretold in prophetic symbols was to increase from year to year, till it culminated at the foot of the cross.

The next we see of Mary is the scene in the Temple where she seeks her son. It shows the social and cheerful nature of the boy, and the love in which he was held, that she should have missed him a whole day from her side without alarm, supposing that he was with the other children of the great family caravans traveling festively homeward from Jerusalem. Not finding him, she returns alarmed to Jerusalem, and, after three days of fruitless search, finds him sitting in the school of the doctors of the Temple. Her agitation and suppressed alarm betray themselves in her earnest and grieved words: "Son, why hast thou dealt thus with us? behold thy father and I have sought thee sorrowing." The answer of Jesus was given with an unconscious artlessness, as a child of heaven might speak. "Why did you seek me? Did you not know I would be at my Father's house?"* This was doubtless one of those peculiar outflashings of an inward light which sometimes break unconsciously from childhood, and it is said, "They understood not the saying." It was but a gleam of the higher nature, and it was gone in a moment; for it is said immediately after that he went down with them unto Nazareth, and was subject to them; but, it is added significantly, "his mother kept all these sayings and pondered them in her heart." Then came twenty years of obscurity and silence, when Jesus lived the plain, literal life of a village mechanic. "Is not this the carpenter, the son of Mary?" they said of him when he appeared in the synagogue of his native village.

How unaccountable to Mary must have appeared that silence! It was as if God had forgotten his promises. The son of her cousin Elisabeth, too, grew up and lived the life of an

* This is said by able critics to be the sense of the original.

anchorite in the desert. It appears from his testimony afterwards that he kept up no personal acquaintance with Jesus, and "knew him not," so that a sign from heaven was necessary to enable him to recognize the Messiah.

From the specimens of the village gossip at the time of Christ's first public teaching in Nazareth, it appears that neither in the mother of Christ nor in Christ himself had his townsfolk seen anything to excite expectation. In his last prayer Jesus says to his Father, "O righteous Father, the world hath not *known* thee." In like manner Nazareth *knew* not Mary and Jesus. "He was in the world, and the world was made by him, and the world *knew* him not."

At last comes the call of John the Baptist; the wave of popular feeling rises, and Jesus leaves his mother to go to his baptism, his great initiation. The descending Spirit, the voice from heaven, ordain him to his work, but immediately the prophetic impulse drives him from the habitation of man, and for more than a month he wanders in the wilderness, on the borders of that spirit-land where he encountered the temptations that were to fit him for his work. We shall see that the whole drift of these temptations was, that he should use his miraculous powers and gifts for personal ends: he should create bread to satisfy the pangs of his own hunger, instead of waiting on the providence of God; he should cast himself from the pinnacles of the Temple, that he might be upborne by angels and so descend among the assembled multitude with the pomp and splendor befitting his station; instead of the toilsome way of a religious teacher, laboring for success through the slowly developing spiritual life of individuals, he should seek the kingdoms of the world and the glory of them, and spread his religion by their power. But, in all the past traditions of the prophetic office, the *supernatural power* was always regarded as a sacred deposit never to be used by its possessor for any private feeling or personal end. Elijah fasted forty days in his wanderings without using this gift to supply his own wants; and Jesus, the greatest of the prophets, was the most utterly and thoroughly possessed with the unselfish spirit of the holy office, and repelled from him with indignation every suggestion of the tempter.

When he returned from his seclusion in the desert, we find him once more in his mother's society, and we see them united in the episode of the marriage at Cana. His mother's mind is, doubtless, full of the mysterious change that has passed upon her son and of triumph in his high calling. She knows that he has received the gift of miraculous power, though as yet he has never used it. It was most human, and most natural, and quite innocent, that after so many years of patient waiting she should wish to see this bright career of miracles begin. His family also might have felt some of the eagerness of family pride in the display of his gifts.

When, therefore, by an accident, the wedding festivities are at a stand, Mary turns to her son with the habit of a mother who has felt for years that she owned all that her son could do, and of a Jewish mother who had always commanded his reverence. She thinks, to herself, that he has the power of working miracles, and here is an opportunity to display it. She does not directly ask, but there is suggestion in the very manner in which she looks to him and says, "They have no wine." Immediately from him, usually so tender and yielding, comes an abrupt repulse, "Woman,* what have I to do with thee? mine hour is not yet come." What sacred vital spot has she touched unaware with her maternal hand? It is, although she knows it not, the very one which had been touched before by the Enemy in the wilderness.

This sacred, mysterious, awful gift of miracles was not his to use for any personal feeling or desire, not to gratify a mother's innocent ambition, or to please the family pride of kindred; and there is the earnestness of a sense of danger in the manner in which he throws off the suggestion, the same abrupt earnestness with which he afterwards rebuked Peter when he pleaded with him to avoid the reproaches and sufferings which lay in his path.

* The address "woman" sounds abrupt and harsh, but in the original language it was a term of respect. Our Lord, in his dying moments, used the same form to his mother, — "Woman, behold thy son."

The whole of this story is not told in full, but it is evident that the understanding between Jesus and his mother was so immediate, that, though he had reproved her for making the suggestion, she was still uncertain whether he might not yet see it consistent to perform the miracle, and so, at once, leaving it to him in meek submission, she said to the servants standing by, "Whatsoever he saith unto you do it." This tone to the servants, assumed by Mary, shows the scene to have occurred in the family of a kinsman, where she felt herself in the position of directress.

After an interval of some time, Jesus commands the servants to fill the watering-pots with water, and performs the desired miracle. We cannot enter into the secret sanctuary of that divine mind, nor know exactly what Jesus meant by saying "Mine hour is not yet come"; it was a phrase of frequent occurrence with him when asked to take steps in his life. Probably it was some inward voice or call by which he felt the Divine will moving with his own, and he waited after the suggestion of Mary till this became clear to him. What he might not do from partial affection, he might do at the Divine motion, as sanctioning that holy state of marriage which the Jewish law had done so much to make sacred. The first miracle of the Christian dispensation was wrought in honor of the family state, which the Mosaic dispensation had done so much to establish and confirm.

The trials of Mary as a mother were still further complicated by the unbelief of her other children in the divine mission of Jesus. His brethren had the usual worldly view of who and what the Messiah was to be. He was to come as a conquering king, with pomp of armies, and reign in Jerusalem. This silent, prayerful brother of theirs, who has done nothing but work at his trade, wander in the wilderness and pray and preach, even though gifted with miraculous power, does not seem in the least to them like a king and conqueror. He may be a prophet, but as the great Messiah they cannot believe in him. They fear, in fact, that he is losing his senses in wild, fanatical expectation.

We have a scene given by St. John where his brethren urge him, if he is the Messiah and has divine power, to go up to Jerusalem and make a show of it at once. The feast of tabernacles is at hand, and his brethren say to him, "Depart hence and go into Judæa, that thy disciples may see the works that thou doest. If thou do these things, *show thyself to the world.* For neither did his brethren believe on him. Then said Jesus, My time is not yet come; but your time is always ready. The world cannot hate you, but me it hateth because I testify of it that the works thereof are evil. Go ye up to this feast. I go not up yet, for my time is not yet full come."

To the practical worldly eye, Jesus was wasting his time and energies. If he was to set up a kingdom, why not go to Jerusalem, work splendid miracles, enlist the chief-priests and scribes, rouse the national spirit, unfurl the standard, and conquer? Instead of that he begins his ministry by choosing two or three poor men as disciples, and going on foot from village to village preaching repentance. He is simply doing the work of a home missionary. True, there come reports of splendid miracles, but they are wrought in obscure places among very poor people, and apparently with no motive but the impulse of compassion and love to the suffering. Then he is exhausting himself in labors, he is thronged by the crowds of the poor and sorrowful, till he has no time so much as to eat. His brethren, taking the strong, coarse, worldly view of the matter, think he is destroying himself, and that he ought to be taken home by his friends with friendly violence till he recover the balance of his mind; as it is said by one Evangelist, "They went out to lay hands on him, for they said, He is beside himself." Thus the prophecy is fulfilling: he is a sign that is spoken against; the thoughts of many hearts are being revealed through him, and the sword is piercing deeper and deeper every day into the heart of his mother. Her heart of heart is touched, — in this son is her life; she is filled with anxiety, she longs to go to him, — they need not lay hands on him; *she* will speak to him, — he who always loved her voice, and for so many years has been subject to her, will surely come back with *her*. In this hour of her life Mary is the type of the trial through which all mothers must pass at the time when they are called on to resign a son to his destiny in the world, and to feel that he is theirs no more; that henceforth he belongs to another life, other duties and affections, than theirs. Without this experience of sorrow Mary would have been less dear to the heart of mortal woman and mother.

Jesus, meanwhile, is surrounded by an eager crowd to whom he is teaching the way to God. He is in that current of joy above all joy where he can see the new immortal life springing up under his touch; he feels in himself the ecstasy of that spiritual vigor which he is awakening in all around him; he is comforting the mourner, opening the eyes of the spiritually blind, and lighting the fire of heavenly love in cold and comfortless hearts. Love without bounds, the love of the shepherd and bishop of souls, flows from him to the poor whom he is enriching. The ecstatic moment is interrupted by a message: "Thy mother and thy brethren stand without, desiring to speak with thee." With a burst of heavenly love he spreads his arms towards the souls whom he is guiding, and says, "Who is my mother and who are my brethren? My mother and my brethren are *these* that hear the Word of God and do it; for whosoever will do the will of my Father in heaven, the same is my brother and sister and mother." As well attempt to imprison the light of the joyous sun in one dwelling as to bound the infinite love of Jesus by one family!

There was an undoubted purpose in the record of these two places where Jesus so positively declares that he had risen to a sphere with which his maternal relations had nothing to do. They were set as a warning and a protest, in advance, against that idolatry of the woman and mother the advent of which he must have foreseen.

In the same manner we learn that, while he was teaching, a woman cried out in enthusiasm, "Blessed be the womb that bore thee, and the paps that thou hast sucked." But he answered, "Yea, rather, blessed are they that hear the Word of God and do it." In the same grave spirit of serious admonition he checked the delight of his disciples when they exulted in miraculous gifts. "Lord, even the devils were subject unto us." "Rejoice not that the devils are subject to you, but rather rejoice that your names are written in heaven."

Undoubtedly an hour was found to console and quiet the fears of his mother so far as in the nature of the case they could be consoled. But the radical difficulty, with her as with his own disciples, lay in the fixed and rooted idea of the temporal Messianic kingdom. There was an awful depth of sorrow before them, to which every day was bringing them nearer. It was pathetic to see how Jesus was moving daily among friends that he loved and to whom he knew that his career was to be one of the bitterest anguish and disappointment. He tried in the plainest words to tell them the scenes of his forthcoming trial, rejection, suffering, death, and resurrection, — words so plain that we wonder any one could hear them and not understand, — and yet it is written, "They understood not his saying. They questioned one with another what the rising from the dead should mean." They discussed offices and stations in the new kingdom, and contended who should be greatest. When the mother of James and John asked the place of honor for her sons, he looked at her with a pathetic patience.

"Ye know not what ye ask. Can ye drink of the cup that I shall drink? Can ye be baptized with my baptism? They said, We are able." He answered, with the scenes of the cross in view, "Ye shall, indeed, drink of the cup I shall drink, and be baptized with my baptism; but to sit on my right hand and my left is not mine to give. It shall be given to them for whom it is prepared of my Father."

We see no more of Mary till we meet her again standing with the beloved John at the foot of the cross. The supreme hour is come; the sword has gone to the depths! All that she hoped is blasted, and all that she feared is come! In this hour, when faith and hope were both darkened, Mary stood by the power of love. *She stood by the cross!* The words are characteristic and wonderful. We see still the same intense, outwardly collected woman who met the salutation of the angel with calm inquiry, and accepted glory and danger with such self-surrender, — silent, firm, sustained in her anguish as in her joy! After years of waiting and hope deferred, after such glorious miracles, such mighty deeds and words, such evident tokens of God's approval, she sees her son forsaken by God and man. To hers as to no other mortal ears must have sounded that death-cry, "My God, my God, why hast *thou* forsaken me?"

But through all, Mary *stood;* she did not faint or fall, — she was resolved to drink of HIS cup to the last bitter dregs. Though the whole world turn against him, though God himself seems to forsake him, she will stand by him, she will love him, she will adore him till death, and after, and forever!

The dying words of Jesus have been collected and arranged by the Church in a rosary, — pearls brought up from the depths of a profound agony, and of precious value in all sorrow. Of those seven last words it is remarkable what a proportion were words for other than himself. The first sharp pang of torture wrung from him the prayer, "Father, forgive them; they know not what they do." The second word was of pardon and comfort to the penitent thief. The third the commendation of his mother to his beloved friend.

If any mortal creature might be said to have entered into the sufferings of the great atonement with Jesus, it was his mother in those last hours. Never has sorrow presented itself in a form so venerable. Here is a depth of anguish which inspires awe as well as tenderness. The magnificent "Stabat Mater," in which the Church commemorates Mary's agony, is an outburst with which no feeling heart can refuse sympathy. We rejoice when again we meet her, after the resurrection, in the company of all the faithful, waiting to receive that promised illumination of the Holy Spirit which solved every mystery and made every doubt clear.

In all this history we see the picture of a woman belonging to that rare and beautiful class who approach the nearest to our ideal of angelic excellence. We see a woman in whom the genius and fire of the poet and prophetess is tempered by a calm and equable balance of the intellect; a woman not only to feel deeply, but to examine calmly and come to just results, and to act with energy befitting every occasion. Hers are the powers which might, in the providence of God, have had a public mission, but they are all concentrated in the nobler, yet secret mission of the mother. She lived and acted in her son, not in herself. There seems to be evidence that both Jesus and his mother had that constitutional delicacy and refinement that made solitude and privacy peculiarly dear, and the hurry and bustle and inevitable vulgarities of a public career a trial. Mary never seems to have sought to present herself as a public teacher; and in the one instance when she sought her son in public, it was from the tremulous anxiety of a mother's affection rather than the self-assertion of a mother's pride. In short, Mary is presented to us as the mother, and the mother alone, seeking no other sphere. Like a true mother she passed out of self into her son, and the life that she lived was in him; and in this sacred self-abnegation she must forever remain, the one ideal type of perfect motherhood.

This entire absence of self-seeking and self-assertion is the crowning perfection of Mary's character. The steadiness, the silent reticence, with which she held herself subject to God's will, waiting calmly on his Providence, never by a hasty word or an imprudent action marring the divine order or seeking to place self in the foreground, is an example which we may all take reverently to our own bosoms.

We may not adore, but we may love her. She herself would not that we turn from her Son to invoke her; but we may tenderly rejoice in the feeling so common in the primitive Church, that in drawing near to Jesus we draw near to all the holy who were dear to him, and so to her, the most blessed among women. We long to know more of this hidden life of Mary on earth, but it is a comfort to remember that these splendid souls with whom the Bible makes us acquainted are neither dead nor lost. If we "hear the Word of God and do it," we may hope some day to rise to the world where we shall find them, and ask of them all those untold things which our hearts yearn to know.

A CHRISTMAS CAROL.

HE shepherds went their hasty way,
And found the lowly stable shed
Where the Virgin-Mother lay:
And now they checked their eager tread,
For to the Babe, that at her bosom clung,
A mother's song the Virgin-Mother sung.

They told her how a glorious light,
Streaming from a heavenly throng,
Around them shone, suspending night;
While, sweeter than a mother's song,
Blessed angels heralded the Saviour's birth,
Glory to God on high! and peace on earth.

She listened to the tale divine,
And closer still the Babe she pressed;
And while she cried, The Babe is mine!
The milk rushed faster to her breast;
Joy rose within her, like a summer's morn:
Peace, peace on earth! the Prince of Peace is born.

Thou Mother of the Prince of Peace,
Poor, simple, and of low estate;
That strife should vanish, battle cease,
Oh! why should this thy soul elate?
Sweet music's loudest note, the poet's story,
Didst thou ne'er love to hear of fame and glory?

And is not War a youthful king,
A stately hero clad in mail?
Beneath his footsteps laurels spring;
Him earth's majestic monarchs hail!

Their friend, their playmate! and his bold bright eye
Compels the maiden's love-confessing sigh.

"Tell this in some more courtly scene,
  To maids and youths in robes of state!
I am a woman poor and mean,
  And therefore is my soul elate.
War is a ruffian, all with guilt defiled,
That from the aged father tears his child!

"A murderous fiend, by fiends adored,
  He kills the sire and starves the son,
The husband kills, and from her board
  Steals all his widow's toil had won;
Plunders God's world of beauty; rends away
All safety from the night, all comfort from the day.

"Then wisely is my soul elate,
  That strife should vanish, battle cease;
I'm poor, and of a low estate,
  The Mother of the Prince of Peace!
Joy rises in me, like a summer's morn;
Peace, peace on earth! the Prince of Peace is born!"

Samuel Taylor Coleridge.

THE VIRGIN MARY TO THE CHILD JESUS.

"But see, the Virgin blest
Hath laid her babe to rest."

MILTON'S *Hymn on the Nativity.*

I.

SLEEP, sleep, mine Holy One!
My flesh, my Lord! — what name? I do not know
A name that seemeth not too high or low,
Too far from me or Heaven.
My Jesus! *that* is best! that word being given
By the majestic angel, whose command
Was softly as a man's beseeching said,
When I and all the earth appeared to stand
In the great overflow
Of light celestial from his wings and head.
Sleep, sleep, my saving One!

II.

And art Thou come for saving, baby-browed
And speechless Being, — art Thou come for saving?
The palm that grows beside our door is bowed
By treadings of the low wind from the south,
A restless shadow through the chamber waving:
Upon its bough a bird sings in the sun;
But Thou, with that close slumber on Thy mouth,
Dost seem of wind and sun already weary.
Art come for saving, O my weary One?

III.

Perchance this sleep, that shutteth out the dreary
Earth-sounds and motions, opens on Thy soul
High dreams on fire with God;

High songs that make the pathways where they roll
More bright than stars do theirs; and visions new
Of Thine eternal nature's old abode.
    Suffer this mother's kiss,
    Best thing that earthly is,
To glide the music and the glory through,
Nor narrow in Thy dream the broad upliftings
    Of any seraph wing!
Thus, noiseless, thus. Sleep, sleep, my dreaming One!

IV.

The slumber of His lips meseems to run
Through *my* lips to mine heart; to all its shiftings
Of sensual life, bringing contrariousness
In a great calm. I feel, I could lie down
As Moses did, and die,* — and then live most.

[*She pauses.*]

I am 'ware of you, heavenly Presences,
That stand with your peculiar light unlost, —
Each forehead with a high thought for a crown,
Unsunned i' the sunshine! I am 'ware. Ye throw
No shade against the wall! How motionless
Ye round me with your living statuary,
While through your whiteness, in and outwardly,
Continual thoughts of God appear to go,
Like light's soul in itself! I bear, I bear,
To look upon the dropt lids of your eyes,
Though their external shining testifies
To that beatitude within which were
Enough to blast an eagle at his sun.
I fall not on my sad clay face before ye;
    I look on His. I know
My spirit, which dilateth with the woe
    Of His mortality,
    May well contain your glory.
    Yea, drop your lids more low, —
Ye are but fellow-worshipers with me!
    Sleep, sleep, my worshiped One!

* It is a Jewish tradition that Moses died of the kisses of God's lips.

V.

We sat among the stalls at Bethlehem.
The dumb kine, from their fodder turning them,
Softened their horned faces
To almost human gazes
Toward the newly born.
The simple shepherds from the star-lit brooks
Brought visionary looks,
As yet in their astonied hearing rung
The strange, sweet angel-tongue.
The magi of the East, in sandals worn,
Knelt reverent, sweeping round,
With long pale beards, their gifts upon the ground, —
The incense, myrrh, and gold,
These baby-hands were impotent to hold.
So, let all earthlies and celestials wait
Upon Thy royal state!
Sleep, sleep, my kingly One!

VI.

I am not proud, — meek angels, ye invest
New meeknesses to hear such utterance rest
On mortal lips, — "I am not proud," — *not proud!*
Albeit in my flesh God sent his Son,
Albeit over Him my head is bowed,
As others bow before Him, still mine heart
Bows lower than their knees. O centuries,
That roll, in vision, your futurities
My future grave athwart, —
Whose murmurs seem to reach me while I keep
Watch o'er this sleep, —
Say of me as the Heavenly said: "Thou art
The blessedest of women!" — blessedest,
Not holiest, not noblest, — no high name,
Whose height misplaced may pierce me like a shame,
When I sit meek in heaven!

VII.

For me, — for me,
God knows that I am feeble like the rest! —

I often wandered forth, more child than maiden,
Among the midnight hills of Galilee,
    Whose summits looked heaven-laden;
Listening to silence, as it seemed to be
God's voice, so soft yet strong, — so fain to press
Upon my heart, as heaven did on the height,
And waken up its shadows by a light,
And show its vileness by a holiness.
Then I knelt down, as silent as the night,
    Too self-renounced for fears,
Raising my small face to the boundless blue
Whose stars did mix and tremble in my tears.
God heard *them* falling after — with his dew.

VIII.

So, seeing my corruption, can I see
This Incorruptible now born of me, —
This fair new Innocence, no sun did chance
To shine on (for even Adam was no child),
Created from my nature all defiled, —
This mystery, from out mine ignorance, —
Nor feel the blindness, stain, corruption, more
Than others do, or *I* did heretofore? —
Can hands wherein such burden pure has been,
Not open with the cry, "Unclean, unclean!"
More oft than any else beneath the skies?
    Ah King! ah Christ! ah Son!
The kine, the shepherds, the abasèd wise,
    Did all less lowly wait
    Than I, upon Thy state! —
    Sleep, sleep, my kingly One!

IX.

Art Thou a king, then? Come, his universe,
    Come, crown me Him a king!
Pluck rays from all such stars as never fling
    Their light where fell a curse,
And make a crowning for this kingly brow! —
What is my word? — Each empyreal star

Sits in a sphere afar
In shining ambuscade:
The child-brow, crowned by none,
Keeps its unchildlike shade.
Sleep, sleep, my crownless One!

X.

Unchildlike shade! — no other babe doth wear
An aspect very sorrowful, as Thou. —
No small babe-smiles my watching heart has seen,
To float like speech the speechless lips between;
No dove-like cooing in the golden air,
No quick, short joys of leaping babyhood.
Alas! our earthly good,
In heaven thought evil, seems too good for Thee:
Yet sleep, my weary One!

XI.

And then the drear, sharp tongue of prophecy,
With the dread sense of things which shall be done,
Doth smite me inly, like a sword, — a sword? —
(*That* "smites the shepherd!") then, I think aloud
The words "despised," — "rejected," — every word
Recoiling into darkness as I view
The DARLING on my knee.
Bright angels, — move not! — lest ye stir the cloud
Betwixt my soul and His futurity!
I must not die, with mother's work to do,
And could not live — and see.

XII.

It is enough to bear
This image still and fair, —
This holier in sleep
Than a saint at prayer:
This aspect of a child
Who never sinned or smiled, —
This presence in an infant's face:

This sadness most like love,
This love than love more deep,
This weakness like omnipotence,
It is so strong to move!
Awful is this watching-place,
Awful what I see from hence, —
A king without regalia,
A God without the thunder,
A child without the heart for play;
Ay, a Creator rent asunder
From his first glory and cast away
On His own world, for me alone
To hold in hands created, crying — SON!

XIII.

That tear fell not on THEE,
Beloved, yet Thou stirrest in Thy slumber!
THOU, stirring not for glad sounds out of number
Which through the vibratory palm-trees run
From summer wind and bird,
So quickly hast Thou heard
A tear fall silently? —
Wak'st Thou, O loving One?

Elizabeth Barrett Browning.

A FRAGMENT.

. . . . .

Blessed among women is thy lot:
But higher meed we yield thee not,
  Nor more than woman's name.

Nor solemn "Hail" to thee we pay,
Nor prayer to thee for mercy pray,
  Nor hymn of glory raise;
Nor thine we deem in God's high throne,
Nor thine the birthright of thy Son,
  The Mediator's praise.

Mother of Jesus, parent dear!
If aught of earthly thou couldst hear,
  If aught of human see;
What pangs thy humble heart must wring,
To know thy Saviour, Lord, and King
  Dishonored thus for thee!

Bishop Mant.

UNIV-
OF

THE WOMAN OF SAMARIA.

DEVEDEUX, *Pinx.* JEHENNE, *Lith.*

THE WOMAN OF SAMARIA.

WE are struck, in the history of our Lord, with the *unworldliness* of his manner of living his daily life and fulfilling his great commission. It is emphatically true, in the history of Jesus, that his ways are not as our ways, and his thoughts as our thoughts. He did not choose the disciples of his first ministry as worldly wisdom would have chosen them. Though men of good and honest hearts, they were neither the most cultured nor the most influential of his nation. We should have said that men of the standing of Joseph of Arimathea or Nicodemus were preferable, other things being equal, to Peter the fisherman or Matthew the tax-gatherer; but Jesus thought otherwise.

And furthermore, he sometimes selected those apparently most unlikely to further his ends. Thus, when he had a mission of mercy in view for Samaria, he called to the work a woman; not such as we should suppose a divine teacher would choose, — not a pre-eminently intellectual or a very good woman, — but, on the contrary, one of a careless life and loose morals and little culture. The history of this person, of the way in which he sought her acquaintance, arrested her attention, gained access to her heart, and made of her a missionary to draw the attention of her people to him, is wonderfully given by St. John. We have the image of a woman — such as many are, social, good-humored, talkative, and utterly without any high moral sense — approaching the well, where she sees this weary Jew reclining to rest himself. He introduces himself to her acquaintance by asking a favor, — the readiest way to open the heart of a woman of that class. She is evidently surprised that he will speak to her, being a Jew, and she a daughter of a despised and hated race. "How is it," she says, "that thou, a Jew, askest drink of me, a woman of Samaria?" Jesus now answers her in that symbolic and poetic strain which was familiar with him: "If thou knewest the gift of God, and who this is that asketh drink of thee, thou wouldst ask of him, and he would give thee living water." The woman sees in this only the occasion for a lively rejoinder. "Sir, thou hast nothing to draw with, and the well is deep; from whence then hast thou that living water?" With that same mysterious air, as if speaking unconsciously from out some higher sphere, he answers, "Whosoever drinketh of this water shall thirst again; but whosoever shall drink of the water that I shall give, shall never thirst. The water that I shall give shall be a well in him springing up to everlasting life."

Impressed strangely by the words of the mysterious stranger, she answers confusedly, "Sir, give me this water, that I thirst not, neither come hither to draw." There is a feeble attempt at a jest struggling with the awe which is growing upon her. Jesus now touches the vital spot in her life. "Go, call thy husband and come hither." She said, "I have no husband." He answers, "Well hast thou said I have no husband; thou hast had five husbands, and he thou now hast is not thy husband; in that saidst thou truly."

The stern, grave chastity of the Jew, his reverence for marriage, strike coldly on the light-minded woman accustomed to the easy tolerance of a low state of society. She is abashed, and hastily seeks to change the subject: "Sir, I see thou art a prophet"; and then she introduces the controverted point of the two liturgies and temples of Samaria and Jerusalem, — not the first nor the last was she of those who seek relief from conscience by discussing doctrinal dogmas. Then, to our astonishment, Jesus proceeds to declare to this woman of light mind and loose morality the sublime doctrines of spiritual worship, to predict the new era which is dawning on the world: "Woman, believe me, the hour cometh when neither in this mountain nor yet in Jerusalem shall ye worship the Father. The hour cometh and now is when the true worshiper shall worship the Father in spirit and in truth, for the Father seeketh such to worship him. God is a spirit, and they that worship him must worship him in spirit and in truth." Then, in a sort of confused awe at his earnestness, the woman says, "I know that Messiah shall come, and when he is come he will tell us all things. Jesus saith unto her, I that speak unto thee am he."

At this moment the disciples returned. With their national prejudices, it was very astonishing, as they drew nigh, to see that their master was in close and earnest conversation with a Samaritan woman. Nevertheless, when the higher and god-like in Jesus was in a state of incandescence, the light and fire were such as to awe them. They saw that he was in an exalted mood, which they dared not question. All the infinite love of the Saviour, the shepherd of souls, was awaking within him; the soul whom he has inspired with a new and holy calling is leaving him on a mission that is to bring crowds to his love. The disciples pray him to eat, but he is no longer hungry, no longer thirsty, no longer weary; he exults in the gifts that he is ready to give, and the hearts that are opening to receive.

The disciples pray him, "Master, eat." He said, "I have meat to eat that ye know not of." They question in an undertone, "Hath any one brought him aught to eat?" He answers, "My meat and my drink is to do the will of Him that sent me, and to finish his work." Then, pointing towards the city, he speaks impassioned words of a harvest which is at hand; and they wonder.

But meanwhile the woman, with the eagerness and bright, social readiness which characterize her, is calling to her townsmen, "Come, see a man that told me all that ever I did. Is not this the Christ?"

What followed on this? A crowd press out to see the wonder. Jesus is invited as an honored guest; he spends two days in the city, and gathers a band of disciples.

After the resurrection of Jesus, we find further fruits of the harvest sown by a chance interview of Jesus with this woman.

In the eighth of Acts we read of the ingathering of a church in a city of Samaria, where it is said that "the people, with one accord, gave heed to the things spoken by Philip, and there was great joy in that city."

One thing in this story impresses us strongly, — the power which Jesus had to touch the divinest capabilities in the unlikeliest subjects. He struck at once and directly for what was highest and noblest in souls where it lay most hidden. As physician of souls he appealed directly to the vital moral force, and it acted under his touch. He saw the higher nature in this woman, and as one might draw a magnet over a heap of rubbish and bring out pure metal, so he from this careless, light-minded, good-natured, unprincipled creature, brought out the suppressed and hidden yearning for a better and higher life. She had no prejudices to keep, no station to preserve; she was even to her own low moral sense consciously a sinner, and she was ready at the kind and powerful appeal to leave all and follow him.

We have no further history of her. She is living now somewhere; but wherever she may be, we may be quite sure she never has forgotten the conversation at the well in Samaria, and the man who "told her all that ever she did."

CHRIST AND THE WOMAN OF SAMARIA.

A Samaritan Woman.

HE sun is hot; and the dry east-wind blowing
Fills all the air with dust. The birds are silent;
Even the little fieldfares in the corn
No longer twitter; only the grasshoppers
Sing their incessant song of sun and summer.
I wonder who those strangers were I met
Going into the city? Galileans
They seemed to me in speaking, when they asked
The short way to the market-place. Perhaps
They are fishermen from the lake; or travelers,
Looking to find the inn. And here is some one
Sitting beside the well; another stranger;
A Galilean also by his looks.
What can so many Jews be doing here
Together in Samaria? Are they going
Up to Jerusalem to the Passover?
Our Passover is better here at Sychem,
For here is Ebal; here is Gerizim,
The mountain where our father Abraham
Went up to offer Isaac; here the tomb
Of Joseph, — for they brought his bones from Egypt
And buried them in this land, and it is holy.

Christus.

Give me to drink.

Samaritan Woman.

How can it be that thou,
Being a Jew, askest to drink of me
Which am a woman of Samaria?
You Jews despise us; have no dealings with us;

Make us a byword; call us in derision
The silly folk of Sychar. Sir, how is it
Thou askest drink of me?

CHRISTUS.

If thou hadst known
The gift of God, and who it is that sayeth
Give me to drink, thou wouldst have asked of him;
He would have given thee the living water.

SAMARITAN WOMAN.

Sir, thou hast naught to draw with, and the well
Is deep! Whence hast thou living water?
Say, art thou greater than our father Jacob,
Which gave this well to us, and drank thereof
Himself, and all his children and his cattle?

CHRISTUS.

Ah, whosoever drinketh of this water
Shall thirst again; but whosoever drinketh
The water I shall give him shall not thirst
Forevermore, for it shall be within him
A well of living water, springing up
Into life everlasting.

SAMARITAN WOMAN.

Every day
I must go to and fro, in heat and cold,
And I am weary. Give me of this water,
That I may thirst not, nor come here to draw.

CHRISTUS.

Go call thy husband, woman, and come hither.

SAMARITAN WOMAN.

I have no husband, Sir.

CHRIST AND THE WOMAN OF SAMARIA.

CHRISTUS.

Thou hast well said
I have no husband. Thou hast had five husbands;
And he whom now thou hast is not thy husband.

SAMARITAN WOMAN.

Surely thou art a Prophet, for thou readest
The hidden things of life! Our fathers worshiped
Upon this mountain Gerizim; and ye say
The only place in which men ought to worship
Is at Jerusalem.

CHRISTUS.

Believe me, woman,
The hour is coming, when ye neither shall
Upon this mount, nor at Jerusalem,
Worship the Father; for the hour is coming,
And is now come, when the true worshipers
Shall worship the Father in spirit and in truth!
The Father seeketh such to worship him.
God is a spirit; and they that worship him
Must worship him in spirit and in truth.

SAMARITAN WOMAN.

Master, I know that the Messiah cometh,
Which is called Christ; and he will tell us all things.

CHRISTUS.

I that speak unto thee am he!

THE DISCIPLES, *returning.*

Behold,
The Master sitting by the well, and talking
With a Samaritan woman! With a woman
Of Sychar, the silly people, always boasting
Of their Mount Ebal, and Mount Gerizim,
Their Everlasting Mountain, which they think

Higher and holier than our Mount Moriah!
Why, once upon the Feast of the New Moon,
When our great Sanhedrim of Jerusalem
Had all its watch-fires kindled on the hills
To warn the distant villages, these people
Lighted up others to mislead the Jews,
And make a mockery of their festival!
See, she has left the Master; and is running
Back to the city!

SAMARITAN WOMAN.

O, come see a man
Who hath told me all things that I ever did!
Say, is not this the Christ?

THE DISCIPLES.

Lo, Master, here
Is food, that we have brought thee from the city.
We pray thee eat it.

CHRISTUS.

I have food to eat
Ye know not of.

THE DISCIPLES, *to each other.*

Hath any man been here,
And brought him aught to eat, while we were gone?

CHRISTUS.

The food I speak of is to do the will
Of Him that sent me, and to finish his work.
Do ye not say, Lo! there are yet four months
And cometh harvest? I say unto you,
Lift up your eyes, and look upon the fields,
For they are white already unto harvest!

From the "DIVINE TRAGEDY," *by H. W. Longfellow.*

THE WOMAN OF SAMARIA.

N the hot noon, for water cool,
She strayed in listless mood:
When back she ran, her pitcher full
Forgot behind her stood.

Like one who followed straying sheep,
A weary man she saw,
Who sat upon the well so deep,
And nothing had to draw.

"Give me to drink," he said. Her hand
Was ready with reply;
From out the old well of the land
She drew him plenteously.

He spake as never man before;
She stands with open ears;
He spake of holy days in store,
Laid bare the vanished years.

She cannot still her throbbing heart;
She hurries to the town,
And cries aloud in street and mart,
"The Lord is here: come down."

Her life before was strange and sad,
Its tale a dreary sound:
Ah! let it go, — or good or bad,
She has the Master found.

Rev. George MacDonald.

HYMN.

LIKE her who on Samaria's ground,
 Beneath a sultry sky,
Oft at the Patriarch's well was found,
 Her weary toil to ply:

Thus we our measured span employ
 In labors, long and vain;
We try each boasted fount of joy,
 And drink and thirst again.

O Thou, who with a pitying heart,
 Didst hear her earnest tale,
To us that living stream impart,
 Whose waters never fail.

So shall our broken cisterns here,
 By fickle dew-drops fed,
No more awake the bitter tear,
 Or bow the sorrowing head.

A holy fountain in the soul,
 Eternally shall rise,
Supplied by those pure streams that roll
 Where pleasure never dies.

JACOB'S WELL.

HERE, after Jacob parted from his brother,
His daughters lingered round this well, new-made;
Here, seventeen centuries after, came another,
And talked with JESUS, wondering and afraid;
Here, other centuries past, the emperor's mother
Sheltered its waters with a temple's shade;
Here, 'mid the falling fragments, as of old,
The girl her pitcher dips within its waters cold.

And Jacob's race grew strong for many an hour,
Then torn beneath the Roman eagle lay;
The Roman's vast and earth-controlling power
Has crumbled like these shafts and stones away;
But still the waters, fed by dew and shower,
Come up, as ever, to the light of day,
And still the maid bends downward with her urn,
Well pleased to see its glass her lovely face return.

And those few words of truth, first uttered here,
Have sunk into the human soul and heart;
A spiritual faith dawns bright and clear,
Dark creeds and ancient mysteries depart;
The hour for God's true worshipers draws near;
Then mourn not o'er the wrecks of earthly art:
Kingdoms may fall, and human works decay,
Nature moves on unchanged, — *Truths* never pass away.

James Freeman Clarke.

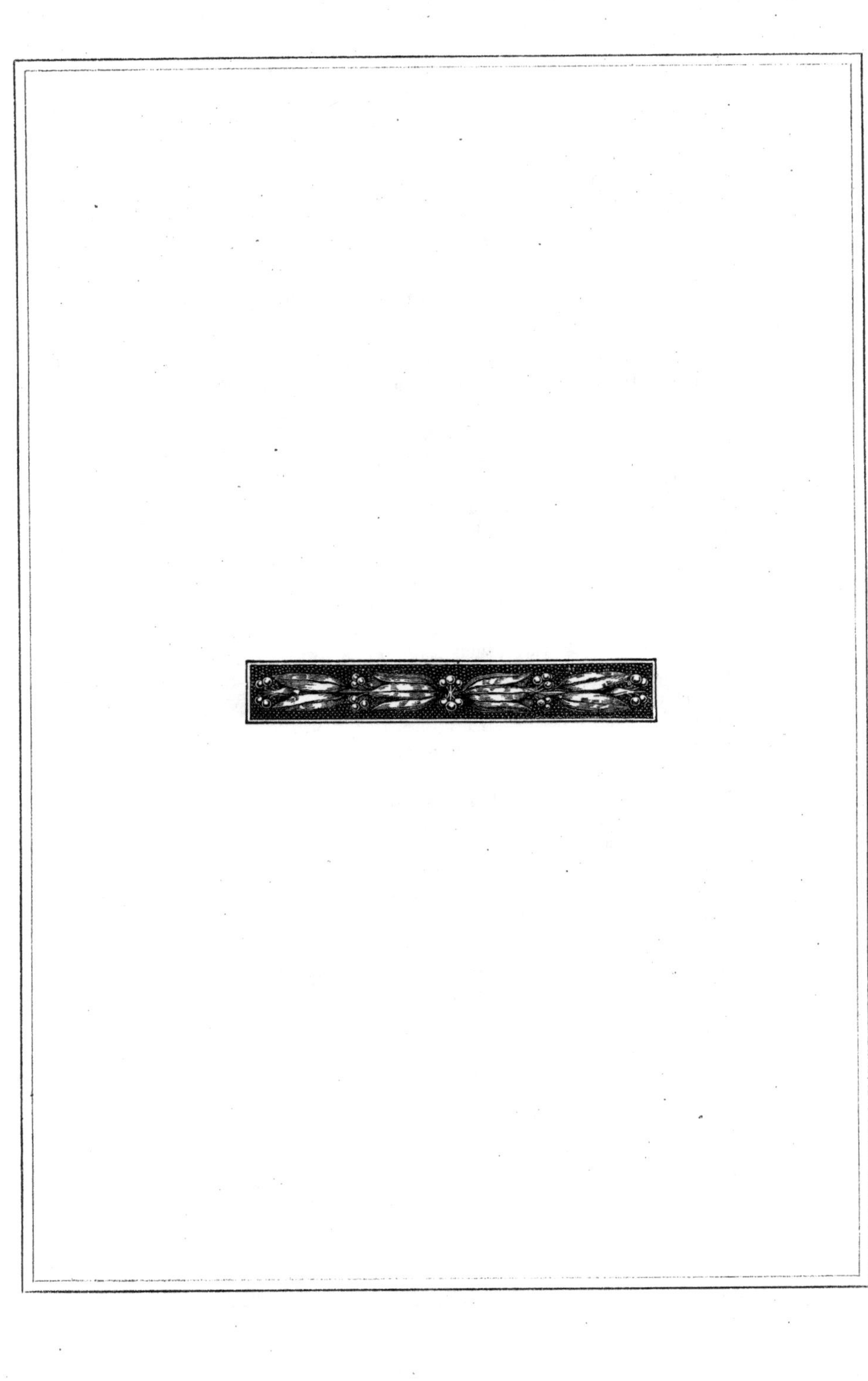

THE WIDOW OF NAIN.

GOODALL, *Pinx.* JEHENNE, *Lith.*

THE WIDOW OF NAIN.

THERE are some incidents in the life of our Lord that come to us with all the force and power of sympathetic revelations of God's character.

The unpitying, unvarying sternness of natural law — cutting, as it constantly does, across the most exquisite nerves of suffering — presents to us a chilling and repulsive idea of the Being who ordained and who upholds law.

Either he is cruel and means to give pain, or he is insensible and does not care for our suffering, or he is so far off and so high up that he neither sees nor feels, — these are all the conclusions that the facts of human life can lead us to in regard to a Deity, if indeed there be one.

But the Bible declares it was the main object and purpose of Christ's life on earth to manifest to us the interior and hidden heart of God. He was to show us God in a human form, under human conditions, with human sympathies; and in this manifestation we see a constant declaration that it is the desire and wish and intention of God to console men under their sorrows. The miracles of Jesus were all so many testimonies that God pities the sufferings of man, and desires and intends to relieve them. They point forward to a stage of development when there shall be no more pain, nor sorrow, nor sickness, neither any more death, but all the former things shall be passed away. They point to a time when the tabernacle of God shall be with men, and God shall dwell with them, and He shall wipe away all tears from their eyes.

The most dreadful, the most hopeless, the most inexorable sorrow is that of death. Nothing is so final, so without hope of retrieval, so utterly full of despair. Yet it was even from this death itself that Jesus at different times snatched the victim, and gave him back to the embraces of friends.

The instances of the raising of the dead by our Lord are three in number, and in each case the subject appears to have been a young person. A little girl in the very dawn of youth was brought back to the embraces of her father and mother; a brother, in the case of Lazarus, was restored to two devoted sisters; and the only son of a widow was given back to his mother.

These actions have more than the force of accidental movements of sympathy. They are to be accepted as protestations from the innermost heart of the great, silent Ruler of Nature, that the anguish and bitterness caused by death among his creatures are not indifferent to him, that it is in his heart finally to put an end to all this sorrow; and this divine representative Man Christ Jesus raises and restores the dead, as a promise of that good time coming when death shall cease and all tears shall be wiped away.

In the first two instances where our Lord is represented as raising the dead, we have no record of anything that he said or did explanatory of the action. When he raised the widow's son at Nain and the ruler's daughter at Capernaum, he said nothing of the philosophy of death or life, and gave no promise of the future. The selecting a widow with an only son as one of the favored instances of mercy was in accordance with the whole spirit of Jewish institutions. By the Mosaic law the widow was made a sacred person. All through the Old Testament, both in the law and the prophets, any act of oppression against a widow is rebuked as the vilest of sins. A special prohibition forbade the taking of a widow's garment as a pledge, and the spirit of this applied to other necessities of life; in multiplied passages the widow was recommended to the special care and consideration of the community.

The case of the widow of Nain was one of the deepest sorrow. She had lost both her husband, and that only son, who was to be in his father's place the staff and stay of her old age; it was sorrow in its bitterest and most hopeless form.

The record of the event is given with the unconscious pathos which everywhere distinguishes the sacred narrative: "And it came to pass that the day after he went into a city called Nain; and many of his disciples went with him, and much people. Now when he came nigh to the gate of the city, behold, there was a dead man carried out, the only son of his mother, and she was a widow; and much people of the city was with her. And when the Lord saw her, he had compassion on her, and said, Weep not. And he came and touched the bier; and they that bare him stood still. And he said unto him, Young man, I say unto thee, Arise. And he that was dead sat up, and began to speak; and he delivered him unto his mother."

We often hear of the sorrows of Jesus; but beyond all others who have lived, he had his hours of joy, and this was doubtless one. To go out amid human suffering with the right and power to relieve it, to give beauty for ashes and a garment of praise for the spirit of heaviness, — this was the joy of Jesus.

Poor in earth's treasures, without a home or place to lay his head, he had in his hands inestimable riches, which could not be bought, but which he freely *gave* to all. He was as one poor, yet making many rich; as having nothing, yet possessing all things.

The silent, self-possessed grandeur of this noble miracle impresses us, it was so evidently a movement, pure and simple, of that depth of Divine compassion which is always invisibly waiting and longing for the hour of consolation to come. The only sons of widows are not dead, — they are gone into that invisible world which is said to be the especial dominion of Him that liveth and was dead, of him that is alive forevermore; and as he gave this one again to his mother, so in that future life he will lay his healing hand on broken ties, and reunite those whom death has parted here, for he is the resurrection and the life, and whoso believeth in him shall never die!

THE WIDOW OF NAIN.

THE dust on their sandals lay heavy and white,
Their garments were damp with the tears of the night,
Their hot feet aweary and throbbing with pain,
As they entered the gates of the city of Nain.

But lo! on the pathway a sorrowing throng
Pressed, mournfully chanting the funeral-song,
And like a sad monotone, ceaseless and slow,
The voice of a woman came laden with woe.

What need, stricken mothers, to tell how she wept?
Ye read by the vigils that sorrow hath kept,
Ye know by the travail of anguish and pain,
The desolate grief of the widow of Nain.

As he who was first of the wayfaring men
Advanced, the mute burden was lowered, and then,
As he touched the white grave-cloths that covered the bier,
The bearers shrank back, but the mother drew near.

Her snow-sprinkled tresses had loosened their strands,
Great tears fell unchecked on the tightly clasped hands;
But hushed the wild sobbing, and stifled her cries,
As Jesus of Nazareth lifted his eyes.

Eyes wet with compassion, as softly they fell, —
Eyes potent to soften grief's tremulous swell,
As sweetly and tenderly, "Weep not," he said,
And turned to the passionless face of the dead.

White, white gleamed his forehead; loose rippled the hair,
Bronze-tinted, o'er temples transparently fair;
And a glory stole up from the earth to the skies,
As he called to the voiceless one, "Young man, arise!"

THE WIDOW OF NAIN.

The hard, rigid outlines grew fervid with breath,
The dull eyes unclosed from the midnight of death;
Weep, weep, happy mother, and fall at his feet:
Life's pale, blighted promise grown hopeful and sweet.

The morning had passed, and the midday heats burned;
Once more to the pathway the wayfarers turned.
The conqueror of kings had been conquered again;
There was joy in the house of the widow of Nain.

Catholic World.

THE WIDOW'S SON.

THE Roman sentinel stood helmed and tall
Beside the gate of Nain. The busy tread
Of comers to the city mart was done,
For it was almost noon, and a dead heat
Quivered upon the fine and sleeping dust,
And the cold snake crept panting from the wall,
And basked his scaly circles in the sun.
Upon his spear the soldier leaned, and kept
His idle watch, and, as his drowsy dream
Was broken by the solitary foot
Of some poor mendicant, he raised his head
To curse him for a tributary Jew,
And slumberously dozed on.

'T was now high noon.
The dull, low murmur of a funeral
Went through the city,—the sad sound of feet
Unmixed with voices,—and the sentinel
Shook off his slumber, and gazed earnestly
Up the wide streets along whose paved way
The silent throng crept slowly. They came on,
Bearing a body heavily on its bier,
And by the crowd that in the burning sun
Walked with forgetful sadness, 't was of one
Mourned with uncommon sorrow. The broad gate
Swung on its hinges, and the Roman bent
His spear-point downwards as the bearers past
Bending beneath their burden. There was one,—
Only one mourner. Close behind the bier,
Crumpling the pall up in her withered hands,
Followed an aged woman. Her short steps
Faltered with weakness, and a broken moan
Fell from her lips, thickened convulsively

As her heart bled afresh. The pitying crowd
Followed apart, but no one spoke to her.
She had no kinsmen. She had lived alone, —
A widow with one son. He was her all, —
The only tie she had in the wide world, —
And he was dead. They could not comfort her.

Jesus drew near to Nain as from the gate
The funeral came forth. His lips were pale
With the noon's sultry heat. The beaded sweat
Stood thickly on his brow, and on the worn
And simple latchets of his sandals lay,
Thick, the white dust of travel. He had come
Since sunrise from Capernaum, staying not
To wet his lips by green Bethsaida's pool,
Nor wash his feet in Kishon's silver springs,
Nor turn him southward upon Tabor's side
To catch Gilboa's light and spicy breeze.
Genesareth stood cool upon the East,
Fast by the sea of Galilee, and there
The weary traveler might bide till eve;
And on the alders of Bethulia's plains
The grapes of Palestine hung ripe and wild;
Yet turned he not aside, but, gazing on
From every swelling mount, he saw afar
Amid the hills the humble spires of Nain,
The place of his next errand, and the path
Touched not Bethulia, and a league away
Upon the East lay pleasant Galilee.

Forth from the city-gate the pitying crowd
Followed the stricken mourner. They came near
The place of burial, and, with straining hands,
Closer upon her breast she clasped the pall,
And with a gasping sob, quick as a child's,
And an inquiring wildness flashing through
The thin gray lashes of her fevered eyes,
She came where Jesus stood beside the way.
He looked upon her, and his heart was moved.
"Weep not!" he said; and as they stayed the bier,
And at his bidding laid it at his feet,

He gently drew the pall from out her grasp
And laid it back in silence from the dead.
With troubled wonder the mute throng drew near,
And gazed on his calm looks. A minute's space
He stood and prayed. Then, taking the cold hand,
He said, "Arise!" And instantly the breast
Heaved in its cerements, and a sudden flush
Ran through the lines of the divided lips,
And with a murmur of his mother's name,
He trembled and sat upright in his shroud.
And, while the mourner hung upon his neck,
Jesus went calmly on his way to Nain.

Nathaniel P. Willis.

RESURRECTION.

"And when the Lord saw her, he had compassion on her, and said unto her, Weep not. And he came and touched the bier; and they that bare him stood still. And he said, Young man, I say unto thee, Arise." — *Luke* vii. 13, 14.

WHO says the wan autumnal sun
Beams with too faint a smile
To light up nature's face again,
And, though the year be on the wane,
With thoughts of spring the heart beguile?

Waft him, thou soft September breeze,
And gently lay him down
Within some circling woodland wall,
Where bright leaves, reddening as they fall,
Wave gayly o'er the waters brown.

And let some grateful arch be there
With wreathèd mullions proud,
With burnished ivy for its screen,
And moss, that glows as fresh and green
As though beneath an April cloud.

Who says the widow's heart must break,
The childless mother sink? —
A kinder, truer voice I hear,
Which, even beside that mournful bier
Whence parents' eyes would hopeless shrink,

Bids weep no more, — O heart bereft,
How strange to thee that sound!
A widow o'er her only son,
Feeling more bitterly alone
For friends that press officious round.

Yet is the voice of comfort heard,
    For Christ has touched the bier, —
The bearers wait with wondering eye,
The swelling bosom dares not sigh,
    But all is still, 'twixt hope and fear.

Even such an awful soothing calm
    We sometimes see alight
On Christian mourners, while they wait
In silence by some churchyard gate
    Their summons to the holy rite.

And such the tones of love which break
    The stillness of that hour,
Quelling th' embittered spirit's strife, —
"The Resurrection and the Life
    Am I; believe, and die no more."

Unchanged that voice, — and though not yet
    The dead sit up and speak,
Answering its call; we gladlier rest
Our darlings on earth's quiet breast,
    And our hearts feel they must not break.

Far better they should sleep awhile
    Within the church's shade,
Nor wake until new heaven, new earth,
Meet for their young immortal birth,
    For their abiding-place be made,

Than wander back to life, and lean
    On our frail love once more.
'T is sweet, as year by year we lose
Friends out of sight, in faith to muse
    How grows in Paradise our store.

Then pass, ye mourners, cheerly on
    Through prayer unto the tomb,
Still, as ye watch life's falling leaf,
Gathering from every loss and grief
    Hope of new spring and endless home.

RESURRECTION.

Then cheerly to your work again
    With hearts new-braced and set
To run, untired, love's blessed race,
As meet for those who face to face
    Over the grave their Lord have met.

John Keble.

THE RAISING OF THE WIDOW'S SON.

EEP not, O mother, sounds of lamentation;
Weep not, O widow, weep not hopelessly!
Strong is His arm, the bringer of salvation!
Strong is the word of God to succor thee!

Bear forth the cold corpse, slowly, slowly bear him;
Hide his pale features with the sable pall;
Chide not the sad one wildly weeping o'er him,
Widowed and childless, she has lost her all.

Why pause the mourners, who forbids our weeping?
Who the dark pomp of sorrow has delayed?
"Set down the bier; — he is not dead, but sleeping:
Young man, arise!" He spake, and was obeyed!

Change then, O sad one, grief to exultation!
Worship and fall before Messiah's knee.
Strong was His arm, the bringer of salvation!
Strong was the word of God to succor thee!

Reginald Heber.

MARY MAGDALENE.

BATONI, *Pinx.*

JEHENNE, *Lith*

MARY MAGDALENE.

ONE of the most splendid ornaments of the Dresden Gallery is the Magdalen of Batoni. The subject has been a favorite among artists, and one sees, in a tour of the various collections of Europe, Magdalens by every painter, in every conceivable style. By far the greater part of them deal only with the material aspects of the subject. The exquisite pathos of the story, the passionate anguish and despair of the penitent, the refinement and dignity of Divine tenderness, are often lost sight of in mere physical accessories. Many artists seem to have seen in the subject only a chance to paint a voluptuously beautiful woman in tears. Titian appears to have felt in this wonderful story nothing but the beauty of the woman's *hair*, and gives us a picture of the most glorious tresses that heart could conceive, perfectly veiling and clothing a very common-place weeping woman. Correggio made of the study only a charming effect of light and shade and color. A fat, pretty, comfortable little body lying on the ground reading, is about the whole that he sees in the subject.

Batoni, on the contrary, seems, by some strange inspiration, to set before us one of the highest, noblest class of women, — a creature so calm, so high, so pure, that we ask involuntarily, How could such a woman ever have fallen? The answer is ready. There is a class of women who fall through what is highest in them, through the noblest capability of a human being, — utter self-sacrificing love. True, we cannot flatter ourselves that these instances are universal, but they do exist. Many women fall through the weakness of self-indulgent passion, many from love of luxury, many from vanity and pride, too many from the mere coercion of hard necessity; but among the sad, unblest crowd there is a class who are the victims of a power of self-forgetting love, which is one of the most angelic capabilities of our nature.

We have shown all along that in the dispensation which prepared the way for the great Messiah and the Christian Era, woman was especially cared for. In all that pertained to the spiritual and immortal nature she was placed on an equality with man, — she could be the vehicle of the prophetic inspiration; as mother she was equally with man enthroned queen of the family; and her sins against chastity were treated precisely as those of man, — as the sin, not of sex, but of a personal moral agent.

The Christian Era, unfolding out of the Mosaic like a rare flower from a carefully cultured stock, brought, in a still higher degree, salvation to woman. The son of Mary was the protector of woman, and one of the earliest and most decided steps in his ministry was his practical and authoritative assertion of the principle, that fallen woman is as capable of restoration through penitence as fallen man, and that repentance should do for a fallen woman whatever it might do for fallen man.

The history of the woman taken in adultery shows how completely that spirit of injustice to woman, which still shows itself in our modern life, had taken possession of the Jewish aristocracy. We hear no word of the guilty *man* who was her partner in crime; we see around Jesus a crowd clamoring for the deadly sentence of the Mosaic law on the woman. Jesus, by one lightning stroke of penetrative omniscience, rouses the dead sense of shame in the accusers, and sends them humbled from his presence, while the sinful woman is saved for a better future.

The absolute divinity of Jesus, the height at which he stood above all men, is nowhere so shown as in what he dared and did for woman, and the godlike consciousness of power with which he did it. It was at a critical period in his ministry, when all eyes were fixed on him in keen inquiry, when many of the respectable classes were yet trembling in the balance whether to accept his claims or no, that Jesus in the calmest and most majestic manner took ground that the sins of a fallen woman were like any other sins, and that repentant love entitled to equal forgiveness. The story so wonderful can be told only in the words of the sacred narrative.

"And one of the Pharisees desired him that he would eat with him, and he went into the Pharisee's house and sat down to meat. And behold a woman in that city which was a sinner, when she knew that Jesus sat at meat in the Pharisee's house, brought an alabaster box of ointment, and stood at his feet behind him, weeping, and began to wash his feet with tears, and did wipe them with the hairs of her head, and kissed his feet and anointed them with the ointment. Now when the Pharisee which had bidden him saw it, he spake within himself, saying, This man, if he were a prophet, would have known who and what manner of woman this is, for she is a sinner. And Jesus answering said unto him, Simon, I have somewhat to say unto thee. He said unto him, Master, say on. There was a certain creditor had two debtors; the one owed him five hundred pence and the other fifty, and when they had nothing to pay he frankly forgave them both. Tell me, therefore, which will love him most. Simon answered and said, I suppose he to whom he forgave most. And he said unto him, Thou hast rightly judged. And he turned to the woman and said unto Simon, Seest thou this woman. I entered into thy house and thou gavest me no water for my feet, but she hath washed my feet with tears and wiped them with the hairs of her head. Thou gavest me no kiss, but this woman, since the time I came in, hath not ceased to kiss my feet. My head with oil thou didst not anoint, but she hath anointed my feet with ointment. Wherefore, I say unto you, her sins, which are many, are forgiven her, for she loved much; but to whom little is forgiven the same loveth little. And he said unto her, Thy sins are forgiven. And they that sat at meat began to say within themselves, Who is this that forgiveth sins also? And he said to the woman, Thy faith hath saved thee; go in peace."

Nothing can be added to the pathos and solemn dignity of this story, in which our Lord assumed with tranquil majesty the rights to supreme love possessed by the Creator, and his sovereign power to forgive sins and dispense favors. The repentant Magdalene became henceforth one of the characteristic figures in the history of the Christian Church. Mary Magdalene became eventually a prominent figure in the mythic legends of the mediæval mythology. A long history of missionary labors and enthusiastic preaching of the gospel in distant regions of the earth is ascribed to her. Churches arose that bore her name, hymns were addressed to her. Even the reforming Savonarola addresses one of his spiritual canticles to St. Mary Magdalene. The various pictures of her which occur in every part of Europe are a proof of the interest which these legends inspired. The most of them are wild and poetic, and exhibit a striking contrast to the concise brevity and simplicity of the New Testament story.

The mythic legends make up a romance in which Mary the sister of Martha and Mary Magdalene the sinner are oddly considered as the same person. It is sufficient to read the chapter in St. John which gives an account of the raising of Lazarus, to perceive that such a confusion is absurd. Mary and Martha there appear as belonging to a family in good standing, to which many flocked with expressions of condolence and respect in time of affliction. And afterwards, in that grateful feast made for the restoration of their brother, we read that so many flocked to the house that the jealousy of the chief priests was excited. All these incidents, representing a family of respectability, are entirely inconsistent with any such supposition. But while we repudiate this extravagance of the tradition, there does seem ground for identifying the Mary Magdalene, who was one of the most devoted followers of our Lord, with the forgiven sinner of this narrative. We read of a company of women who followed Jesus and ministered to him. In the eighth chapter of Luke he is said to be accompanied by "certain women which had been healed of evil spirits and infirmities," among whom is mentioned "Mary called Magdalene," as having been a victim of demoniacal possession. Some women of rank and fortune also are mentioned as members of the same company: "Joanna the wife of Chusa, Herod's steward, and Susanna, and many others who ministered to him of their substance." A modern commentator thinks it improbable that Mary Magdalene could be identified with the "sinner" spoken of by St. Luke, because women of standing like Joanna and Susanna would not have received one of her class to their company. We ask why not? If Jesus had received her, had forgiven and saved her; if *he* acknowledged previously her grateful ministrations, — is it likely that they would reject her? It was the very peculiarity and glory of the new kingdom that it had a better future for sinners, and for sinful woman as well as sinful man. Jesus did not hesitate to say to the proud and prejudiced religious aristocracy of his day, "The publicans and harlots go into the kingdom of heaven before you." We cannot doubt that the loving Christian women who ministered to Jesus received this penitent sister as a soul absolved and purified by the sovereign word of their Lord, and henceforth there was for her a full scope for that ardent, self-devoting power of her nature which had been her ruin, and was now to become her salvation.

Some commentators seem to think that the dreadful demoniacal possession which was spoken of in Mary Magdalene proves her not to have been identical with the woman of St. Luke. But on the contrary, it would seem exactly to account for actions of a strange and unaccountable wickedness, for a notoriety in crime that went far to lead the Pharisees to feel that her very touch was pollution. The story is symbolic of what is too often seen in the fall of woman. A noble and beautiful nature wrecked through inconsiderate prodigality of love, deceived, betrayed, ruined, often drifts like a shipwrecked bark into the power of evil spirits. Rage, despair, revenge, cruelty, take possession of the crushed ruin that should have been the home of the sweetest affections. We are not told when or where the healing word was spoken that drove the cruel fiends from Mary's soul. Perhaps before she entered the halls of the Pharisee, while listening to the preaching of Jesus, the madness and despair had left her. We can believe that in his higher moods virtue went from him, and there was around him a holy and cleansing atmosphere from which all evil fled away, — a serene and healing purity which calmed the throbbing fever of passion and gave the soul once more the image of its better self.

We see in the manner in which Mary found her way to the feet of Jesus the directness and vehemence, the uncalculating self-sacrifice and self-abandon, of one of those natures which, when they move, move with a rush of undivided impulse; which, when they love, trust all, believe all, and are ready to sacrifice all. As once she had lost herself in this self-abandonment, so now at the feet of her God she gains all by the same power of self-surrender.

We do not meet Mary Magdalene again till we find her at the foot of the cross, sharing the last anguish of our Lord and his mother. We find her watching the sepulcher, preparing sweet spices for embalming. In the dim gray of the resurrection morning she is there again, only to find the sepulcher open and the beloved form gone. Everything in this last scene is in consistency with the idea of the passionate self-devotion of a nature whose sole life is in its love. The disciples, when they found not the body, went away; but Mary stood without at the sepulcher weeping, and as she wept she stooped down and looked into the sepulcher. The angels said to her, "Woman, why weepest thou? She answered, Because they have taken away my Lord, and I know not where they have laid him." She then turns and sees through her tears dimly the form of a man standing there. "Jesus saith unto her, Woman, why weepest thou? whom seekest thou? She, supposing him to be the gardener, saith unto him, Sir, if thou have borne him hence, tell me where thou hast laid him, and I will go and take him away. Jesus saith unto her, Mary! She turned herself and said unto him, Rabboni, — Master!"

In all this we see the characteristic devotion and energy of her who loved much because she was forgiven much. It was the peculiarity of Jesus that he saw the precious capability of every nature, even in the very dust of defilement. The power of devoted love is the crown-jewel of the soul, and Jesus had the eye to see where it lay trampled in the mire, and the strong hand to bring it forth purified and brightened. It is the deepest malignity of Satan to degrade and ruin souls through love. It is the glory of Christ, through love, to redeem and restore.

In the history of Christ as a teacher, it is remarkable, that, while he was an object of enthusiastic devotion to so many women, while a band of them followed his preaching and ministered to his wants and those of his disciples, yet there was about him something so entirely unworldly, so sacredly high and pure, that even the very suggestion of scandal in this regard is not to be found in the bitterest vituperations of his enemies of the first two centuries.

If we compare Jesus with Socrates, the moral teacher most frequently spoken of as approaching him, we shall see a wonderful contrast. Socrates associated with courtesans, without passion and without reproof, in a spirit of half-sarcastic, philosophic tolerance. No quickening of the soul of woman, no call to a higher life, came from him. Jesus is stern and grave in his teachings of personal purity, severe in his requirements. He was as intolerant to sin as he was merciful to penitence. He did not extenuate the sins he forgave. He declared the sins of Mary to be *many*, in the same breath that he pronounced her pardon. He said to the adulterous woman whom he protected, "Go, sin no more." The penitents who joined the company of his disciples were so raised above their former selves, that, instead of being the shame, they were the glory of the new kingdom. St. Paul says to the first Christians, speaking of the adulterous and impure, "Such were some of you, but ye are washed, but ye are sanctified, but ye are justified in the name of the Lord Jesus, and by the Spirit of God."

The tradition of the Church that Mary Magdalene was an enthusiastic preacher of Jesus seems in keeping with all we know of the strength and fervor of her character. Such love must find expression, and we are told that when the first persecution scattered the little church at Jerusalem, "they that were scattered went everywhere, preaching the word." Some of the most effective preaching of Christ is that of those who testify in their own person of a great salvation. "He can save to the uttermost, for he has saved ME," is a testimony that often goes more straight to the heart than all the arguments of learning. Christianity had this peculiarity over all other systems, that it not only forgave the past, but made of its bitter experiences a healing medicine; so that those who had sinned deepest might have therefrom a greater redeeming power. "When thou art converted, strengthen thy brethren," was the watchword of the penitent.

The wonderful mind of Goethe has seized upon and embodied this peculiarity of Christianity in his great poem of Faust. The first part shows the Devil making of the sweetest and noblest affection of the confiding Margaret a cruel poison to corrupt both body and soul. We see her driven to crime, remorse, shame, despair, — all human forms and forces of society united to condemn her, when with a last cry she stretches her poor hands to heaven and says, "Judgment of God, I commend myself to you"; and then falls a voice from heaven, "She is judged; she is saved."

In the second part we see the world-worn, weary Faust passing through the classic mythology, vainly seeking rest and finding none; he seeks rest in a life of benevolence to man, but fiends of darkness conflict with his best aspirations, and dog his steps through life, and in his dying hour gather round to seize his soul and carry it to perdition. But around him is a shining band. Mary the mother of Jesus, with a company of purified penitents, encircle him, and his soul passes, in infantine weakness, to the guardian arms of Margaret, — once a lost and ruined woman, now a strong and pitiful angel, — who, like a tender mother, leads the new-born soul to look upon the glories of heaven, while angel-voices sing of the victory of good over evil: —

"All that is transient
Is but a parable;
The unattainable
Here is made real.
The indescribable
Here is accomplished;
The eternal womanly
Draws us upward and onward."

MARY MAGDALENE.

THE TOWER OF MAGDALA.

MARY MAGDALENE.

COMPANIONLESS, unsatisfied, forlorn,
I sit here in this lonely tower, and look
Upon the lake below me, and the hills
That swoon with heat, and see as in a vision
All my past life unroll itself before me.
The princes and the merchants come to me,
Merchants of Tyre and princes of Damascus,
And pass, and disappear, and are no more;
But leave behind their merchandise and jewels,
Their perfumes, and their gold, and their disgust.
I loathe them, and the very memory of them
Is unto me as thought of food to one
Cloyed with the luscious figs of Dalmanutha!
What if hereafter, in the long hereafter
Of endless joy or pain, or joy in pain,
It were my punishment to be with them
Grown hideous and decrepit in their sins,
And hear them say: Thou hast brought us here,
Be unto us as thou hast been of old!

I look upon this raiment that I wear,
These silks, and these embroideries, and they seem
Only as cerements wrapped about my limbs!
I look upon these rings thick set with pearls
And emerald and amethyst and jasper,
And they are burning coals upon my flesh!
This serpent on my wrist becomes alive!
Away, thou viper! and away, ye garlands,
Whose odors bring the swift remembrance back
Of the unhallowed revels in these chambers!

But yesterday, — and yet it seems to me
Something remote, like a pathetic song
Sung long ago by minstrels in the street, —
But yesterday, as from this tower I gazed,
Over the olive and the walnut trees,
Upon the lake and the white ships, and wondered
Whither and whence they steered, and who was in them,
A fisher's boat drew near the landing-place
Under the oleanders, and the people
Came up from it, and passed beneath the tower,
Close under me. In front of them, as leader,
Walked one of royal aspect, clothed in white,
Who lifted up his eyes, and looked at me,
And all at once the air seemed filled and living
With a mysterious power, that streamed from him,
And overflowed me with an atmosphere
Of light and love. As one entranced I stood,
And when I woke again, lo! he was gone;
So that I said: Perhaps it is a dream.
But from that very hour the seven demons
That had their habitation in this body
Which men call beautiful, departed from me!

This morning, when the first gleam of the dawn
Made Lebanon a glory in the air,
And all below was darkness, I beheld
An angel, or a spirit glorified,
With wind-tossed garments walking on the lake.
The face I could not see, but I distinguished
The attitude and gesture, and I knew
'T was he that healed me. And the gusty wind
Brought to mine ears a voice, which seemed to say:
Be of good cheer! 'T is I! Be not afraid!
And from the darkness, scarcely heard, the answer:
If it be thou, bid me come unto thee
Upon the water! And the voice said: Come!
And then I heard a cry of fear: Lord, save me!
As of a drowning man. And then the voice:
Why didst thou doubt, O thou of little faith!
At this all vanished, and the wind was hushed,
And the great sun came up above the hills,
And the swift-flying vapors hid themselves

In caverns among the rocks! O, I must find him
And follow him, and be with him forever!

Thou box of alabaster, in whose walls
The souls of flowers lie pent, the precious balm
And spikenard of Arabian farms, the spirits
Of aromatic herbs, ethereal natures
Nursed by the sun and dew, not all unworthy
To bathe his consecrated feet, whose step
Makes every threshold holy that he crosses;
Let us go forth upon our pilgrimage,
Thou and I only! Let us search for him
Until we find him, and pour out our souls
Before his feet, till all that 's left of us
Shall be the broken caskets, that once held us!

THE HOUSE OF SIMON THE PHARISEE.

A Guest, *at table.*

Are ye deceived? Have any of the Rulers
Believed on him? or do they know indeed
This man to be the very Christ? Howbeit
We know whence this man is, but when the Christ
Shall come, none knoweth whence he is.

Christus.

Whereunto shall I liken, then, the men
Of this generation? and what are they like?
They are like children sitting in the markets,
And calling unto one another, saying:
We have piped unto you, and ye have not danced;
We have mourned unto you, and ye have not wept!
This say I unto you, for John the Baptist
Came neither eating bread nor drinking wine;
Ye say he hath a devil. The Son of Man
Eating and drinking cometh, and ye say:
Behold a gluttonous man, and a wine-bibber;
Behold a friend of publicans and sinners!

A GUEST, *aside to* SIMON.

Who is that woman yonder, gliding in
So silently behind him?

SIMON.

It is Mary,
Who dwelleth in the Tower of Magdala.

THE GUEST.

See, how she kneels there weeping, and her tears
Fall on his feet; and her long, golden hair
Waves to and fro and wipes them dry again.
And now she kisses them, and from a box
Of alabaster is anointing them
With precious ointment, filling all the house
With its sweet odor!

SIMON, *aside.*

O, this man, forsooth,
Were he indeed a Prophet, would have known
Who and what manner of woman this may be
That toucheth him! would know she is a sinner!

CHRISTUS.

Simon, somewhat have I to say to thee.

SIMON.

Master, say on.

CHRISTUS.

A certain creditor
Had once two debtors; and the one of them
Owed him five hundred pence; the other, fifty.
They having naught to pay withal, he frankly

Forgave them both. Now tell me which of them
Will love him most?

SIMON.

He, I suppose, to whom
He most forgave.

CHRISTUS.

Yea, thou hast rightly judged.
Seest thou this woman? When thine house I entered,
Thou gavest me no water for my feet,
But she hath washed them with her tears, and wiped them
With her own hair! Thou gavest me no kiss;
This woman hath not ceased, since I came in,
To kiss my feet! My head with oil didst thou
Anoint not; but this woman hath anointed
My feet with ointment. Hence I say to thee,
Her sins, which have been many, are forgiven,
For she loved much.

THE GUESTS.

O, who, then, is this man
That pardoneth also sins without atonement?

CHRISTUS.

Woman, thy faith hath saved thee! Go in peace!

From the "DIVINE TRAGEDY," *by H. W. Longfellow.*

MARY MAGDALENE.

WITH eyes aglow, and aimless zeal,
She hither, thither, goes;
Her speech, her motions, all reveal
A mind without repose.

She climbs the hills, she haunts the sea,
By madness tortured, driven;
One hour's forgetfulness would be
A gift from very Heaven.

The night brings sleep, sleep new distress;
The anguish of the day
Returns as free, in darker dress,
In more secure dismay.

The demons blast her to and fro;
She has no quiet place;
Enough a woman still to know
A haunting dim disgrace.

Hers in no other eyes confide
For even a moment brief;
With restless glance they turn aside,
Lest they betray her grief.

A human touch! a pang of death!
And in a low delight
Thou liest, waiting for new breath,
For morning out of night.

MARY MAGDALENE.

Thou risest up: the earth is fair,
  The wind is cool and free;
Is it a dream of hell's despair
  Dissolves in ecstasy?

Did this man touch thee? Eyes divine
  Make sunrise in thy soul;
Thou seest love and order shine:
  His health hath made thee whole.

What matter that the coming time
  Will stain thy virgin name!
Will call thine agony thy crime,
  And count thy madness blame!

Let the reproach of men abide!
  He shall be well content
To see not seldom by his side
  Thy head serenely bent.

Thou, sharing in the awful doom,
  Shalt help thy Lord to die;
And, mourning o'er his empty tomb,
  First share his victory.

Rev. George MacDonald.

MARY MAGDALENE.

AT THE DOOR OF SIMON THE PHARISEE.

[To accompany a drawing in which Mary is represented as having left a festal procession, and as ascending by a sudden impulse the steps of the house where she sees Christ. Her lover has followed her, and is trying to turn her back.]

"WHY wilt thou cast the roses from thine hair?
Nay, be thou all a rose, — wreath, lips, and cheek.
Nay, not this house, — that banquet-house we seek;
See how they kiss and enter; come thou there.
This delicate day of love we two will share
Till at our ear love's whispering night shall speak.
What, sweet one, — hold'st thou still the foolish freak?
Nay, when I kiss thy feet they 'll leave the stair."

"O, loose me! See'st thou not my Bridegroom's face
That draws me to him? For his feet my kiss,
My hair, my tears, he craves to-day; — and O,
What words can tell what other day and place
Shall see me clasp those blood-stained feet of his?
He needs me, calls me, loves me, — let me go!"

Dante Gabriel Rossetti.

MARY MAGDALENE.

FROM THE SPANISH.

LESSED, yet sinful one, and broken-hearted!
The crowd are pointing at the thing forlorn,
In wonder and in scorn!
Thou weepest days of innocence departed;
Thou weepest, and thy tears have power to move
The Lord to pity and love.

The greatest of thy follies is forgiven,
Even for the least of all the tears that shine
On that pale cheek of thine.
Thou didst kneel down to him who came from heaven,
Evil and ignorant, and thou shalt rise
Holy, and pure, and wise.

It is not much that to the fragrant blossom
The ragged brier should change; the bitter fir
Distill Arabian myrrh;
Nor that, upon the wintry desert's bosom,
The harvest should rise plenteous, and the swain
Bear home the abundant grain.

But come and see the bleak and barren mountains
Thick to their tops with roses; come and see
Leaves on the dry dead tree:
The perished plant, set out by living fountains,
Grows fruitful, and its beauteous branches rise,
Forever, towards the skies.

William Cullen Bryant.

THE PENITENT'S OFFERING.

THOU that with pallid cheek,
And eyes in sadness meek,
And faded locks that humbly swept the ground,
From their long wanderings won,
Before the all-healing Son,
Didst bow thee to the earth, O lost and found!

When thou wouldst bathe his feet
With odors richly sweet,
And many a shower of woman's burning tear,
And dry them with that hair
Brought low the dust to wear
From the crowned beauty of its festal year,

Did he reject thee then,
While the sharp scorn of men
On thy once bright and stately head was cast?
No, from the Saviour's mien
A solemn light serene
Bore to thy soul the peace of God at last.

For thee their smiles no more
Familiar faces wore;
Voices, once kind, had learned the stranger's tone.
Who raised thee up and bound
Thy silent spirit's wound?
He, from all guilt the stainless, he alone!

But which, O erring child,
From home so long beguiled,
Which of thine offerings won those words of Heaven,

THE PENITENT'S OFFERING.

That o'er the bruised reed,
Condemned of earth to bleed,
In music passed, "Thy sins are all forgiven"?

Was it that perfume, fraught
With balm and incense, brought
From the sweet woods of Araby the blest?
Or that fast-flowing rain
Of tears which not in vain
To him who scorned not tears thy woes confessed?

No, not by these restored
Unto thy Father's board,
Thy peace that kindled joy in heaven was made;
But costlier in his eyes
By that blest sacrifice,
Thy heart, thy full deep heart before him laid.

Felicia Hemans.

MARY MAGDALENE.

HEN blessed Mary wiped her Saviour's feet
(Whose precepts she had trampled on before),
And wore them for a jewel on her head,
Shewing his steps should be the street
Wherein she henceforth evermore,
With pensive humbleness, would live and tread:

She being stained herself, why did she strive
To make him clean who could not be defiled?
Why kept she not her tears for her own faults,
And not his feet? Though we could dive
In tears, like seas; our sins are piled
Deeper than they, in words, and works, and thoughts.

Dear soul, she knew who did vouchsafe and deign
To bear her filth; and that her sins did dash
E'en God himself; wherefore she was not loath,
As she had brought wherewith to stain,
So to bring in wherewith to wash:
And yet in washing one she washėd both.

George Herbert.

SONNETS.

I. ANOINTING CHRIST'S FEET.

THERE was a mournfulness in angel eyes,
That saw thee, woman! bright in this world's train,
Moving to pleasure's airy melodies,
Thyself the idol of the enchanted strain.
But from thy beauty's garland, brief and vain,
When one by one the rose-leaves had been torn,
When thy heart's core had quivered to the pain
Through every life-nerve sent by arrowy scorn;
When thou didst kneel to pour sweet odors forth
On the Redeemer's feet, with many a sigh,
And showering tear-drop, of yet richer worth
Than all those costly balms of Araby;
Then was there joy, a song of joy in heaven,
For thee, the child won back, the penitent forgiven!

II. AT THE SEPULCHER.

WEEPER! to thee how bright a morn was given
After thy long, long vigil of despair,
When that high voice which burial rocks had riven,
Thrilled with immortal tones the silent air!
Never did clarion's royal blast declare
Such tale of victory to a breathless crowd,
As the deep sweetness of *one* word could bear
Into thy heart of hearts, O woman! bowed
By strong affection's anguish! — one low word —
"*Mary!*" — and all the triumph wrung from death
Was thus revealed! and thou, that so hadst erred,

So wept, and been forgiven, in trembling faith
Didst cast thee down before the all-conquering Son,
Awed by the mighty gift thy tears and love had won!

III. BEARING TIDINGS OF THE RESURRECTION.

THEN was a task of glory all thine own,
Nobler than e'er the still small voice assigned
To lips in awful music making known
The stormy splendors of some prophet's mind.
"Christ is arisen!" by thee, to wake mankind,
First from the sepulcher those words were brought!
Thou wert to send the mighty rushing wind
First on its way, with those high tidings fraught, —
"*Christ is arisen!*" Thou, *thou*, the sin-enthralled,
Earth's outcast, Heaven's own ransomed one, wert called
In human hearts to give that rapture birth:
O, raised from shame to brightness! — there doth lie
The tenderest meaning of *His* ministry,
Whose undespairing love still owned the spirit's worth.

Felicia Hemans.

TO ST. MARY MAGDALENE.

MID the white spouses of the Sacred Heart,
After its Queen, the nearest, dearest, thou;
Yet the auréola around thy brow
Is not the Virgin's. Thine a throne apart.
Nor yet, my Saint, does faith-illumined art
Thy hand with palm of martyrdom endow;
And when thy hair is all it will allow
Of glory to thy head, we do not start.
O more than virgin in thy penitent love!
And more than martyr in thy passionate woe!
How should thy sisters equal thee above
Who knelt not with thee on the gory sod?
Or where the crown our worship could bestow
Like that long gold that wiped the feet of God?

Catholic World.

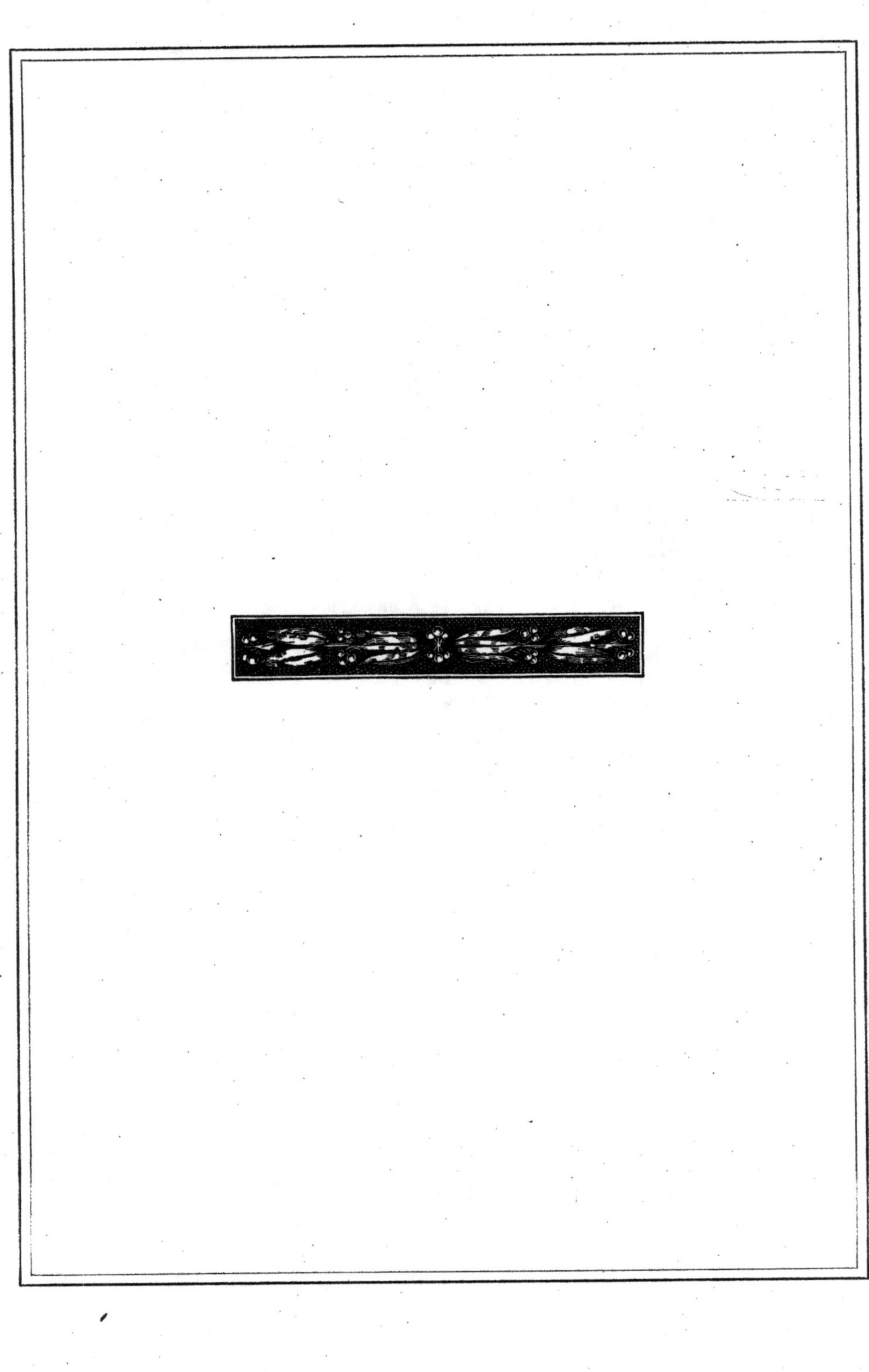

THE DAUGHTER OF HERODIAS.

VERNET-LECOMTE, *Pinx.* JEHENNE, *Lith.*

THE DAUGHTER OF HERODIAS.

IN the great drama of the history of Jesus many subordinate figures move across the stage, indicated with more or less power by the unconscious and artless simplicity of the narrative. Among these is the daughter of Herodias, whose story has often been a favorite subject among artists as giving an opportunity of painting female beauty and fascination in affinity with the deepest and most dreadful tragedy.

Salome was the daughter of Herodias, who was a woman of unbridled passions and corrupt will. This Herodias had eloped from her husband Philip, son of Herod the Great, to marry her step-uncle, Herod Antipas, who forsook for her his lawful wife, the daughter of the king of Arabia. Herod appears in the story of the Gospels as a man with just enough conscience and aspiration after good to keep him always uneasy, but not enough to restrain from evil.

When the ministry of John powerfully excited the public mind, we are told by St. Mark that "Herod feared John, knowthat he was a just man and holy, and he observed him, and when he heard him he did many things and heard him gladly."

The Jewish religion strongly cultivated conscience and a belief in the rewards and punishments of a future life, and the style of John's preaching was awful and monitory. "Behold the axe is laid at the root of the tree, and whatsoever tree doth not bring forth good fruit shall be hewn down and cast into the fire." There was no indulgence for royal trees; no concession to the divine right of kings to do evil. John was a prophet in the spirit and power of Elijah; he dwelt in the desert, he despised the power and splendor of courts, and appeared before kings as God's messenger, to declare his will and pronounce sentence of wrath on the disobedient. So without scruple he denounced the adulterous connection of his royal hearer, and demanded that Herod should put away the guilty woman as the only condition of salvation. Herod replied, as kings have been in the habit of replying to such inconvenient personal application of God's laws: he shut John up in prison. It is said in St. Mark that Herodias had a quarrel against him, and would have killed him, but she could not. The intensity of a woman's hatred looks out through this chink of the story as the secret exciting power to the man's slower passions. She would have had him killed had she been able to have her way; she can only compass his imprisonment for the present, and she trusts to female importunities and blandishments to finish the vengeance. The hour of opportunity comes. We are told in the record: "And when a convenient day came, Herod on his birthday made a supper to his lords and high captains and chief estates of Galilee."

One of the entertainments of the evening was the wonderful dancing of Salome, the daughter of his paramour. We have heard in the annals of the modern theatre into what inconsiderate transports of rapture crowned heads and chief captains and mighty men of valor have been thrown by the dancing of some enthroned queen of the ballet; and one does not feel it incredible, therefore, that Herod, who appeared to be nervously susceptible to all kinds of influences, said to the enchantress, "Ask me whatsoever thou wilt, and I will give it thee; and he sware unto her after the pattern of Ahasuerus to Esther, saying, Whatsoever thou shalt ask of me I will give it thee, to the half of my kingdom." And now the royal tigress, who has arranged this snare and watched the king's entrance into the toils, prepares to draw the noose. Salome goes to her mother and says, "What shall I ask?" The answer is ready. Herodias said, with perfect explicitness, "Ask for the head of John the Baptist." So the graceful creature trips back into the glittering court circle, and, bowing her flower-like head, says in the sweetest tones, "Give me here John the Baptist's head in a charger."

The narrative says very artlessly, "And the king was sorry, but for his oath's sake, and for the sake of them that sat with him at meat, he would not refuse her, and immediately the king sent an executioner and commanded his head to be brought, and he went and beheaded him in prison!"

What wonderful contrasted types of womanhood the Gospel history gives! We see such august and noble forms as Elisabeth, the mother of the Baptist, and Mary, the mother of Jesus, by the side of this haughty royal adulteress and her beautiful daughter. The good were the lower, and the bad the higher class of that day. Vice was enthroned and triumphant, while virtue walked obscure by hedges and byways; a dancing girl had power to take away the noblest life in Judæa, next to that which was afterward taken on Calvary.

No throb of remorse that we know of ever visited these women, but of Herod we are told that when afterwards he heard of the preaching and mighty works of Jesus, he said, "It is John the Baptist that I slew. He is risen from the dead, therefore mighty works do show forth themselves in him."

In the last scenes of our Lord's life we meet again this credulous, superstitious, bad man. Pilate, embarrassed by a prisoner who alarmed his fears and whom he was troubled to dispose of, sent Jesus to Herod. Thus we see the licentious tool and slave of a bad woman has successively before his judgment-seat the two greatest men of his age and of all ages. It is said Herod received Jesus gladly, for he had a long time been desirous to see him, for he hoped some miracle would be done by him. But he was precisely of the class of whom our Lord spoke when he said, "An adulterous generation seeketh a sign, and there shall no sign be given them." God has no answer to give to wicked, unrepentant curiosity, and though Herod questioned Jesus in many words he answered him nothing. Then we are told, "Herod with his men of war set Jesus at naught, and mocked him, and arrayed him in a gorgeous robe, and sent him again to Pilate." And this was how the great ones of the earth received their Lord.

SALOME, THE DAUGHTER OF HERODIAS.

I. BEFORE THE GATES OF MACHÆRUS.

MANAHEM.

WELCOME, O wilderness, and welcome, night
And solitude, and ye swift-flying stars
That drift with golden sands the barren heavens,
Welcome once more! The Angels of the Wind
Hasten across the desert to receive me;
And sweeter than men's voices are to me
The voices of these solitudes; the sound
Of unseen rivulets, and the far-off cry
Of bitterns in the reeds of water-pools.
And lo! above me, like the Prophet's arrow
Shot from the eastern window, high in air
The clamorous cranes go singing through the night.
O ye mysterious pilgrims of the air,
Would I had wings that I might follow you!

I look forth from these mountains, and behold
The omnipotent and omnipresent night,
Mysterious as the future and the fate
That hangs o'er all men's lives! I see beneath me
The desert stretching to the Dead Sea shore,
And westward, faint and far away, the glimmer
Of torches on Mount Olivet, announcing
The rising of the Moon of Passover.
Like a great cross it seems, on which suspended,
With head bowed down in agony, I see
A human figure! Hide, O merciful heaven,
The awful apparition from my sight!

And thou, Machærus, lifting high and black
Thy dreadful walls against the rising moon,

Haunted by demons and by apparitions,
Lilith, and Jezerhara, and Bedargon,
How grim thou showest in the uncertain light,
A palace and a prison, where King Herod
Feasts with Herodias, while the Baptist John
Fasts, and consumes his unavailing life!
And in thy court-yard grows the untithed rue,
Huge as the olives of Gethsemane,
And ancient as the terebinth of Hebron,
Coeval with the world. Would that its leaves
Medicinal could purge thee of the demons
That now possess thee, and the cunning fox
That burrows in thy walls, contriving mischief!

Music is heard from within.

Angels of God! Sandalphon, thou that weavest
The prayers of men into immortal garlands,
And thou, Metatron, who dost gather up
Their songs, and bear them to the gates of heaven,
Now gather up together in your hands
The prayers that fill this prison, and the songs
That echo from the ceiling of this palace,
And lay them side by side before God's feet!

He enters the castle.

II. HEROD'S BANQUET-HALL.

MANAHEM.

THOU hast sent for me, O King, and I am here.

HEROD.

Who art thou?

MANAHEM.

Manahem, the Essenian.

HEROD.

I recognize thy features, but what mean
These torn and faded garments? On thy road

Have demons crowded thee, and rubbed against thee,
And given thee weary knees? A cup of wine!

MANAHEM.

The Essenians drink no wine.

HEROD.

What wilt thou, then?

MANAHEM.

Nothing.

HEROD.

Not even a cup of water?

MANAHEM.

Nothing.

Why hast thou sent for me?

HEROD.

Dost thou remember
One day when I, a school-boy in the streets
Of the great city, met thee on my way
To school, and thou didst say to me: Hereafter
Thou shalt be King?

MANAHEM.

Yea, I remember it.

HEROD.

Thinking thou didst not know me, I replied:
I am of humble birth; whereat, thou, smiling,
Didst smite me with thy hand, and saidst again:
Thou shalt be King; and let the friendly blows
That Manahem hath given thee on this day
Remind thee of the fickleness of fortune.

MANAHEM.

What more?

HEROD.

No more.

MANAHEM.

Yea, for I said to thee:
It shall be well with thee if thou love justice
And clemency towards thy fellow-men.
Hast thou done this, O King?

HEROD.

Go, ask my people.

MANAHEM.

And then, foreseeing all thy life, I added:
But these thou wilt forget; and at the end
Of life the Lord will punish thee.

HEROD.

The end!
When will that come? For this I sent to thee.
How long shall I still reign? Thou dost not answer!
Speak! shall I reign ten years?

MANAHEM.

Thou shalt reign twenty,
Nay, thirty years. I cannot name the end.

HEROD.

Thirty? I thank thee, good Essenian!
This is my birthday, and a happier one
Was never mine. We hold a banquet here.
See, yonder are Herodias and her daughter.

MANAHEM, *aside.*

'T is said that devils sometimes take the shape
Of ministering angels, clothed with air,
That they may be inhabitants of earth,
And lead man to destruction. Such are these.

HEROD.

Knowest thou John the Baptist?

MANAHEM.

Yea, I know him;
Who knows him not?

HEROD.

Know, then, this John the Baptist
Said that it was not lawful I should marry
My brother Philip's wife, and John the Baptist
Is here in prison. In my father's time
Matthias Margaloth was put to death
For tearing the golden eagle from its station
Above the Temple Gate, — a slighter crime
Than John is guilty of. These things are warnings
To intermeddlers not to play with eagles,
Living or dead. I think the Essenians
Are wiser, or more wary, are they not?

MANAHEM.

The Essenians do not marry.

HEROD.

Thou hast given
My words a meaning foreign to my thought.

MANAHEM.

Let me go hence, O King!

HEROD.

Stay yet awhile,
And see the daughter of Herodias dance.
Cleopatra of Jerusalem, my mother,
In her best days was not more beautiful.

Music. THE DAUGHTER OF HERODIAS *dances.*

O, what was Miriam dancing with her timbrel,
Compared to this one!

MANAHEM, *aside.*

O thou Angel of Death,
Dancing at funerals among the women,
When men bear out the dead! The air is hot
And stifles me! O for a breath of air!
Bid me depart, O King!

HEROD.

Not yet. Come hither,
Salome, thou enchantress! Ask of me
Whate'er thou wilt; and even unto the half
Of all my kingdom, I will give it thee,
As the Lord liveth!

DAUGHTER OF HERODIAS, *kneeling.*

Give me here the head
Of John the Baptist on this silver charger!

HEROD.

Not that, dear child! I dare not; for the people
Regard John as a prophet.

DAUGHTER OF HERODIAS.

Thou hast sworn it.

HEROD.

For mine oath's sake, then. Send unto the prison;
Let him die quickly. O accursed oath!

MANAHEM.

Bid me depart, O King!

HEROD.

Good Manahem,
Give me thy hand. I love the Essenians.
He 's gone and hears me not! The guests are dumb,
Awaiting the pale face, the silent witness.

The lamps flare; and the curtains of the doorways
Wave to and fro as if a ghost were passing!
Strengthen my heart, red wine of Ascalon!

III. UNDER THE WALLS OF MACHÆRUS.

MANAHEM, *rushing out.*

AWAY from this Palace of sin!
The demons, the terrible powers
Of the air, that haunt its towers
And hide in its water-spouts,
Deafen me with the din
Of their laughter and their shouts
For the crimes that are done within!

Sink back into the earth,
Or vanish into the air,
Thou castle of despair!
Let it all be but a dream
Of the things of monstrous birth,
Of the things that only seem!
White Angel of the Moon,
Onafiel! be my guide
Out of this hateful place
Of sin and death, nor hide
In yon black cloud too soon
Thy pale and tranquil face!

A trumpet is blown from the walls.

Hark! hark! It is the breath
Of the trump of doom and death,
From the battlements overhead
Like a burden of sorrow cast
On the midnight and the blast,
A wailing for the dead,
That the gusts drop and uplift!
O Herod, thy vengeance is swift!
O Herodias, thou hast been
The demon, the evil thing,

That in place of Esther the Queen,
In place of the lawful bride,
Hast lain at night by the side
Of Ahasuerus the king!

The trumpet again.

The Prophet of God is dead!
At a drunken monarch's call,
At a dancing-woman's beck,
They have severed that stubborn neck,
And into the banquet-hall
Are bearing the ghastly head!

A body is thrown from the tower.

A torch of lurid red
Lights the window with its glow;
And a white mass as of snow
Is hurled into the abyss
Of the black precipice,
That yawns for it below!
O hand of the Most High,
O hand of Adonai!
Bury it, hide it away
From the birds and beasts of prey,
And the eyes of the homicide,
More pitiless than they,
As thou didst bury of yore
The body of him that died
On the mountain of Peor!

Even now I behold a sign,
A threatening of wrath divine,
A watery, wandering star,
Through whose streaming hair, and the white
Unfolding garments of light,
That trail behind it afar,
The constellations shine!
And the whiteness and brightness appear
Like the Angel bearing the Seer
By the hair of his head, in the might
And rush of his vehement flight.

And I listen until I hear
From fathomless depths of the sky
The voice of his prophecy
Sounding louder and more near!

Malediction! malediction!
May the lightnings of heaven fall
On palace and prison wall,
And their desolation be
As the day of fear and affliction,
As the day of anguish and ire,
With the burning and fuel of fire,
In the Valley of the Sea!

From the "DIVINE TRAGEDY," *by H. W. Longfellow.*

THE DAUGHTER OF HERODIAS.

MOTHER! I bring thy gift;
Take from my hand the dreaded boon, I pray!
Take it; the still, pale sorrow of the face
Hath left upon my soul its living trace,
Never to pass away, —
Since from these lips one word of idle breath
Blanched that calm face; O mother, this is death!

What is it that I see
From all the pure and settled features gleaming?
Reproach! reproach! My dreams are strange and wild;
Mother! hadst thou no pity on thy child?
Lo! a celestial smile seems softly beaming
On the hushed lips, — my mother, canst thou brook
Longer upon thy victim's face to look?

Alas! at yestermorn
My heart was light, and to the viol's sound
I gayly danced, while crowned with summer flowers,
And swiftly by me sped the flying hours,
And all was joy around:
Not *death!* O mother, could I say thee nay?
Take from thy daughter's hand thy boon away!

Take it! my heart is sad,
And the pure forehead hath an icy chill;
I dare not touch it, for avenging Heaven
Hath shuddering visions to my fancy given,
And the pale face appalls me, cold and still,
With the closed lips. O, tell me, could I know
That the pale features of the dead were so?

I may not turn away
From the charmed face; and I have heard his name
Even as a prophet by his people spoken.
And that high brow, in death, bears seal and token
Of one whose words were flame:
O holy teacher! couldst thou rise and live,
Would not these hushed lips whisper, "I forgive"?

Away with lute and harp,
With the glad heart forever, and the dance!
Never again shall tabret sound for me!
O fearful mother! I have brought to thee
The silent dead, with his rebuking glance,
And the crushed heart of one to whom are given
Wild dreams of judgment and offended Heaven.

Lucy Hooper.

MARTHA AND MARY.

BOULANGER, *Pinx.* JEHENNE, *Lith.*

MARTHA AND MARY.

THE dramatic power of the brief Bible narratives is one of their most wonderful characteristics. By a few incidents, a word here and there, they create a vivid image of a personality that afterwards never dies from our memory. The women of Shakespeare have been set upon the stage with all the accessories of dress, scenery, and the interpreting power of fine acting, and yet the vividness of their personality has not been equal to that of the women of the Bible.

Mary and Martha, the two sisters of Bethany, have had for ages a name and a living power in the Church. Thousands of hearts have throbbed with theirs; thousands have wept sympathetic tears in their sorrows and rejoiced in their joy. By a few simple touches in the narrative they are so delicately and justly discriminated that they stand for the representatives of two distinct classes. Some of the ancient Christian writers considered them as types of the active and the contemplative aspects of religion. Martha is viewed as the secular Christian, serving God in and through the channels of worldly business, and Mary as the more peculiarly religious person, devoted to a life of holy meditation and the researches of heavenly truth. The two were equally the friends of Jesus. Apparently, the two sisters with one brother were an orphan family, united by the strongest mutual affection, and affording a circle peculiarly congenial to the Master.

They inhabited a rural home just outside of Jerusalem; and it seems that here, after the labors of a day spent in teaching in the city, our Lord found at evening a home-like retreat where he could enjoy perfect quiet and perfect love. It would seem, from many touches in the Gospel narrative, as if Jesus, amid the labors and applauses and successes of a public life, yearned for privacy and domesticity, — for that home love which he persistently renounced, to give himself wholly to mankind. There is a shade of pathos in his answer to one who proposed to be his disciple and dwell with him: "Foxes have holes; the birds of the air have nests; but the Son of Man hath not where to lay his head." This little orphan circle, with their quiet home, were thus especially dear to him, and it appears that this was his refuge during that last week of his life, when he knew that every day was bringing him nearer to the final anguish.

It is wonderful how sharply and truly, in a narrative so brief, the characters of Martha and Mary are individualized. Martha, in her Judæan dress and surroundings, is, after all, exactly such a good woman as is often seen in our modern life, — a woman primarily endowed with the faculties necessary for getting on in the world, yet sincerely religious. She is energetic, business-like, matter-of-fact, strictly orthodox, and always ready for every emergency. She lives in the present life strongly and intensely, and her religion exhibits itself through regular forms and agencies. She believes in the future life orthodoxly, and is always prompt to confess its superior importance as a matter of doctrine, though prone to make material things the first in practice. Many such women there are in the high places of the Christian Church, and much good they do. They manage fairs, they dress churches, they get up religious festivals, their names are on committees, they are known at celebrations. They rule their own homes with activity and diligence, and they are justly honored by all who know them. Now, nothing is more remarkable in the history of Jesus than the catholicity of his appreciation of character. He never found fault with natural organization, or expected all people to be of one pattern. He did not break with Thomas for being naturally a cautious doubter, or Peter for being a precipitate believer; and it is specially recorded in the history of this family that Jesus loved Martha. He understood her, he appreciated her worth, and he loved her.

In Mary we see the type of those deeper and more sensitive natures who ever aspire above and beyond the material and temporal to the eternal and divine; souls that are seeking and inquiring with a restlessness that no earthly thing can satisfy, who can find no peace until they find it in union with God.

In St. Luke we have a record of the manner in which the first acquaintance with this family was formed. This historian says: "A woman named Martha received him at her house." Evidently the decisive and salient power of her nature caused her to be regarded as mistress of the family. There was a grown-up brother in the family; but this house is not called the house of Lazarus, but the house of Martha, — a form of speaking the more remarkable from the great superiority or leadership which ancient customs awarded to the male sex. But Martha was one of those natural leaders whom everybody instinctively thinks of as the head of any house they may happen to belong to. Her tone toward Mary is authoritative. The Mary-nature is a nature apt to appear to disadvantage in physical things. It is often puzzled, and unskilled, and unready in the details and emergencies of a life like ours, which so little meets its deepest feelings and most importunate wants. It acquires skill in earthly things only as a matter of discipline and conscience, but is always yearning above them to something higher and divine. A delicacy of moral nature suggests to such a person a thousand scruples of conscientious inquiry in every turn of life, which embarrass directness of action. To the Martha-nature, practical, direct, and prosaic, all these doubts, scruples, hesitations, and unreadinesses appear only as pitiable weaknesses.

Again, Martha's nature attaches a vast importance to many things which, in the view of Mary, are so fleeting and perishable, and have so little to do with the deeper immortal wants of the soul, that it is difficult for her even to remember and keep them in sight. The requirements of etiquette, the changes and details of fashion, the thousand particulars which pertain to keeping up a certain footing in society and a certain position in the world, — all these Martha has at her fingers' ends. They are the breath of her nostrils, while Mary is always forgetting, overlooking, and transgressing them. Many a Mary has escaped into a convent, or joined a sisterhood, or worn the plain dress of the Quaker, in order that she might escape from the exaction of the Marthas of her day, "careful [or, more literally, *full of care*] and troubled about many things."

It appears that in her way Martha was a religious woman, a sincere member of the Jewish Church, and an intense believer. The preaching of Christ was the great religious phenomenon of the times, and Martha, Mary, and Lazarus joined the crowd who witnessed his miracles and listened to his words. Both women accepted his message and believed his Messiahship, — Martha, from the witness of his splendid miracles; Mary, from the deep accord of her heart with the wonderful words he had uttered. To Martha he was the King that should reign in splendor at Jerusalem, and raise their nation to an untold height of glory; to Mary he was the answer to the eternal question, — the Way, the Truth, the Life, for which she had been always longing.

Among many who urge and press hospitality, Martha's invitation prevails. A proud home is that, when Jesus follows her, — her prize, her captive. The woman in our day who has captured in her net of hospitalities the orator, the poet, the warrior, — the star of all eyes, the central point of all curiosity, desire, and regard, — can best appreciate Martha's joy. She will make an entertainment that will do credit to the occasion. She revolves prodigies of hospitality. She invites guests to whom her acquisition shall be duly exhibited, and all is hurry, bustle, and commotion. But Mary follows him, silent, with a fluttering heart. His teaching has aroused the divine longing, the immortal pain, to a throbbing intensity; a sweet presentiment fills her soul, that she is near One through whom the way into the Holiest is open, and now is the hour. She neither hears nor sees the bustle of preparation; but apart, where the Master has seated himself, she sits down at his feet, and her eyes, more than her voice, address to him that question and that prayer which are *the* question and the *one great reality* of all this fleeting, mortal life.

The question is answered; the prayer is granted. At his feet she becomes spiritually clairvoyant. The way to God becomes clear and open. Her soul springs toward the light; is embraced by the peace of God, that passeth understanding. It is a soul-crisis, and the Master sees that in that hour his breath has unfolded into blossom buds that had been struggling in darkness. Mary has received in her bosom the "white stone with the new name, which no man knoweth save him that receiveth it," and of which Jesus only is the giver. As Master and disciple sit in that calm and sweet accord, in which giver and receiver are alike blessed, suddenly Martha appears and breaks into the interview, in a characteristically imperative sentence: "Lord, dost thou not care that my sister hath left me to serve alone? Bid her, therefore, that she help me."

Nothing could more energetically indicate Martha's character than this sentence. It shows her blunt sincerity, her conscientious, matter-of-fact worldliness, and her dictatorial positiveness. Evidently, here is a person accustomed to having her own way and bearing down all about her; a person who believes in herself without a doubt, and is so positive that her way is the only right one that she cannot but be amazed that the Master has not at once seen as she does. To be sure, this is in her view the Christ, the Son of God, the King of Israel, the human being whom in her deepest heart she reverences; but no matter, she is so positive that she is right that she does not hesitate to say her say, and make her complaint of him as well as of her sister. People like Martha often arraign and question the very Providence of God itself when it stands in the way of their own plans. Martha is sure of her ground. Here is the Messiah, the King of Israel, at her house, and she is getting up an entertainment worthy of him, slaving herself to death for him, and he takes no notice, and most inconsiderately allows her dreamy sister to sit listening to him, instead of joining in the preparation.

The reply of Jesus went, as his replies were wont to do, to the very root-fault of Martha's life, the fault of all such natures: "Martha, Martha! thou art careful and troubled about many things, but *one* thing is needful, and Mary hath chosen that good part which shall not be taken from her." The Master's words evidently recognize that in that critical hour Mary had passed a boundary in her soul history, and made an attainment of priceless value. She had gained something that could never be taken from her; and she had gained it by that single-hearted devotion to spiritual things which made her prompt to know and seize the hour of opportunity.

The brief narrative there intermits; we are not told how Martha replied, or what are the results of this plain, tender faithfulness of reproof. The Saviour, be it observed, did not blame Martha for her nature. He did not blame her for not being Mary; but he did blame her for not restraining and governing her own nature and keeping it in due subjection to higher considerations. A being of brighter worlds, he stood looking on Martha's life,—on her activities and bustle and care; and to him how sorrowfully worthless the greater part of them appeared! To him they were mere toys and playthings, such as a child is allowed to play with in the earlier, undeveloped hours of existence; not to be harshly condemned, but still utterly fleeting and worthless in the face of the tremendous eternal realities, the glories and the dangers of the eternal state.

It must be said here that all we know of our Lord leads us to feel that he was not encouraging and defending in Mary a selfish, sentimental indulgence in her own cherished emotions and affections, leaving the burden of necessary care on a sister who would have been equally glad to sit at Jesus's feet. That was not his reading of the situation. It was that Martha, engrossed in a thousand cares, burdened herself with a weight of perplexities of which there was no need, and found no time and had no heart to come to him and speak of the *only*, the *one* thing that endures beyond the present world. To how many hearts does this reproof apply? How many who call themselves Christians are weary, wasted, worn, drained of life, injured in health, fretted in temper, by a class of anxieties so purely worldly that they can never bring them to Jesus, or if they do, would meet first and foremost his tender reproof, "Thou art careful and troubled about many things; there is but *one* thing really needful. Seek that good part which shall never be taken away."

What fruit this rebuke bore will appear as we further pursue the history of the sister. The subsequent story shows that Martha was a brave, sincere, good woman, capable of yielding to reproof and acknowledging a fault. There is precious material in such, if only their powers be turned to the highest and best things.

It is an interesting thought that the human affection of Jesus for one family has been made the means of leaving on record the most consoling experience for the sorrows of bereavement that sacred literature affords. Viewed merely on the natural side, the intensity of human affections and the frightful possibilities of suffering involved in their very sweetness present a fearful prospect when compared with that stony inflexibility of natural law, which goes forth crushing, bruising, lacerating, without the least apparent feeling for human agony.

The God of nature appears silent, unalterable, unsympathetic, pursuing general good without a throb of pity for individual suffering; and that suffering is so unspeakable, so terrible! Close shadowing every bridal, every cradle, is this awful possibility of death that may come at any moment, unannounced and inevitable. The joy of this hour may become the bitterness of the next; the ring, the curl of hair, the locket, the picture, that to-day are a treasure of hope and happiness, to-morrow may be only weapons of bitterness that stab at every view. The silent inflexibility of God in upholding laws that work out such terrible agonies and suffering is something against which the human heart moans and chafes through all ancient literature. "The gods envy the happy," was the construction put upon the problem of life as the old sages viewed it.

But in this second scene of the story of the sisters of Bethany we have that view of God which is the only one powerful enough to soothe and control the despair of the stricken heart. It says to us that behind this seeming inflexibility, this mighty and most needful upholding of law, is a throbbing, sympathizing heart, — bearing with us the sorrow of this struggling period of existence, and pointing to a perfect fulfillment in the future.

The story opens most remarkably. In the absence of the Master, the brother is stricken down with deadly disease. Forthwith a hasty messenger is dispatched to Jesus. "Lord, he whom thou lovest is sick." Here is no prayer expressed; but human language could not be more full of all the elements of the best kind of prayer. It is the prayer of perfect trust, — the prayer of love that has no shadow of doubt. If only we let Jesus know we are in trouble, we are helped. We need not ask, we need only say, "He whom thou lovest is sick," and he will understand, and the work will be done. We are safe with him.

Then comes the seeming contradiction — the trial of faith — that gives this story such a value: "Now Jesus loved Martha and her sister and Lazarus. When, *therefore*, he heard that he was sick, he abode two days in the same place where he was." Because he loved them, he delayed; because he loved them, he resisted that most touching appeal that heart can make, — the appeal of utter trust. We can imagine the wonder, the anguish, the conflict of spirit, when death at last shut the door in the face of their prayers. Had God forgotten to be gracious? Had he in anger shut up his tender mercy? Did not Jesus love them? Had he not power to heal? Why then had he suffered this? Ah! this is exactly the strait in which thousands of Christ's own beloved ones must stand in the future; and Mary and Martha, unconsciously to themselves, were suffering with Christ in the great work of human consolation. Their distress and anguish and sorrow were necessary to work out a great experience of God's love, where multitudes of anguished hearts have laid themselves down as on a pillow of repose, and have been comforted.

Something of this is shadowed in the Master's words: "This sickness is not unto death, but for the glory of God, — that the Son of God might be glorified thereby." What was that glory of God? Not most his natural power, but his sympathetic tenderness, his loving heart. What is the glory of the Son of God? Not the mere display of power, but power used to console, in manifesting to the world that this cruel *death* — the shadow that haunts all human life, that appalls and terrifies, that scatters anguish and despair — is *not* death, but the gateway of a brighter life, in which Jesus shall restore love to love, in eternal reunion.

In the scene with the sisters before the Saviour arrives, we are struck with the consideration in which the family is held. This house is thronged with sympathizing friends, and, as appears from some incidents afterwards, friends among the higher classes of the nation. Martha hears of the approach of Jesus, and goes forth to meet him.

In all the scene which follows we are impressed with the dignity and worth of Martha's character. We see in the scene of sorrow that Martha has been the strong, practical woman, on whom all rely in the hour of sickness, and whose energy is equal to any emergency. We see her unsubdued by emotion, ready to go forth to receive Jesus, and prompt to meet the issues of the moment. We see, too, that the appreciation of the worth of her character, which had led him to admonish her against the materialistic tendencies of such a nature, was justified by the fruits of that rebuke. Martha had grown more spiritual by intercourse with the Master, and as she falls at Jesus's feet, the half-complaint which her sorrow wrings from her is here merged in the expression of her faith: "Lord, if thou hadst been here my brother had not died; but I know that even now, whatsoever thou wilt ask of God, God will give it to thee. Jesus saith unto her, Thy brother shall rise again." Like every well-trained religious Jew of her day, Martha was versed in the doctrine of the general resurrection. That this belief was a more actively operating motive with the ancient Jewish than with the modern Christian Church of our day, is attested by the affecting history of the martyrdom of the mother and her seven sons in the Book of Maccabees. Martha therefore makes prompt answer, "I know that he shall rise again in the resurrection at the last day." Jesus answered her in words which no mere mortal could have uttered,—words of a divine fullness of meaning,—"I am the Resurrection and the Life: he that believeth in me, though dead, shall live, and whosoever believeth in me is immortal."

In these words he claims to be the great source of Life,—the absolute Lord and Controller of all that relates to life, death, and eternity; and he makes the appeal to Martha's faith: "Believest thou this?" "Yea, Lord," she responds, "I believe thou art the Christ of God that should come into the world." And then she runs and calls her sister secretly, saying, "The Master is come and calleth for thee." As a majestic symphony modulates into a tender and pathetic minor passage, so the tone of the narrative here changes to the most exquisite pathos. Mary, attended by her weeping friends, comes and falls at Jesus's feet, and sobs out: "Lord, if thou hadst been here my brother had not died!"

It indicates the delicate sense of character which ever marked the intercourse of our Lord, that to this helpless, heart-broken child prostrate at his feet he addresses no appeal to reason or faith. He felt within himself the overwhelming power of that tide of emotion which for the time bore down both reason and faith in helpless anguish. With such sorrow there was no arguing, and Jesus did not attempt argument; for the story goes on: "When Jesus saw her weeping, and the Jews also weeping that came with her, he groaned in spirit and was troubled; and he said, Where have ye laid him? And they said, Lord, come and see. Jesus wept." Those tears interpreted for all time God's silence and apparent indifference to human suffering; and wherever Christ is worshiped as the brightness of the Father's glory and the express image of his person, they bear witness that the God who upholds the laws that wound and divide human affections still feels with us the sorrow which he permits. "In all our afflictions he is afflicted."

And now came the sublime and solemn scene when he who had claimed to be Resurrection and Life made good his claim. Standing by the grave he called, as he shall one day call to all the dead: "Lazarus, come forth!" And here the curtain drops over the scene of restoration.

We do not see this family circle again till just before the final scene of the great tragedy of Christ's life. The hour was at hand, of suffering, betrayal, rejection, denial, shame, agony, and death; and with the shadow of this awful cloud over his mind, Jesus comes for the last time to Jerusalem. To the eye of the thoughtless, Jesus was never so popular, so beloved, as at the moment when he entered the last week of his life at Jerusalem. Palm branches and flowers strewed his way, hosannas greeted him on every side, and the chief-priests and scribes said, "Perceive ye how ye prevail nothing? Behold the world is gone after him!" But the mind of Jesus was wrapped in that awful shade of the events that were so soon to follow.

He passes out, after his first day in Jerusalem, to Bethany, and takes refuge in this dear circle. There they make him a feast, and Martha served, but Lazarus, as a restored treasure, sits at the table. Then took Mary a pound of ointment, very precious, and anointed the head of Jesus, and anointed his feet with the ointment, and wiped them with her hair.

There is something in the action that marks the poetic and sensitive nature of Mary. Her heart was overburdened with gratitude and love. She longed to give something, and how little was there that she could give! She buys the most rare, the most costly of perfumes, breaks the vase, and sheds it upon his head. Could she have put her whole life, her whole existence, into that fleeting perfume and poured it out for him, she gladly would have done it. That was what the action said, and what Jesus understood. Forthwith comes the criticism of Judas: "What a waste! It were better to give the money to the poor than to expend it in mere sentimentalism." Jesus defended her with all the warmth of his nature, in words tinged with the presentiment of his approaching doom: "Let her alone; she is come aforehand to anoint my body for the burial." Then, as if deeply touched with the reality of that love which thus devoted itself to him, he adds, "Wheresoever this Gospel shall be preached throughout the world, there shall what this woman hath done be had in remembrance." The value set upon pure love, upon that unconsidering devotion which gives its best and utmost freely and wholly, is expressed in these words. A loving God seeks love; and he who thus spoke is he who afterward, when he appeared in glory, declared his abhorrence of lukewarmness in his followers: "I would thou wert cold or hot; because thou art lukewarm I will spew thee out of my mouth." It is significant of the change which had passed upon Martha that no criticism of Mary's action in this case came from her. There might have been a time when this inconsiderate devotion of a poetic nature would have annoyed her and called out remonstrance. In her silence we feel a sympathetic acquiescence.

After this scene we meet the family no more. Doubtless the three were among the early watchers upon the resurrection morning; — doubtless they were of the number among whom Jesus stood after the resurrection, saying, "Peace be unto you"; — doubtless they were of those who went out with him to the Mount of Olives when he was taken up into heaven; and doubtless they are now with him in glory: for it is an affecting thought that no human personality is ever lost or to be lost. In the future ages it may be our happiness to see and know those whose history has touched our hearts so deeply.

One lesson from this history we pray may be taken into every mourning heart. The Apostle says that Jesus upholds all things by the word of his power. The laws by which accident, sickness, loss, and death are constantly bringing despair and sorrow to sensitive hearts, are upheld by that same Jesus who wept at the grave of Lazarus, and who is declared to be Jesus Christ, the same yesterday and forever. When we see the exceeding preciousness of human love in his eyes, and realize his sympathetic nature, and then remember that he is

RESURRECTION AND LIFE, can we not trust him with our best beloved, and look to him for that hour of reunion which he has promised?

The doctrine of the resurrection of the body is a precious concession to human weakness and human love. How dear the outward form of our child, — how distressing to think we shall never see it again! But Christ promises we shall. Here is a mystery. St. Paul says, that as the seed buried in the earth is to the new plant or flower, so is our present mortal body to the new immortal one that shall spring from it. It shall be our friend, our child, familiar to us with all that mysterious charm of personal identity, yet clothed with the life and beauty of the skies; and then the Lord God will wipe away all tears from all faces.

AT BETHANY.

MARTHA *busy about household affairs.* MARY *sitting at the feet of* CHRISTUS.

MARTHA.

SHE sitteth idly at the Master's feet,
And troubles not herself with household cares.
'T is the old story. When a guest arrives
She gives up all to be with him; while I
Must be the drudge, make ready the guest-chamber,
Prepare the food, set everything in order,
And see that naught is wanting in the house.
She shows her love by words, and I by works.

MARY.

O Master! when thou comest, it is always
A Sabbath in the house. I cannot work;
I must sit at thy feet; must see thee, hear thee!
I have a feeble, wayward, doubting heart,
Incapable of endurance or great thoughts,
Striving for something that it cannot reach,
Baffled and disappointed, wounded, hungry;
And only when I hear thee am I happy,
And only when I see thee am at peace!

Stronger than I, and wiser, and far better
In every manner, is my sister Martha.
You see how well she orders everything
To make thee welcome; how she comes and goes,
Careful and cumbered ever with much serving,
While I but welcome thee with foolish words!
Whene'er thou speakest to me, I am happy;
When thou art silent, I am satisfied.
Thy presence is enough. I ask no more.
Only to be with thee, only to see thee,

Sufficeth me. My heart is then at rest.
I wonder I am worthy of so much.

MARTHA.

Lord, dost thou care not that my sister Mary
Hath left me thus to wait on thee alone?
I pray thee, bid her help me.

CHRISTUS.

Martha, Martha,
Careful and troubled about many things
Art thou, and yet one thing alone is needful!
Thy sister Mary hath chosen that good part,
Which never shall be taken away from her!

From the "DIVINE TRAGEDY," *H. W. Longfellow.*

THE SISTERS OF BETHANY.

MARTHA.

ITH joyful pride her heart is high:
Her humble chambers hold
The Man prophetic destiny
Long centuries hath foretold.

Poor, is he? Yes, and lowly born:
Her woman-soul is proud
To know and hail the coming morn
Before the eyeless crowd.

At her poor table will he eat?
He shall be servéd there
With honor and devotion meet
For any king that were.

'T is all she can; she does her part,
Profuse in sacrifice;
Nor knows that in her unknown heart
A better offering lies.

But many crosses she must bear;
Her plans are turned and bent;
Do all she can, things will not wear
The form of her intent.

With idle hands, and drooping lid,
See Mary sit at rest!
Shameful it was her sister did
No service for their guest.

But Martha one day Mary's lot
  Must share with hands and eyes;
Must — all her household cares forgot —
  Sit down as idly wise.

Erelong they both in Jesus' ear
  Shall make the self-same moan:
"Lord, if thou only hadst been here,
  My brother had not gone."

Then once will Martha set her word,
  Yet once, to bar his ways,
Crying, "By this he stinketh, Lord;
  He hath been dead four days."

When Lazarus drags his trammeled clay
  Forth with half-opened eyes,
Her buried best will hear, obey,
  And with the dead man rise.

MARY.

She sitteth at the Master's feet
  In motionless employ;
Her ears, her heart, — her soul complete
  Drinks in the tide of joy.

Ah! who but her the glory knows
  Of life, pure, high, intense,
Whose holy calm breeds awful shows
  Beyond the realm of sense!

In her still ear, his thoughts of grace
  Incarnate are in voice;
Her thoughts, the people of the place
  Receive them, and rejoice.

WOMAN IN SACRED HISTORY.

Her eyes, with heavenly reason bright,
  Are on the ground cast low;
It is his words of truth and light
  That sets them shining so.

But see! a face is at the door
  Whose eyes are not at rest;
A voice breaks in on wisest lore
  With petulant request.

"Lord," Martha says, "dost thou not care
  She lets me serve alone?
Tell her to come and take her share."
  Still Mary's eyes shine on.

Calmly she lifts a questioning glance
  To him who calmly heard;
The merest sign, she 'll rise at once,
  Nor wait the uttered word.

The other, standing by the door,
  Waits too what he will say.
His "Martha, Martha" with it bore
  A sense of coming *nay.*

Gently her troubled heart he chid;
  Rebuked its needless care;
Methinks her face she turned and hid
  With shame that bordered prayer.

What needful thing is Mary's choice,
  Nor shall be taken away?
There is but one, — 't is Jesus' voice;
  And listening she shall stay.

O, joy to every doubting heart,
  Doing the thing it would,
When He, the holy, takes its part,
  And calls its choice the good!

Rev. George MacDonald.

MARY'S CHOICE.

JESUS, engrave it on my heart,
That thou the one thing needful art;
I could from all things parted be,
But never, never, Lord, from thee.

Needful is thy most precious blood,
Needful is thy correcting rod,
Needful is thy indulgent care,
Needful thy all-prevailing prayer.

Needful thy presence, dearest Lord,
True peace and comfort to afford;
Needful thy promise to impart
Fresh life and vigor to my heart.

Needful art thou to be my stay
Through all life's dark and thorny way;
Nor less in death thou 'lt needful be,
To bring my spirit home to thee.

Then needful still, my God, my King,
Thy name eternally I 'll sing;
Glory and praise be ever his,
The one thing needful, Jesus is.

Anon.

THE BETTER PART.

LOVE divine, how sweet thou art!
When shall I find my willing heart
All taken up by thee?
I thirst, I faint, I die to prove
The greatness of redeeming love,
The love of Christ to me.

Stronger his love than death or hell;
Its riches are unsearchable;
The first-born sons of light
Desire in vain its depths to see;
They cannot reach the mystery,
The length and breadth and height.

God only knows the love of God;
O that it now were shed abroad
In this poor stony heart!
For love I sigh, for love I pine;
This only portion, Lord, be mine,—
Be mine this better part.

Forever would I take my seat
With Mary at the Master's feet;
Be this my happy choice;
My only care, delight, and bliss,
My joy, my heaven on earth, be this,—
To hear the Bridegroom's voice.

Anon.

SONNETS.

I. MARY AT THE FEET OF CHRIST.

OH! blest beyond all daughters of the earth!
What were the Orient's thrones to that low seat,
Where thy hushed spirit drew celestial birth?
Mary! meek listener at the Saviour's feet!
No feverish cares to that divine retreat
Thy woman's heart of silent worship brought,
But a fresh childhood, heavenly truth to meet,
With love, and wonder, and submissive thought.
Oh! for the holy quiet of thy breast,
'Midst the world's eager tones and footsteps flying!
Thou, whose calm soul was like a well-spring lying
So deep and still in its transparent rest,
That e'en when noontide burns upon the hills,
Some one bright solemn star all its lone mirror fills.

II. THE SISTERS OF BETHANY AFTER THE DEATH OF LAZARUS.

ONE grief, one faith, O sisters of the dead!
Was in your bosoms,—thou, whose steps, made fleet
By keen hope fluttering in the heart which bled,
Bore thee, as wings, the Lord of life to greet;
And thou, that duteous in thy still retreat
Didst wait his summons,—then with reverent love
Fall weeping at the blest Deliverer's feet,
Whom e'en to heavenly tears thy woe could move.
And which to *Him*, the All-Seeing and All-Just,
Was loveliest, that quick zeal, or lowly trust?
Oh! question not, and let no law be given
To those unveilings of its deepest shrine,
By the wrong spirit made in outward sign:
Free service from the heart is all in all to Heaven.

III. THE MEMORIAL OF MARY.

"Verily I say unto you, Wheresoever this gospel shall be preached in the whole world, there shall also this, that this woman hath done, be told for a memorial of her." — MATTHEW xxvi. 13. See, also, JOHN xii. 3.

THOU hast thy record in the monarch's hall,
And on the waters of the far mid-sea;
And where the mighty mountain-shadows fall,
The Alpine hamlet keeps a thought of thee:
Where'er, beneath some Oriental tree,
The Christian traveler rests, — where'er the child
Looks upward from the English mother's knee,
With earnest eyes in wondering reverence mild,
There art thou known, — where'er the Book of Light
Bears hope and healing, there, beyond all blight,
Is borne thy memory, and all praise above;
O, say what deed so lifted thy sweet name,
Mary! to that pure, silent place of fame?
One lowly offering of exceeding love.

Felicia Hemans.

MARY.

HER eyes are homes of silent prayer,
Nor other thought her mind admits
But he was dead, and there he sits,
And He that brought him back is there.

Then one deep love doth supersede
All other, when her ardent gaze
Roves from the living brother's face
And rests upon the Life indeed.

All subtle thought, all curious fears,
Borne down by gladness so complete,
She bows, she bathes the Saviour's feet
With costly spikenard and with tears.

Thrice blest whose lives are faithful prayers,
Whose loves in higher love endure;
What souls possess themselves so pure,
Or is there blessedness like theirs?

Alfred Tennyson.

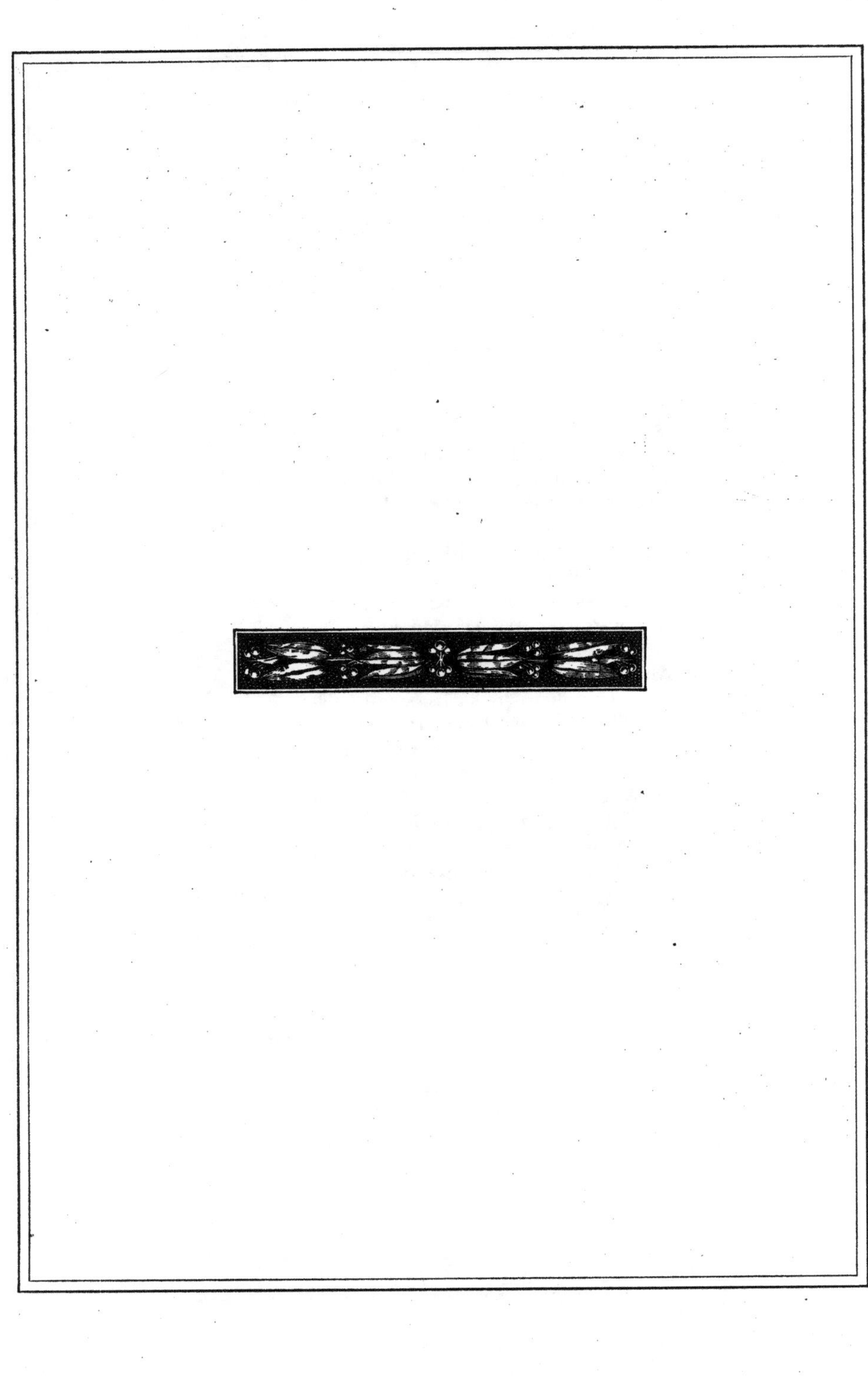

THE WIDOW'S MITE.

DUBUFE, *Pinx.* JEHENNE, *Lith.*

THE WIDOW'S MITE.

THE great peculiarity of the Bible is its unworldliness, — its contempt of what men usually care for, its care for what men usually despise. It is the book of the neglected, the suffering, the forgotten. This care of the lowly is asserted of the God of the Bible with a peculiar majesty of language: "For thus saith the high and lofty One that inhabiteth eternity, whose name is Holy: I dwell in the high and holy place, with him also that is of a contrite and humble spirit, to revive the heart of the contrite ones."

One of the most painful feelings of the heart is the sense of personal insignificance. To have the soul full of emotions that nobody cares for; to love and admire those who we are sensible can neither know nor regard our love; to long in some way to do something for a great and noble cause, and feel utterly poor and powerless, — be conscious that the utmost we can give and do is of no account, — is a smothering sorrow which would have no outlet were there not such a God as the Bible reveals.

The temple of the living God in Jerusalem was a miracle of riches and splendor. Tacitus speaks of it as a prodigy of opulence, celebrated through the world. It flamed like a constellation on the distant view of the tribes going up to worship in Jerusalem, a mountain of white marble and glittering gold. The pride and wealth of the returning Jews, whom the great festivals brought up to Jerusalem, were all the while enriching the treasury with magnificent offerings from every known land. The Jews were a trading people, scattered through all lands of the earth, who brought back, when they returned to their national festivals, contributions from all the riches of the world.

An incident of the life of Jesus shows him sitting by, watching the rich and prosperous as they went up and cast their offerings in; and he judged and valued very differently from any human spectator. "And looking up, he saw the rich men casting their gifts into the treasury. And he saw also a poor widow casting therein two mites, and he said, Of a truth I say unto you that this poor widow hath cast in more than they all. For all these have, of their abundance, cast in unto the offerings of God, but she of her penury hath cast in all the living she hath."

Here is the secret history of a life which mirrors thousands. A widow with none to work for her, poor, pinched to make the ends of life meet, restricted to the plainest food and scantiest clothing, and yet with all longing to do a little something for her country and her God! Patriotic and pious feeling burned in her heart; her two poor little mites could scarcely be more in the great splendid treasury than two snowflakes in the ocean, but she wanted to give them. Perhaps she did not hear the words of Jesus, and only went away with the feeling of a loving heart that she had done what she could.

But these words of Jesus were like the bread which he gave to feed the multitude. They were gathered up and stored in the record, that they might in all ages be food of encouragement for humble, unseen, faithful laborers in God's work. The words, "SHE HATH DONE WHAT SHE COULD," are meant for thousands whom the world knew not then and for thousands whom it knows not now. For example: In this house is an aged, bedridden woman, old and blind, utterly dependent on the care of a nurse; to be taken up, washed, dressed, fed like a helpless infant. But her mind remains strong and active, and day and night, through the dark and lonely hours, her thoughts travel towards the sanctuary where once she worshiped with the people of God. She keeps track of all the good works that are doing in the world; she is an eager, sympathetic listener, and counts all that is done for Christ's cause as so much personal gain. But the prayers of helplessness are the only aid she can give. During dark days and long wakeful night hours she lies praying, "Thy kingdom come, thy will be done;" she prays for this and that good cause; she prays for her church, for her minister, for her Christian friends, for her children and relatives; she prays because she cannot help it. But all this while she has the feeling, "What a poor, helpless, worthless creature I am! Why am I kept in a world where I can do nothing and am only a burden?" But in the eyes of Jesus those constant prayers of her weakness are so many offerings falling into the treasury of the temple; noiseless as snowflakes, uncounted in the world's estimate of forces, they are counted by him, and he says, "*She hath done what she could.*" Those silent prayers may be dearer in his eyes and in the eyes of witnessing angels than bursts of eloquence and floods of noisy zeal that attract the attention of the world.

In the town of Brunswick, Maine, is shown the lonely cottage where an old negro woman once lived, supported through days of helplessness by the alms of her neighbors. Yet the prayers of this woman, her example of patient suffering, the witness she was able to bear to the sustaining power of religious faith, caused her to be a blessing to the town and a power in the church. Her patient endurance, her loving spirit, and her prayers were offerings cast into the treasury that brought forth more good than the service of many more gifted and educated.

And so, through all the ranks and orders of this busy world, the eye of Jesus is on the *unnoticed* workers and givers. In this respect the service of God differs from all other service. In human affairs the small workers are overlooked. It is the general, the governor, the orator, the poet, that gets the praise and is supposed to do the work. The poor common soldier that fell and bled to death uncomplaining and alone is not remembered, the glory goes to the officer who planned the battle. The poor widow who gave her only son to die for his country is forgotten in the hour of triumph and glory.

But in Christ's final triumph there will be no such overlooking. He tells us that not so much as the gift of a cup of cold water shall lose its reward. As he saw the pearl of great price in the silent gift of this poor widow, so he is still going forth a "merchantman seeking goodly pearls," and in the day when he shall make up his jewels, how many such obscure and neglected offerings will be brought to light!

The tenderness of Jesus for the widow is often shown in his

history. The law of Moses manifests a special care over the helplessness of widowhood, and the Jews were taught both by the law and the prophets to regard the widow as peculiarly under God's protection. Jesus was the ideal Jew of his times. All that was tender and humane in the institutes of Moses shone forth in him with an added grace and benignity. Hence we find so many instances of his peculiar care for this class of helpless sufferers: it was the only son of a widow that he called back from the dead; it was a poor widow besetting an unjust judge that was his illustration of the prevailing force of prayer; he indignantly denounces those who devour widows' houses. It is inferred from many incidents in the sacred narrative that his own mother was left a widow before the beginning of his public career, and thus personal knowledge of the trials of such added to his feeling.

The name of the woman in this little story is not told us. She drifts before us as the type of a great class never wanting in life, —the poor, hard-working, little-regarded widow,—and what was said of her may be the comfort of thousands. It may have been among the blest surprises of heaven, after this woman passed the golden gate, to find her poor little offerings garnered up in God's loving remembrance, as we keep the plaything our sick and suffering child gives us as its last love-gift. This generous God, who thus cares for the least and lowest, is the God revealed in Jesus. "He is our God forever; he will be our guide until death."

THE WIDOW'S MITE.

T is the fruit of waking hours,
When others are asleep,
When moaning round the low thatched roof
The winds of winter creep.

It is the fruit of summer days
Passed in a gloomy room,
When others are abroad, to taste
The pleasant morning bloom.

'T is given from a scanty store,
And missed while it is given;
'T is given, for the claims of earth
Are less than those of Heaven.

Few, save the poor, feel for the poor;
The rich know not how hard
It is to be of needful food
And neebful rest debarred.

Their paths are paths of plenteousness;
They sleep on silk and down,
And never think how heavily
The weary head lies down.

They know not of the scanty meal,
With small pale faces round;
No fire upon the cold, damp hearth,
When snow is on the ground.

They never by their window sit
And see the gay pass by;
Yet take their weary work again,
Though with a mournful eye.

The rich, they give — they miss it not;
A blessing cannot be
Like that which rests, thou widowed one,
Upon thy gift and thee!

Letitia E. Landon.

THE WIDOW'S OFFERING.

"She of her penury hath cast in all the living that she had."

STRONG in faith! thus cheerfully to fling,
With unreluctant hand, thine earthly all
Upon God's altar! Did no fear appall,
No dread arise of future suffering,
Of anguish such as poverty may bring
To the worn frame, o'ertasked? No, — for between
Thy faith and God no cloud did intervene.
Thou couldst not doubt the fullness of that Spring
Whence flowed thy sure supply! Thrice happy thou,
On whose unquestioning faith the Saviour's eye
Looked and approved! Thy record is on high, —
And taught by thee, my doubting soul shall bow,
And own with shame its former fears unjust,
Clinging henceforth to God in perfect trust.

William H. Burleigh.

THE VALUE OF A LITTLE.

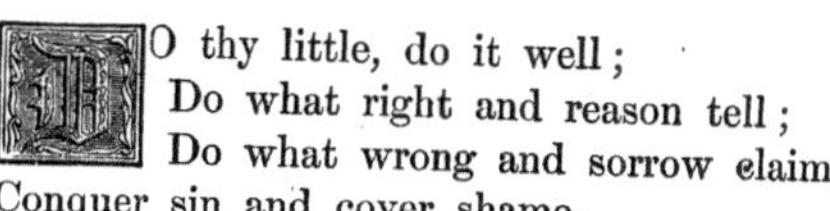

DO thy little, do it well;
Do what right and reason tell;
Do what wrong and sorrow claim,
Conquer sin and cover shame.

Do thy little, though it be
Dreariness and drudgery;
They whom Christ apostles made,
"Gathered fragments" when he bade.

Do thy little: never mind
Though thy brethren be unkind,
Though the men who ought to smile
Mock and taunt thee for a while.

Do thy little: never fear
While thy Saviour standeth near;
Let the world its javelins throw,
On thy way undaunted go.

Do thy little: God hath made
Million leaves for forest shade;
Smallest stars their glory bring;
God employeth everything.

Do thy little; and when thou
Feelest on thy pallid brow,
Ere has fled the vital breath,
Cold and damp the sweat of death, —

Then the little thou hast done,
Little battles thou hast won,

Little masteries achieved,
Little want with care relieved,
Little words in love expressed,
Little wrongs at once confessed,
Little favors kindly done,
Little toils thou didst not shun,
Little graces meekly worn,
Little slights with patience borne, —

These shall crown the pillowed head,
Holy light upon thee shed;
These are treasures that shall rise
Far beyond the smiling skies.

Anonymous.

THE TWO MITES.

TWO mites, two drops, yet all her house and land,
Fall from a steady heart, though trembling hand;
The other's wanton wealth flows high and brave,
The other cast away, she only gave.

Richard Crashaw.

LYDIA.

BROCHART, *Pinx.* JEHENNE, *Lith.*

WOMEN OF THE APOSTOLIC CHURCH.

THE Christian Church developed as blossom and fruit of the Jewish one. It took all that centuries of growth and care had done for human society, and, giving to it a warmer soil and higher culture, developed from it a richer and higher life.

The Jewish dispensation had already allotted to woman a position of great respect and consideration. We have seen in these studies, that, according to the usages of the Mosaic dispensation, woman could equally with man be recognized as a recipient of the Divine gift of prophecy, and through this recognized as an authoritative teacher. We have seen, indeed, the sister of Moses associated with him in the prophetic office during the time that the Jewish system was being consolidated, and spoken of in the prophetic writings as sent of God equally with her brothers Moses and Aaron: "I sent before you Moses and Aaron and Miriam."

It appears in the history of our Lord, that the customs of society in relation to the sacred or religious offices of women were such that it gave no scandal and excited no comment that a band of pious women accompanied the preaching tours of Jesus through Palestine. The probability seems to be that under his direction they were agents in that ministry of consolation which he declared to be his peculiar mission.

When we consider how little it has been the study and office of so-called Christian ecclesiastical power to comfort the poor and sorrowful, it excites a sort of wonder, in view of the first declaration which our Lord made of the purpose of his mission, at Nazareth, that this and nothing else was mentioned.

"The Spirit of the Lord God is upon me, because he hath appointed me to preach the good news to the poor, — he hath sent me to heal the broken-hearted, to preach deliverance to the captives and recovering of sight to the blind, to set at liberty them that are bruised."

In this ministry of mercy it was particularly right and meet that women should be associated. We find, from the record of the Evangelist, that these women, some of them of high position and of liberal means, gave contributions to the common stock out of which the traveling mission was supported. It also appears, from incidental mention, that Jesus not only helped the suffering by miraculous power, but that out of the family purse, which was kept for common expenses, he was wont to give alms to the poor, so that at the Last Supper his enigmatical words to Judas were supposed by them to refer to some deed of almsgiving.

In the fact that the progress of the mission family of the Lord through the country was so largely one of relief and consolation, we see a still further reason why it excited no remark or scandal. These women were so evidently laborers for others, helpers and comforters of the distressed and suffering, their life was so unselfish and devoted to the good of others, that no one felt disposed to speak against them. They were holy women, — a recognized order in the old Jewish church, rising into a recognized order in the Christian life with the development of the larger liberty of Christianity.

In the very first sermon preached after the resurrection of Jesus, the first public announcement of the genius of the new dispensation, the Apostle Peter quotes the words of the prophet Joel: "It shall come to pass in the last days, saith God, that I will pour out my spirit upon all flesh, and your sons and your daughters shall prophesy; and on my servants and on my handmaids I will pour out my spirit, and they shall prophesy."

After the resurrection, when the disciples assembled together to pray for the promised gift of the Holy Spirit, these holy women are especially mentioned as being present, with Mary the mother of Jesus at their head.

Subsequently in the history of the apostolic labors we come

upon traces of these devout women, who seemed to share the mission labors of the Apostles, or to minister as deaconesses in individual churches. They were sometimes married women, who traveled with and shared the labors of their husbands. Such a pair were Priscilla and Aquila, who are frequently noticed in the Book of Acts. The name of the wife is generally put first, perhaps from the fact that the woman was the more energetic of the two; and it appears, from the narrative in Acts, that Priscilla and Aquila were both united in the theological training of the eloquent Apollos, whom they "took," and to whom they expounded the way of God more perfectly. Paul first stayed with this pair in Corinth, working with them at their common business of tent-making. On the Apostle's departure from Corinth the faithful pair accompanied him on his missionary labors, and remained with him awhile at Ephesus, where they met with Apollos. Afterwards it appears, from Romans xvi. 3, that this couple had settled themselves in Rome, where they are once more mentioned by the Apostle as his "helpers in Christ Jesus": he adds, "Who for my life have laid down their own necks; unto whom not only I give thanks, but all the churches of the Gentiles."

In the same chapter of Romans we find mention of another holy woman holding a definite rank in the Church: "I commend unto you Phœbe our sister, which is a deaconess of the church at Cenchrea." Cenchrea was the seaport of Corinth, and it is probable that the churches of Corinth and Cenchrea were identical. Phœbe, it appears, traveled independently, and came with a recognized position to the Christian Church at Rome; and the manner in which the Apostle speaks of her sufficiently defines the work of her office: "She hath been a succorer of many, and of myself also."

The Apostle goes on sending messages to other members of the Christian body, among which occurs this: "Greet Mary, who bestowed much labor upon us. Salute Andronicus and Junia, my fellow-prisoners. Salute Triphena and Triphosa, who labor in the Lord. Salute the beloved Persis, who labored much in the Lord. Salute Julia and Nereus and his sister."

We have also in the Acts the account of Dorcas, whose sudden death, putting an end to a fruitful ministry of consolation, caused mourning through the church at Joppa, and who was miraculously restored to life by the Apostle Peter.

Here we have the image of the Christian woman of those days, with the poor weeping around her lifeless body and showing sorrowfully the coats and garments she made for them while she was yet living.

We have a somewhat minute account of Lydia, a distinguished convert, made by the preaching of the Apostle Paul at Philippi.

It appears from the story that a colony of Jews were established at Philippi, a city of Macedonia, and that the worship of the synagogue was held there on the Sabbath day. The Apostle's narrative says: "On the Sabbath day we went out of the city by the river-side, to a place where prayer was wont to be made; and we sat down and spake unto the women that resorted thither. And a certain woman named Lydia, a seller of purple, of the city of Thyatira, which worshiped God, heard us, whose heart the Lord opened that she attended to the things that were spoken by Paul. And when she was baptized with her household, she said, If ye have judged me to be faithful to the Lord, come unto my house and abide there. And she constrained us."

And now occurred an event of striking import. There was in the city a girl who, in our modern times, would be called a medium, and who, as such mediums do in our days, brought her masters much gain by soothsaying. This girl followed Paul and his associates through the streets, crying aloud, "These men are the servants of the most high God, which show unto us the way of salvation."

It is recorded that so far from wishing to avail himself of such testimony in his mission, Paul was grieved, and turned and said to the spirit which possessed her, "I command thee in the name of Jesus Christ to come out of her," and he came out the same hour. And when her masters saw that the hope of their gains was gone, they raised a popular tumult, and led the Apostles before a magistrate; and they were scourged and cast into prison.

When they had been miraculously delivered from the prison they returned again to the house of Lydia, where they remained some time, comforting and strengthening the disciples.

This is all we know of the history of Lydia. Renan, in his "Apostles," conjectures a marriage between her and St. Paul, founding the idea on St. Paul's assertion, "Have we not a right to lead about a sister, a wife?"

He seems to think and assume with an easy air of knowledge, that, because St. Paul asserted his right to have a wife, and because Lydia would have made a good one, there is therefore no doubt of the fact, and with a singular ignoring (for a critic) of all lack of evidence, he alludes to it forthwith as a historical verity too well known to need proof.

In the Epistle to the Corinthians, St. Paul expresses a deliberate choice of a single life, not from any superstitious or ascetic notions of the superior purity of such a life, but simply as enabling him with less distraction to devote himself to the missionary work. So far as there is any evidence, therefore, it is in favor of Paul's celibacy. In this same epistle he asserts his right, if he saw fit, to lead about a sister, a wife, as well as other Apostles, or as the brother of the Lord, or Cephas. But he asserts his right to that which at the same time he disclaims on grounds of higher expediency. Life is too short, affords too little rest in such a work as he projects, to leave space for family ties. "The time is short," he says; "it remaineth that those that have wives be as though they had none, and they that weep as though they wept not, and they that rejoice as though they rejoiced not."

Of the somewhat striking figure of Lydia, then, we can only make out thus much, — a vigorous, large-hearted, Greek woman, perhaps and probably of Jewish parentage, and evidently a convert to the Jewish religion, who embraced Christianity at once, and became in a large and generous sense a ministering mother in the Church.

That there was afterwards a church in her native city of Thyatira may have been the consequence of her Christian enthusiasm and zeal, but there is no further distinct record of the fact. She was a trader in purple and fine linen; probably her traffic had its center in Thyatira, and she visited Philippi in the way of trade, where she met the Apostle and received the new religion.

One such woman as she seems in the history to be, so prompt, so energetic, so courageous and fearless, gifted with wealth and a vigorous temperament, and enkindled with religious fervor, is quite a sufficient cause to account for the existence of a Christian church in Thyatira. But there is not in the Acts of the Apostles, nor in all the Epistles of Paul, a single fact or incident which would lead us to suppose any wifely companionship with Paul on her part. She was a noble and efficient fellow-worker, however, and may have been one of the women afterwards mentioned in the Epistle to the Philippians, who labored with him in the gospel in that place, and whose names were in "the Book of Life."

DORCAS.

IF I might guess, then guess I would:
Amid the gathered folk
This gentle Dorcas one day stood,
And heard what Jesus spoke.

She saw the woven, seamless coat,—
Half envious for his sake;
"O happy hands," she said, "that wrought
That honored thing to make!"

Her eyes with longing tears grow dim;
She never can come nigh,
To work one service poor for Him
For whom she glad would die!

But hark! he speaks a mighty word:
She hearkens now indeed!
"When did we see thee naked, Lord,
And clothe thee in thy need?

"The King shall answer, Inasmuch
As to my brothers ye
Did it,—even to the least of such,—
Ye did it unto me."

Home, home she went, and plied the loom,
And Jesus' poor arrayed.
She died,—they wept about the room
And showed the coats she made.

Rev. George Macdonald.

"A WOMAN"—"A DISCIPLE."

Acts ix. 36.

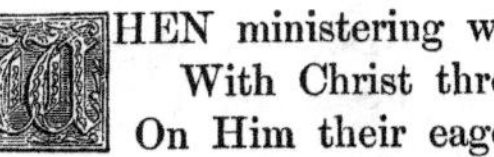

HEN ministering women went
With Christ through Galilee,
On Him their eager service spent,
Their substance lavished free,
We know not if there went with these
Discipleship to claim;
Enough, we know thy ministries
Did win for thee the name.

"Woman"—"Disciple"—for good deeds,
Wrought by thy loving hands,
That ministered to lowly needs,
Thy name on record stands,
Embalmed in fragrant love and tears
And everlasting praise,
That down to our far distant years
Doth fresh memorials raise.

Woman! Disciple! still the same
Christ claims your ministering;
Still tender, fearless, over shame
Your love's fair garment fling!
Still let your helpful hands be swift
To bless and beautify;
The lowest services do lift
Up to His throne on high.

Anonymous.

ST. PAUL AND LYDIA.

"And on the sabbath we went out of the city by a river-side, where prayer was wont to be made; and we sat down, and spake unto the women that resorted thither." — *Acts* xvi. 13.

ETHINKS that holy man,
Well pleased, creation's page would scan;
And loved in Nature's beauteous face
Her Maker's lineaments to trace:
For this he fled the noisy street,
The balm of evening's breath to greet, —
To sun him in the smile that glowed
From yonder western sky,
And half forget the dark abode
Of man and misery.
Soft and sweet are the sounds that then
Steal out from copse-wood, fold, and glen;
Those mellow voices that commingle
With the small brooklet's silver song,
That, dancing down o'er rock and shingle,
Carols its happiness along.

But sadly Paul addressed his friend, —
"Hear'st thou that vesper-hymn ascend,
Pealing into the radiant skies
Its pure and sinless sacrifice?
Alas, to miss those strains among
The accents of the human tongue!"
"Nay," Silas cried, "e'en now methought
Echoes of gentlest speech I caught!
And list again! more sweet and clear
They melt upon my listening ear:
'T is woman's voice, — that liquid tone
An angel might not blush to own; —
O that an angel's theme were given
To notes so harmonized with heaven!

But haste we thither! not in vain
Is breathed on high that votive strain;
The heart that owns devotion's power
In such a scene, at such an hour,
Needs but a glimpse of clearer light
To guide its wandering homage right."

'Twas a lone spot, that shrine of prayer, —
Some river-nymph's deserted haunt,
Whose sacred springlet, diamond clear,
Welled bubbling from its rocky font;
And near, all lovely in decay,
A little shrine and altar lay; —
Ay, lovely! though the Grecian maid
No more in summer's spoils arrayed
The light Ionian colonnade;
For nature's wild and simple taste
Had well those withering gifts replaced;
Perennial chaplets court the breeze,
Festooned along the crumbling frieze;
Or, climbing up each shattered shaft,
Gayly the purple blossoms laughed;
Or from the walls peeped shy between
The ivy's everlasting green.

A moment paused the pilgrim twain
Upon the threshold of the fane:
A moment, fixed as by a spell,
They listened to the choral swell;
And, O, how wakened memory's chords
Made answer to those thrilling words!

Psalm.

How lovely is thy dwelling-place,
O Lord our God!
Our spirit longs and faints to trace
The courts thy saints have trod.

ST. PAUL AND LYDIA.

The sparrow and the swallow there
Have found a nest:
Ah, why are we forbid to share
That holy place of rest?

The great and holy One on high
Inhabiteth eternity,
Nor needs a human shrine;
Yet, Spirit, boundless as thou art,
Within the meek and contrite heart
Thy presence deigns to shine!

'T were long to tell what greeting passed;
And how the twilight hours fled fast,
And still, with eager eye and ear,
That simple band pressed round to hear;
And how the Apostle wove
With whatsoe'er in woman's breast
Wakes deep and tender interest
His wondrous tale of love.
He told, how in that awful hour
Of Satan's brief permitted power,
When Vengeance on her victim's head
Her seven-fold vials sternly shed,
When foes the hand of menace shook,
And friends betrayed, denied, forsook,
Then woman, meekly constant still,
Followed to Calvary's fatal hill;—
Yes, followed where the boldest failed,
Unmoved by threat or sneer;
For faithful woman's love prevailed
O'er helpless woman's fear.

In sorrow and in peril tried,
She was the last to quit his side;
And, when the bloody scene was closed,
And low in dust her friend reposed,
The first was she to seek his tomb,
With balm of Araby's perfume:
She fondly thought that honored form
To rescue from the loathsome worm;

And little dreamed, how death in vain
Had cast his adamantine chain
O'er One who came his might to quell
Even in his gloomiest citadel.
And high reward her zeal hath won:
"Woman!" She started at the tone;—
"Mary!" She turned,—beheld,—adored;—
'T was He, to life and her restored.

Thus on the pure and patient mind,
Quiet in joy, in grief resigned,
Fraught with rich blessing from above,
Beams the benignest smile of love;
E'en as the lake's unruffled breast
Makes pillow for the sunbeam's rest,
While waves, in wild disorder driven,
Roll dark beneath the clearest heaven.
O woman! though thy fragile form
Bows like the willow to the storm,
Ill-suited in unequal strife
To brave the ruder scenes of life;
Yet, if the power of grace divine
Find in thy lowly heart a shrine,
Then, in thy very weakness strong,
Thou winn'st thy noiseless course along:
Weaving thy influence with the ties
Of sweet domestic charities,
And softening haughtier spirits down
By happy contact with thine own.

Yes! all were blest, whose every sense
Drank in the heaven-taught eloquence;
For, ah! my feeble strain doth wrong
To speech so liquid and so strong,
Bearing the willing soul along
    Upon its powerful stream:
Yet one a holier bliss confessed,—
One, to whose meek and placid breast
No human eloquence addressed
    The great Apostle's theme:

ST. PAUL AND LYDIA.

God opened Lydia's heart to feel
And bow beneath his own appeal:
He cleared the mists of doubt away,
Poured in fair truth's celestial day;
And all the trembling soul subdued
To hope and love and gratitude.
Not idle were the tears that glistened,
As silently she sat and listened, —
Such streams as fancy bids to flow
At tale of visionary woe, —
They issued from the warm heart's spring,
Affection's earnest offering,
And told her speechless thanks to Heaven
For mercy found, and sin forgiven.

When all their homeward way had ta'en
She lingered in the lonely fane,
And humbly urged her kind request, —
"O, were it worthy of such quest,
Deign, holy pilgrims, deign to share
My quiet roof, and homely fare!"
And there they sojourned, pleased awhile
To bask in friendship's grateful smile.
How sweet at morn or evening's close
The mutual prayer and praise arose!
What thoughts of heavenly peace had birth
In converse round that happy hearth!
And when on each devoted head
The pure baptismal stream was shed,
The eternal spirit winged its flight
To seal and bless the solemn rite!
In sooth that home was hallowed ground;
Hope spread her rainbow wings around,
And cheered with ever-smiling face
The adopted family of grace.

From "ST. PAUL AT PHILIPPI," *by Rev. Thos. E. Hankinson.*

WOMEN OF SCRIPTURE.

YOUR tents are desolate; your stately steps,
Of all their choral dances have not left
One trace beside the fountains; your full cup
Of gladness and of trembling, each alike
Is broken: yet, amidst undying things,
The mind still keeps your loveliness, and still
All the fresh glories of the early world
Hang round you in the spirit's pictured halls,
Never to change!

Felicia Hemans.

APPENDIX.

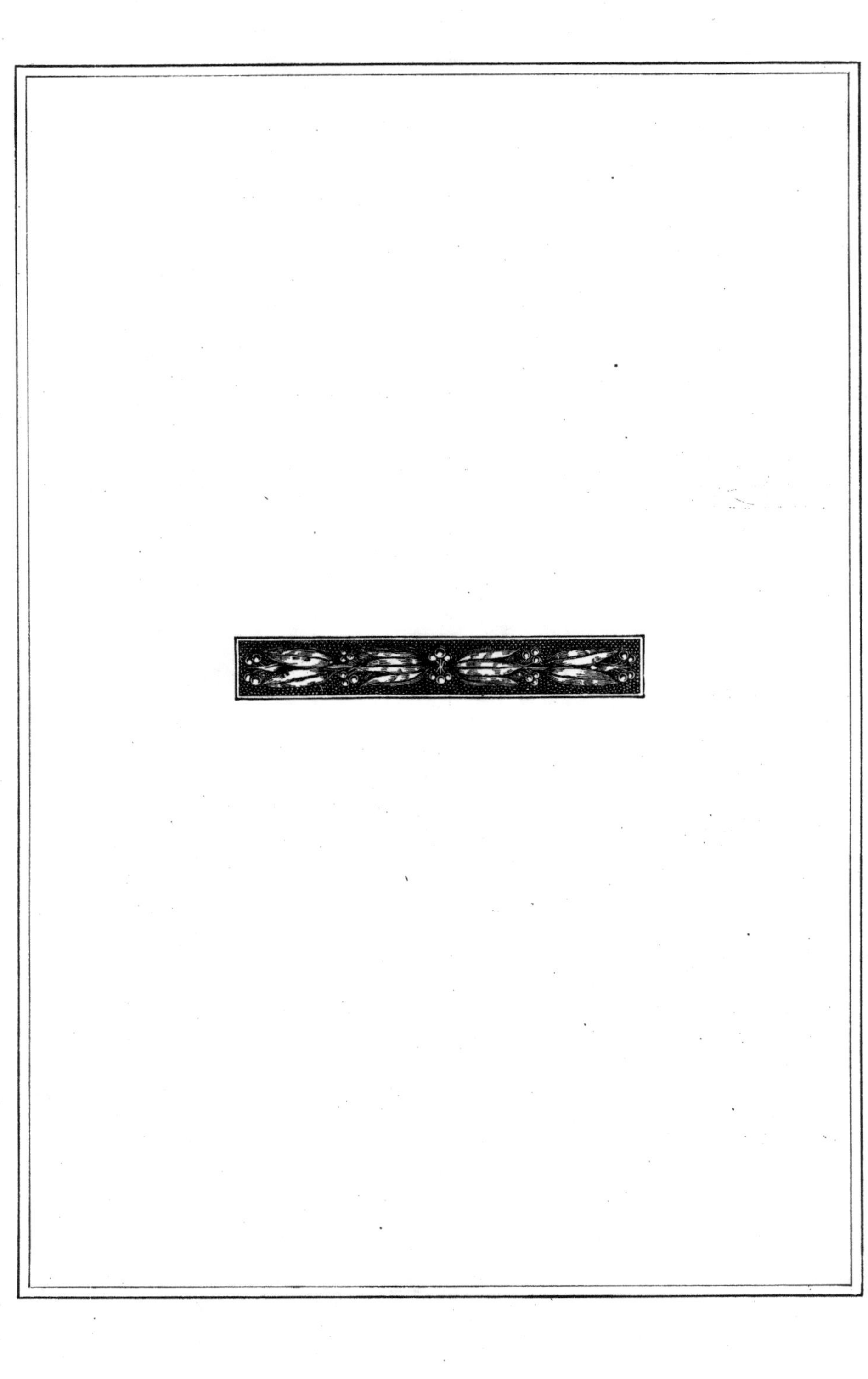

DESCRIPTIVE LIST OF ILLUSTRATIONS.

THE notable characters among the women of Bible history present so attractive and variable a theme for pictorial representation, that they have been several times grouped in book form, both in Europe and America, within the past twenty years. The freshness of the present publication, therefore, consists, not in the subject, but in its mode of treatment.

In seeking material to illustrate Mrs. Stowe's interesting sketches, two purposes have been kept in view: first, the securing of a series of pictures which, by a judicious selection among different schools and epochs of art, might give a more original and less conventional presentation of the characters than could be had were all the illustrations conceived by the same mind, or executed by the same hand; and, secondly, the choice of such pictorial subjects as were well adapted to reproduction in colors, so as to represent as perfectly as possible, by the rapidly maturing art of oil color-printing, the real ideas of the painters. The guiding principles of selection have been *aptness of design* and a rich *variety of effect.*

It will be seen that, in pursuit of this purpose, some pictures of world-wide renown have been here reproduced in whole or in part, — the desirable being always limited by the practicable: examples of these are the beautiful "Magdalen" of BATONI, and the main portion of that most wonderful of all pictures, the "Sistine Madonna" of RAPHAEL. The only possible excuse for abridging this glorious design is the desire to give some slight idea of its color-effect to the thousands who have known it only through engravings, and who could never know it otherwise, unless in some such way as this. Among our illustrations are copies of celebrated paintings of more modern date, by the great painters of France, Germany, and England: such as PAUL DELAROCHE'S graceful scene on the Nile, where Miriam watches little Moses, exposed in the bulrushes; HORACE VERNET'S terrible "Judith with the Head of Holofernes"; BAADER'S remorseless "Delilah"; and GOODALL'S lovely picture of "Mary, the Mother of Our Lord," with her offering of two doves in the Temple. Of still another class are those which have been adapted, because of their appositeness, to illustrate subjects for which they were not originally painted: of these, LANDELLE'S "Fellah Woman" well shows the Oriental style and youthful sweetness of *Rebekah* at the fountain; and the "Dancing-Girl" of VERNET-LECOMTE may fairly represent the costume and beauty of Salome, the *Daughter of Herodias.* In addition to these varieties, the sixteen plates include several which were designed and painted expressly for this work. One of the most pleasing is "Ruth," by DEVEDEUX of Paris. It is accounted also a special advantage that the "Queen Esther" and the "Martha and Mary"—two very striking and effective pictures—are from the studio of BOULANGER, who shares with Gérome the highest eminence as a delineator of the peculiar and beautiful features of the Orient.

In order to give some idea of the care taken in the reproduction of these subjects, it may be stated that (except where the original paintings themselves were accessible) in every case an accurate copy in oils was painted by a skillful artist, and this, together with photographs from the original pictures, the best impressions of the best engravings, etc., formed the basis on which JEHENNE, the artist-lithographer, founded his conscientious work. Each subject is produced by a series of color-printings. The delicacy and difficulty of this art may be better appreciated by remembering that, while the painter has always at hand his palette, with its numberless pigments and shades of color, for the patient elaboration of the picture, the lithographer has to analyze the work which has thus grown up by infinite touches under the painter's brush, and must study to concentrate as much as possible the effects of each single color in a single stone, — which can print or touch the picture but once. The final effect is of course produced by the superposition of colors and shades of color one upon another. It requires an artistic sensibility and training by no means ordinary, to detect in a painting the three or four reds, the varying yellows, the different blues, the several shades of gray, etc., and to put them upon different stones, each accurately correct in position and true in tone and intensity; so that, when printed one upon another, to the number of fifteen, twenty, and sometimes thirty and forty, separate stones, they shall in the general effect reproduce the original painting, in all its harmonies and contrasts, with its subtle variations of color, tint, and shade. The art which can thus transfer the painter's minute and painful toil to the breadth and rapidity of mechanical reproduction, making accessible to thousands the great creations of genius, instead of leaving them imprisoned in the single copy which only the rich purchaser may possess, is itself an art, and claims recognition of the lovers of art.

Below is a descriptive list of these illustrations, with notices of their subjects, and the artists by whom they were originally executed.

No. I. *Mary the Mother of Jesus.* Frederick Goodall (England; b. 1822).

This is one of the few modern pictures of the Virgin which are at once original and fine. The Mariolatry of the Roman Catholic Church imparted a pure and sweet element to the artistic pursuits of the devoted monks and pious painters of the fifteenth century, and by the general demand for altar-pieces and church pictures of the Virgin or the Holy Family, impelled even the most worldly to aim in that direction, thus giving the impulse of an age to the study of a single subject; but this has been superseded by the broader and more general culture of the present day, which fills the art-world with an infinitude of subjects. The production of a fine picture of the Virgin at this day, therefore, is something very unusual. Goodall's picture embodies a most exquisite conception, and in its engraved form has had a large popularity, while receiving high praise from the critics. This presentation of the Virgin, going into the temple with her offering of two doves, is one of the most delicate and beautiful of the entire series. The exceeding simplicity of the design and coloring gives it an effect of purity, while the face is tender, thoughtful, and in every way attractive. The softness of the drapery and the gentle gradations of light are special features of this most charming subject.

II. *Sara the Princess.* CHARLES BROCHART (Paris, France; b. 1829).

This is a well-chosen subject, from the easel of an artist who has taken high rank in the modern Oriental school of French painters. Brochart is especially well known as a painter of beautiful female faces. Greeks, Turks, Persians, Syrians, — all the races of the Levant, — furnish him types of his pictures. In the present subject (an original painting for the book) is depicted "Sara the Princess," the nomad queen, wife of the wealthy Abram, — the "woman fair to look upon." The repose of manner, the placid, dignified beauty of the face and form, the picturesqueness of costume, and the romantic features of the Eastern landscape background, — with its well and palm-trees, its flocks and tents, its long stretch of desert and distant boundary of mountains, — combine to make an attractive and characteristic picture. Perhaps its most marked trait is the rich and agreeable harmony of color which pervades it; producing, at once, a very pleasing effect and a singularly truthful representation of the atmospheric warmth and glow of the land of the palm.

III. *Hagar and Ishmael.* CHRISTIAN KOEHLER (Werben, Germany; b. 1809, d. 1861).

This picture is strong and expressive, rather than attractive. The depth of the greenish-blue sky and the barrenness of the indicated landscape give an intensity to the conception of the desolate mother, clasping passionately her sturdy and unconscious little outcast son. It is, indeed, as Mrs. Stowe calls it, "a striking pendant to the picture of Sara the Princess," for Hagar the Slave is the embodiment of all that is despairing and forlorn. Koehler, the artist, is prominent among the painters of the Düsseldorf school, which during the past fifty years has filled a large place in the history of European art. That little town at the junction of the Düssel and the Rhine, although important as a center of railway and river traffic, has gained its chief name as the birthplace of the artist Cornelius and the poet Heine, and as the seat of one of the most eminent of German art-schools. The original painting of the present subject is now in the Civic Gallery of Düsseldorf. It was painted at Leinwand in 1843.

IV. *Rebekah the Bride.* CHARLES LANDELLE (Laval, France; b. 1815).

This is another of those charming subjects which the enterprise and graceful art of the French have brought from the Orient. Landelle, from whom several of our illustrations have been taken, has always been especially successful in his treatment of Eastern scenes, having spent years in his studies around the farther shores of the Mediterranean Sea, both in Syria and Africa. The original painting at present under consideration (1866) is entitled "Femme Fellah," and represents one of the young women of the Nubian tribe of Fellahs, resting at the well before taking upon her head the earthen water-pot which she has just filled. The costume is rich and appropriate, while the lovely face and figure may well be used to illustrate the maidenly grace of "Rebekah at the Fountain."

V. *Leah and Rachel.* JEAN FRANÇOIS PORTAËLS (Vilvorde, Belgium; b. 1820).

Like others of the Belgian artists, Portaëls found in Paris a more brilliant and successful patronage than his own little country could afford; though Belgium boasts of some very choice collections of art. Portaëls is not a remarkably original genius, but his pictures always show thought and care. In the Bible story, Leah, the "tender-eyed," became the wife of Jacob seven years before he attained the hand of his chosen love, Rachel the "beautiful." The fruitful motherhood of Leah is suggested by the merry boy climbing over her shoulders, while Rachel's gentle face shows the sadness which afterwards became almost an agony of grief, and found utterance in her supplication, "Give me children, or I die." The grouping is natural, simple, and effective.

VI. *Miriam and Moses.* PAUL DELAROCHE (France; b. 1797, d. 1856).

This is one of the most famous designs of one of the most fertile artists of France. Delaroche, who began his studies as a landscape-painter, soon abandoned that field and betook himself to the more congenial pursuit of historic art. A genius of natural force, he adopted a style equally free from the formalities of the classic school (represented by David), which was just passing away, and the romantic school, which was just coming up. His rather melancholic turn of mind, while it led him generally to select, from the great multitude of striking scenes in modern history, subjects of a somber tone (like his "Joan of Arc in Prison," "Strafford on the Way to the Scaffold," "Marie Antoinette before the Revolutionary Tribunal," etc.), did not hinder him from a wonderful mastery of his art in all the elements of correct drawing, effective color, and power of composition, nor from the attainment of more scholarly and professional knowledge than most of his associates, who greatly venerated his opinions and his work. In his riper later years, he occasionally took up subjects from sacred history; and among these was the picture under consideration. The original painting has often been engraved, but its freshness and beauty are best shown by reproducing its soft and delicate coloring. The careful sister, watching through the rushes, and the indistinct form of the mother on the bank above, are in exquisite contrast to the quietude of the babe in his basket on the waters of the placid Nile.

VII. *Deborah.* Charles Landelle (Laval, France; b. 1815).

This is from a painting of Velleda, the great prophetess of the Druids of ancient Gaul, and is admirably adapted to represent the splendid vigor and earnestness of the Prophetess of Israel. The background of the original painting shows the gloomy, murky depths of a cavern, while the sacrificial flame burns on an altar of hewn rock. These accessories have been somewhat modified, and a wholesomer atmosphere of sunlight and verdure are given, to better suggest the *locale* of the Syrian land. But the grand form, the noble face, and the inspired attitude of the original figure have been scrupulously retained, as true indications of the prophetic fire.

VIII. *Delilah.* Louis Marie Baader (Lannion, France).

A most ungrateful subject, here portrayed with singular strength and concentration of purpose. It is a peculiar combination, both in color and in the grouping and suggestiveness of details. The time selected by the artist appears to have been just after the shearing of Samson's hair by the wily woman, for some curling jetty locks lie on the floor; and the upset chair seems to indicate the sudden but futile resistance which had been made by the disendowed athlete before he was led out bound by the Philistines. The cold, hard look of the face and the unrelenting will expressed by the slender but steady arm and the firm, supporting hand, half buried in the cushion, instantly compel the attention of the beholder, while the harmonious variety of color in the accessory draperies and furniture supports the interest of the central figure, without detracting from its power. On the whole, this is one of the most striking illustrations in the series.

IX. *Jephtha's Daughter.* Hugues Merle (St. Marcelin, France).

Whatever may have been the desolate fate to which the daughter of the stern Jewish chieftain was devoted, there can be no doubt of the sweetness, the gentleness, and the heroic fidelity of her filial love. The tender beauty of the maiden represented in the illustration is admirably expressive of the character; the face is earnest and shaded by a certain sadness in the eyes, while yet there is no mark of rebellion or discontent at the rash vow, the fulfilment of which she has gone with her companions into the mountains to bewail. This is an adaptation from one of Merle's most beautiful pictures. He has always been especially noted for his success in depicting children and young girls, and in the present instance he has certainly obtained a very charming effect.

X. *Hannah and Samuel.* Charles Brochart (Paris, France; b. 1829).

This is a subject painted for the book. "The Praying Mother," who in the depths of her intense desire for children had promised to devote to the Lord the man-child for which she pleaded, brought her little son Samuel — "asked of God" — when about three years of age and left him in the Temple, consecrated for a lifetime to the service of Jehovah. The pious, devotional spirit of the woman appears in the quiet face and reverent eyes, and the expression of happy gratitude and contentment, although she has come to yield up forever the child of her prayers and vows. The little fellow whom she tenderly holds to her breast has a clear-eyed, intelligent, interesting face, and the beholder instinctively feels that he is a child of no ordinary qualities, and one not unlikely to hear the mysterious voice calling him to the high and holy duties of his after life. The last and greatest of the Judges and one of the most favored of the Prophets of that wonderful Jewish line was sent to the world through a beautiful childhood. The faces of both mother and boy are full of appropriate feeling, while the chaste and simple accessories enrich without overloading the picture.

XI. *Ruth.* Louis Devedeux (Paris, France; b. 1845).

The author of this fancy of the gentle and faithful Moabite (a picture painted for this volume) is one of the rising young painters of France, having already taken several medals under the severe critical awards of the Parisian annual *Salon des Beaux Arts.* The grace and modesty of both face and figure in this picture of Ruth are enhanced by the delicacy of the color, which is rich, but so quiet in tone that it is not in the slightest degree obtrusive. The costume is simple, but effective; the grace with which the fine fair drapery is thrown over the head and around the neck and shoulders charmingly enhances the maidenly action of the entire figure. There is one pretty touch of nature, to which a French or

Italian or Oriental artist, with an observing eye, would almost irresistibly be led, though an English or American painter would never think of it, — the brilliant eyes of the poppy, shining out from amid the grain. This is one of the most beautiful features of the grain-fields of warm countries, and it is used in this picture with admirable effect.

XII. *Abigail.* CHARLES BROCHART (Paris, France; b. 1829).

The noble and generous nature which impelled Abigail to withstand the brutal fury of her husband, and even in that age of violence to dare disobedience to his wicked commands, is admirably portrayed in this attractive picture. The woman who was beautiful enough and rich enough in womanly virtues to win the heart of David, the warrior, singer, poet, king, the most brilliant man of his day, and the one who has left a more potent influence upon the ages than any other of his nation (save his "greater Son"), must have been possessed of rarely attractive qualities. The subject has given the artist opportunity to make a fine and striking picture, in which he has perhaps given prominence rather to the hospitable impulses of Abigail, in her offering of provision and refreshment to the famished soldier-band.

XIII. *The Witch of Endor.* CHARLES BROCHART (Paris, France; b. 1829).

Contrary to the traditional conception of the woman who "had a familiar spirit," by which she is generally represented as a hideous old hag, more frightful to look upon than the ghosts she summoned from the other world, BROCHART has here taken a bold departure and given this Witch some semblance of *witchery*, by making her young, beautiful, and intelligent. The picture presents her as herself terrified by the apparition she evoked, which was a spirit of loftier mien than those she had been accustomed to traffic with; as the author says, she "cast her line into the infinite shadows, and was somewhat appalled by what it brought up." The self-confidence customary with such people has disappeared, and we see only the startled woman, who, having arrayed herself for the artifices of her calling, has found her spells more potent than she expected, and, crying with a loud voice, starts back in affright from the dread shade of the Prophet-Judge.

XIV. *Jezebel.* CHARLES BROCHART (Paris, France; b. 1829).

The crafty, cruel, heathen queen, who with her wiles and her superior spirit for so many years ruled Ahab the king, and sucked the blood of Israel, is a subject easy to misconceive. Perhaps the first impression of such a character would suggest a large masculine frame, with great physical power. But a closer study of history and of nature will show how much more probable is the conception of the artist, — a slender, compact body, with small but graceful arms, firm but beautifully shaped hands, eyes to flash hatred or beam calculating kindness, a mouth capable of the compression of cruel will or the more dangerous smile of craft; a dress elegant in material, lustrous in jewels and costly fabrics, and exquisite in the faultless harmony of its color and arrangement. Jezebel was of the *Vivien* order of women, who are wicked, not because of temptation, but from simple love of wickedness. They seem to come upon the earth originally inspired by the Spirit of Evil, — their chief joy being to exercise their intelligence and power in utter badness.

XV. *The Captive Maid.* Charles Landelle (Laval, France; b. 1815).

There is perhaps nothing of special note in this charming and graceful picture of Landelle's. It is one of his favorite subjects of the Oriental type, the original being called "A Young Girl of Tanger." The little maid of the captive Israelites was evidently one who had made herself respected and liked; for when she suggested that Naaman, the greatest lord of the Syrian court and chief of its armies, should go to seek out a prophet of her despised and despoiled countrymen, her advice was acted upon. The picture shows a beautiful, gentle face, a graceful form, and a thoroughly Eastern type of person and costume.

XVI. *Queen Esther.* Gustave Rodolphe Clarence Boulanger (Paris, France; b. 1824).

Of all the Orientalists of the modern French school, Gérome is probably the most brilliant and renowned. Next to him, and indeed almost his equal, is Boulanger, who has several times accompanied his famous *confrère* to the East, where they refill their portfolios with new faces and costumes and scenes, to be wrought up into new pictures. Having just returned from one of these trips, Mons. Boulanger was fortunately able promptly to respond to the demand for two original designs for the present work. *Queen Esther* is one of these. The proud and serene beauty of the face, the dignity of the form and bearing, and the simple richness and elegance of the costume, make this a notable picture. The calm brow, steady eyes, and "level-fronting eyelids," together with the somewhat lofty poise of the head, show the conscious strength of the brave woman who took her own life in her hand when facing an Oriental despot in behalf of her enslaved countrymen. The pearl-tipped golden coronet, the rich details of the costume, the grace of the hands, and the regular beauty of the face, convey a sense of the woman's weapons, — the queen's power over her lord. Although the background is devoid of almost everything save the somber shadow which gives relief to the figure, the imagination easily supplies the haughty king, the throng of courtiers, and the crowd of suppliant Jews behind their queen.

XVII. *Judith.* Horace Vernet (France; b. 1789, d. 1863).

This artist (whose full name was Emile Jean Horace) was born of a race of artists; his fathers for four generations having attained eminence as painters, while he himself led a life of almost unvarying success, and died the recognized head of his profession. His early army life gave him a marked advantage in knowledge and the attainment of a brilliant realism in his military pictures; which, as the glory of France was his chief inspiration, were for many years almost his only works. During the reign of Louis Philippe he was commissioned to paint for one of the grand halls of the royal palace at Versailles a series of pictures celebrating the French military successes in Algeria; a task which led him to make several journeys to Northern Africa and to Palestine, for the correct study of facial types, scenery, costume, etc. This was the most fertile period of his life, and produced among other things a notable series of Scriptural subjects; one of which — *Judith and Holofernes* — furnishes the illustration of that subject in this volume. Artists have always been fond of this strong subject; but none have so well succeeded in rendering the beauty of the intrepid Jewess, combined with her resolution and force of character. The horror of the old woman who holds the dreadful basket to receive the head is finely contrasted with the superb sternness of Judith's face and action; just as the illuminated, gorgeous tapestry of the tyrant's tent is rebuked by the quiet sky and the steady shining of the stars. It is a grand composition; graphic in design, perfect in detail, effective in coloring. No wonder it has become famous.

XVIII. *The Sistine Madonna.* Raphael Sanzio (Urbino, Italy; b. 1483, d. 1520).

There can be no doubt that the Sistine Madonna of Raphael is the grandest picture in the world. The artist was one of those few happy men who, gifted alike with genius, energy, perseverance, and an amiable disposition, enter early on their life-work, achieve instant success, and pursue a continuous ascending grade of wealth and honor until death. His works range from the simplest portraits to the most elaborate compositions, from easel-paintings to vast architectural plans and decorations, frescos, cartoons, altar-pieces, — the variety is marvelous, the execution of the highest excellence. To crown all, his private character was very noble. Mrs. Jameson says: "We may reflect with pleasure that nothing rests on surer evidence than the admirable qualities of Raphael; that no earthly renown was ever so unsullied by reproach, so justified by merit, so confirmed by concurrent opinion, so established by time."

Of his great paintings, his last, "The Transfiguration," now in the Vatican Gallery, is by many regarded as the grandest; but, on the whole, the palm is given by most to this wondrous-eyed Madonna, with her babe, so supernatural and yet so very human, in her arms. The picture was painted for the Convent of St. Sixtus, at Piacenza,—whence its name. To quote again that admirable authority, Mrs. Jameson: "It represents the Virgin standing in a majestic attitude; the infant Saviour enthroned in her arms; and around her head a glory of innumerable cherubs melting into light. Kneeling before her, we see on one side St. Sixtus, on the other Santa Barbara, and beneath her feet two heavenly cherubs gaze up in adoration. In execution, as in design, this is probably the most perfect picture in the world. It is painted throughout by Raphael's own hand; and as no sketch or study of any part of it was ever known to exist, and as the execution must have been, from the thinness and delicacy of the color, wonderfully rapid, it is supposed that he painted it at once upon the canvas,—a *creation* rather than a picture." It is a vast canvas, and by its very size is impressive; the surrounding angel heads, and figures of St. Sixtus and Santa Barbara, have been omitted from this reproduction. But it is, after all, not so much the grandeur of the figures, the symmetry and grace of the composition and grouping, the bright beauty of the cherub faces, or the masterly skill in design and finish and atmosphere of color, though all these are admirable; it is, above all things, the wonderful expression of the two faces, the Mother and Child. "And Mary kept these things and pondered them in her heart"; it is a thoughtful face, happy and yet "pondering" the strange things that had come upon her. For the child's face, it is a perpetual miracle; it is indeed a babe, and yet there is in the eyes a far-seeing look, and on the face an expression of such deep wisdom, combined with infantile simplicity, that it affords a never-ending study. The present reproduction is but a meager suggestion of this great work. Fortunately, through some fine engravings (notably Steinla's, by all odds the best), the picture is in general form and intent tolerably familiar. The original painting hangs in the Dresden Gallery.

XIX. *The Woman of Samaria.* Emil Vernet-Lecomte (Paris, France; b. 1821).

This is one of the admirable Eastern subjects of the modern French school, and has been deemed a singularly apposite illustration of the woman at the well, to whom the Saviour talked. The easy poise of the figure, the steadiness of the head and right hand, and the strength of the face, indicate the self-reliance and confidence of a woman who has seen much of life; while the listless forgetfulness of the left hand, holding the water-jar, and the earnest gaze of the eyes, show the awakened mind and fixed attention of the listener. Vernet-Lecomte has been one of the most enterprising and successful of the French Orientalists; his pictures always glow with the warmth and color of the East.

XX. *The Widow of Nain.* Frederick Goodall (England; b. 1822).

This is a powerful picture. Although it is, for its present purpose, an adaptation, the expression of absolute and heart-breaking desolation which it portrays tells a definite story. There have been other modes of treating this subject, most of them giving the rather revolting scene of the dead man in his winding-sheet arising from the bier, while the life-giving Master stands by, and the weeping relatives and friends throng confusedly around. But besides the limitations of space, which preclude any such extended composition from this series, we have preferred, on other accounts, the single striking figure, which, after all, embodies in itself the central and dominating sentiment of the widowed and bereaved mother. Some one controlling thought must be the life of every picture. The joy and sorrow of this history are too widely contrasted to admit of both being presented on a single canvas.

XXI. *Mary Magdalene.* Pompeo Girolamo Batoni (Lucca, Italy; b. 1708, d. 1781).

This beautiful and every way noble work is kept alive in constant reproduction. Lithograph, wood-engraving, steel line-engraving, mezzotint, — there is hardly a mode of copying which has not been resorted to for the purpose of multiplying it in all its graceful lines and admirable proportions, while the number of actual oil-paintings which have been carefully elaborated from the original is probably greater than has been inspired by any other of the "great Masters," excepting always Raphael's three world-renowned pictures of the Virgin, — the "Sistine Madonna," the "Madonna della Seggiola," and "La Belle Jardinière." The Magdalen of Batoni is one of the few paintings which fairly compete with the masters of the fifteenth and sixteenth centuries on their own ground; for, though it is a picture of the eighteenth century, painted during the decadence of European and especially of Italian art, it is very much after the style of the older artists, and it is brought into direct comparison with the similar expression of this same subject by Correggio, in the same gallery at Dresden. In this competition it easily holds its own, if, indeed, it does not bear away the palm. Correggio has by far the greater name, for his pictures are among the choicest treasures of the principal galleries of Europe; but in this subject, the freedom and boldness of the treatment seem to dwarf the more delicate and weaker rendering of Correggio, while in color and expression Batoni is fully the equal of the older and more famous master.

XXII. *The Daughter of Herodias.* Emil Vernet-Lecomte (Paris, France; b. 1821).

As stated in the remarks prefatory to this list, this plate has been taken to represent one of the types of Eastern beauty and a costume appropriate to the subject. It is known as "L'Almée" (The Dancing-Girl), and since it was painted, in 1869, it has gained quite a fame as characteristic of the artist and of the school to which he belongs. Travelers in the East find so little change in dress and manners, as also boats, houses, tools, instruments, and modes of life, from those of twenty centuries ago, that we need not go far astray in taking a dancing-girl of the present day, in that ancient land, to suggest the dress which the dancing Salome may have assumed in order to please the voluptuous king and obtain the request of her revengeful mother. Viewed simply as a work of art, also, the picture is pleasing. The dress is simple, graceful, and rich; the attitude is easy and modest; and the face is agreeable in feature and expression.

XXIII. *Martha and Mary.* Gustave Rudolph Clarence Boulanger (Paris, France; b. 1824).

Thoroughly effective and original, the hand of a master is to be seen in every line. The artist, who was a pupil of Paul Delaroche, carried off, at the age of twenty-five, the "Grand Prize of Rome," the ambition of every art student in the French and Italian schools. His grand earlier successes were in the classical field; but of late years he has (as already remarked) devoted himself more particularly to the Orient; and Arabia, Egypt, Syria, Turkey, and the Levant in general, have been illustrated by his glowing pencil. In this picture, the dark beauty and spirited action of Martha, the serene repose of Mary's figure, and the sweetness of her face and her quietude of manner under the fiery reproaches of her elder sister, the characteristic contrast of color in the dresses of the two, the suggested coolness of the vine-embowered porch, and the general harmony of line, design, and color, are well worthy of observation. The fact that it was designed and painted for this volume by the great Orientalist, gives to the picture an additional value and interest.

XXIV. *The Widow's Mite.* ÉDOUARD DUBUFE (Paris, France; b. 1819).

This painter has achieved for himself a splendid record. His first studies were made with his father, CLAUDE MARIE DUBUFE, who had attained eminence as a portrait painter (b. 1790; d. 1864); but later, he had the great advantage of tuition by DELAROCHE, the acknowledged master of the French school of thirty years ago. He began exhibiting his pictures in the annual *Salon des Beaux Arts* at the age of twenty-one (obtaining a medal), and shortly afterwards gave his attention to subjects of religious sentiment. But after five years of this, successful as he was, he turned his talents into the channel where his father had become famous, and has given France a most admirable series of portraits of her public men and women, — renowned in the arts, in war, in politics, in society. During this period, however, he has not lost sight of imaginative art, but has made his name known throughout the world by such works as "The Prodigal Son," and the picture here reproduced, "The Widow's Mite." This group, without doubt, is from the life; it bears all the marks of reality, without, however, any of the hard, unsympathetic treatment of realism. The thoughtful and rather sad face of the poor woman, beautiful with the gentle joy of helping others poorer than herself; the unconscious babe asleep on her shoulder; the bright blond beauty of the little girl who with cheerful look watches the last penny of her mother's little store — "all her living" — as it drops into the treasury-coffer; and the half-roguish, half-shy little boy standing close under the protecting hand of his elder sister, — these form a group rarely surpassed in grace or interest. The color is managed with especial skill, the mother's somber robes being well contrasted with the brighter tints of the children's clothing, though all are evidently worn and old. The gleam of brilliant effect from the tumbled red cap in the little fellow's hand is a marvel of cleverness, and the general management of the light, softly illumining what would otherwise be a rather cold and chilly picture, is most admirable.

XXV. *Lydia the Hospitable.* CHARLES BROCHART (Paris, France; b. 1829).

From among the "Women of the Apostolic Church" treated of in the text, it was necessary to select some prominent character. Probably no other, save perhaps Dorcas, the typical figure of charitable industry, stands forth so distinctly as *Lydia.* A woman of Greek nationality, yet rescued from the sensuous habits of her race and time by the influence of Christianity and its strenuous spiritual and moral teaching as enforced by the Apostle Paul, Lydia appears chiefly as a clear-headed, generous-hearted woman of wealth, who, embracing the new religion with earnestness, was happy in throwing open her house for the entertainment of its wandering Apostles, — they leaving home and kindred to "endure hardship as good soldiers" among strangers and foreigners, for the cause they so nobly served; she welcoming them with cheerful hospitality to her home and giving them efficient aid in their work. The illustration aims only to set forth this idea; its intrinsic beauty of color and design are too obvious to need pointing out.

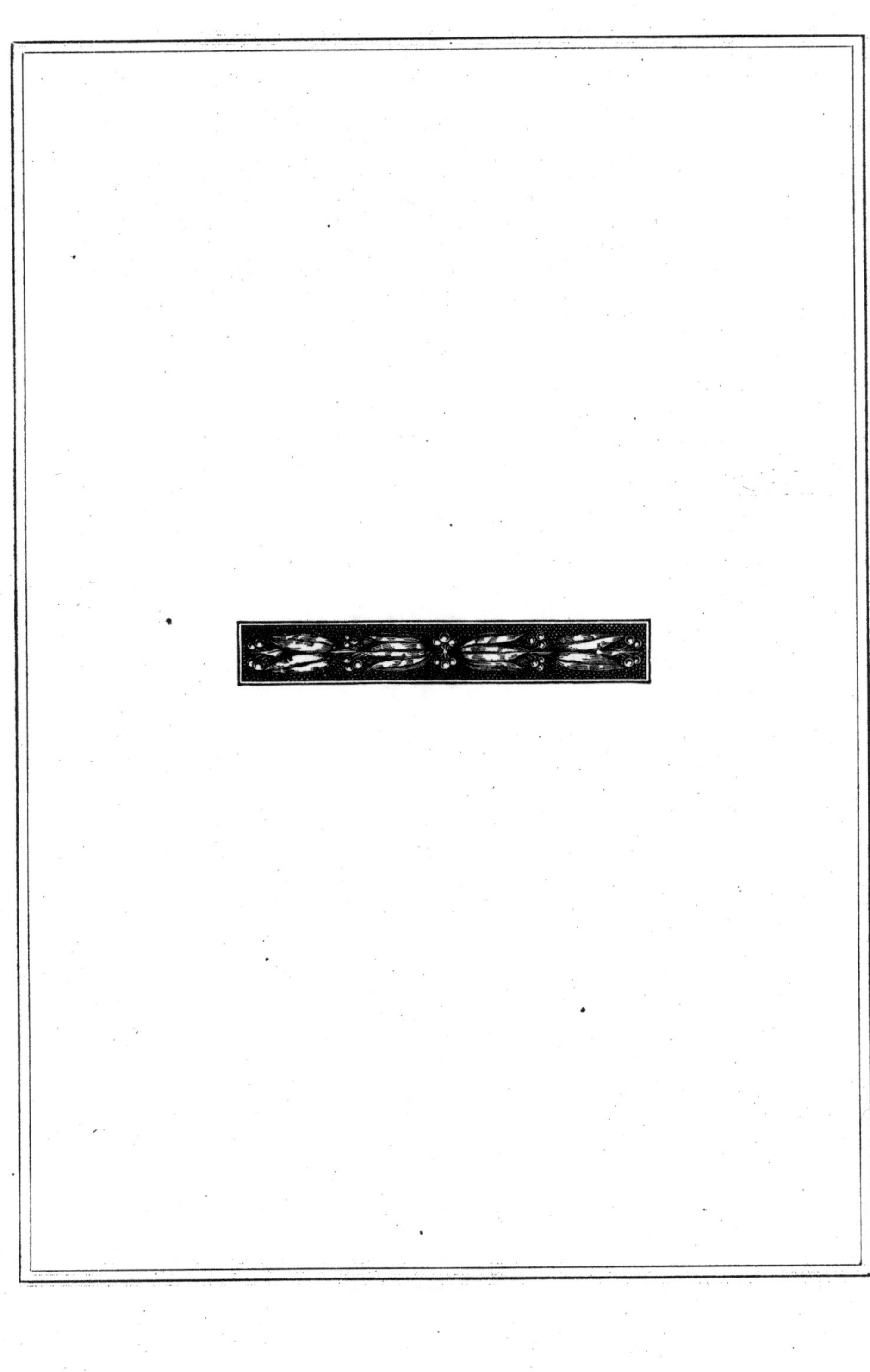

INDEX TO FIRST LINES

OF THE POETRY IN THIS VOLUME.

INDEX TO FIRST LINES.

www.ingramcontent.com/pod-product-compliance
Lightning Source LLC
LaVergne TN
LVHW020914110826
845150LV00004B/672

* 9 7 8 1 4 2 5 5 5 5 8 1 8 *